# One Billion Seconds

So love connecting with you, George & Pamela! Thanks for sharing the journey!

Poppy & Gryff

# One Billion Seconds

There's Still Time to Discover Love

~

**New Edition**

*Poppy and Geoff Spencer CPC*

ISBN: 0692910751
ISBN 13: 9780692910757
Library of Congress Control Number: 2017909798
Legacy Publishing, Sarasota, FL

*We dedicate this book—our legacy of love—to our children: Kimmy, Kelly, Jonathon, George, and Molly; our parents: Valerie and George, and Jean and George. Although our fathers are no longer with us, their gentle and loving souls are in our hearts every day.*

# Prologue

~⁀

I HAVE THE ABILITY TO look at someone and, in a matter of seconds, know what they're like.

I'm *that* good.

I embrace the old proverb: "The eyes are the window to the soul." All cultures say it. The French say the eyes are the mirror of the soul: *Les yeux sont le miroir de l'âme.*

I'm a student of eyes. Their color. Shape. Eyebrows and lashes. Their sparkle. Their emptiness. And their ability to spill emotion. Eyes show a life of belonging and connection. Or a life of loneliness and exile.

My first instinct is to search someone's eyes. Whether they're the eyes of my colleagues, or the eyes of the individuals assigned to me.

My name is Jesse Rader. My role in the organization: to choreograph relationships.

Selected out of a few hundred for this position, I'm best described as a relationship observer—present with the people whom we choreograph, yet they're unable to see or hear us.

I watch people. Look for good fits—compatibility. When they're stuck, I offer them a little nudge. An inspiration. A shove in the right direction.

My psychological profile revealed that I excelled in assessing people—that I had the ability to identify and understand their unique strengths and talents. The report also showed giftedness in many areas. I received a ten on positivism—always upbeat. I shined in relational studies. Passionate about my work. Ambitious. The remark I enjoyed the most? My exceptional skill with timing.

My supervisor had told me I connected people faster and more often than anyone else. He'd said that of all the candidates, I'd shown mastery in the art of timing—I always gave a gentle nudge at just the right moment.

When I place two people together, I help them step back to view their behaviors—to see what actions impeded their progress. So the relationship has a chance to flourish on its own.

In my two-year internship, I directed a dozen romantic journeys. My goal was always the same: to connect people to each other. And, of course, to have success.

This is the story of my first assignment after I graduated. My first real job.

Two upper-class college students, Poppy and Geoff, appeared to be a perfect match for each other. Assigned to choreograph these two, I did not have the option to create their initial matchup. Too bad, because I know I'm really good at it.

My supervisor, Phillip—whom I have never met face-to-face—had predetermined my couple. As a newbie, I'd received one assignment, already established. My couple attended a college in central Florida—Rollins College.

Phillip had given me a scroll with the necessary information; the scroll was how he communicated with me. Its thin aluminum case looked like rolled parchment. Quite efficient. Genius, really. If I wanted a detail, some background info on my couple, I pulled the scroll from the top and the bottom, and the information appeared. Instantly.

My two perfectly matched. The only difference was a few months of age. I looked at the personality assessments of Poppy and Geoff. These two aligned as an exact fit.

*I probably won't need the scroll much,* I thought. *Or our old manual. It's the same stuff we covered in my internship.*

*Maybe other choreographers need extra time with the scroll. Not me. I'll learn a lot more from people's eyes than from the scroll.*

PART I

# First Love

# CHAPTER 1

# Just a Glance

~〜ૐ

## 1977

I DECIDED TO JUMP-START MY work, go to Rollins right away. *I can peek at the scroll anytime*, I thought.

On September 7, 1977, I arrived to begin my career as a choreographer. Just after Labor Day, a Wednesday. Before I got to the campus, I glanced at my scroll. I wanted some background information on Florida. I assumed it flat. With orange groves and beaches. Low-rise condos. Tourists and retirees.

The town of Winter Park revealed nothing of the sort. The homes—a mix of pastels—sky blue, pale green, and light pink. Styled like Key West. And colonials with wraparound porches, shaded by huge oaks. Brick-lined streets with Park Avenue as the main artery. Charming boutiques. Five-star restaurants. A museum that held Tiffany-stained glass. At the end of Park Avenue was the town's crown jewel, Rollins College.

The private, co-ed liberal arts college looked like an oasis.

Lake Virginia bordered the back of the campus, its shoreline shaped like a parenthesis. Blue-green water. Azure. Under a cloudless sky. The center of campus featured a massive grass square—Mills Lawn—the Green. Around the lawn, a walkway led to various buildings and included some historical stones with names on them. The stones apparently signified the birthplace of each person. Aristotle, Abraham Lincoln, George Washington. Hundreds more. I imagined my name here someday.

*I need to get the lay of the land. Look for some good spots to bring my couple together. Nudgeable locations.*

Lush foliage covered the hundred-year-old campus, and stucco buildings connected by arched breezeways—loggias—led students to classrooms and dorms. Garnet roof tiles sat on top of the Spanish-style buildings. The sun looked like it was playing an endless game of hide-and-seek with the oaks and palms. Definitely a B&B setting. Breathtaking and beautiful. It looked more like a resort than an institution of higher learning. I sat on the grass at the edge of Lake Virginia, near the pool.

I checked my scroll for some background on my couple. Where they lived, what classes they had. Their schedule, interests. Where and when I'd have the opportunity to nudge them together.

Poppy and Geoff had returned as upperclassmen at Rollins. In my review of Poppy, I discovered her roots in Milwaukee, Wisconsin. She'd followed in her mother's footsteps, both as a Rollins student and as a Kappa Alpha Theta sorority member.

Last month, she'd traveled to Europe with her grandfather. A two-and-a-half-week trip. They'd flown over on the Concorde, which was faster than the speed of sound. They'd visited Paris, London, Rome, and Athens. On the final leg, they'd sailed home from Cherbourg, France. First-class on the luxury ocean liner the *Queen Elizabeth II*.

Prior to her Europe jaunt, she'd finished a successful summer internship at an ad agency in Milwaukee. She'd been promised the position of Assistant Creative Art Director upon her graduation.

Well-liked by her peers, Poppy had a lot of dating experience with guys, both at home and at college, yet none of them were guys I would've picked for a fine art major with a passion for psychology.

I continued reading.

Poppy's file described her personality as outgoing. A big heart and a great capacity to love. Close with her family, adored by her parents and her grandfather. One of her grandfather's qualities that resonated with her: a love for family. Unconditional.

A worksheet popped up on my scroll. The well-being success chart that measured seven key elements; those critical markers that showed success in a relationship. Individuals needed to be good on their own before they're good together. The seven traits: confidence, happiness, optimism, humor, empathy, resilience, and gratitude. We assigned marks for total well-being—a minus, a check, or a plus.

I gave Poppy all plus marks.

In my internship, I never gave all plusses. *But there it is. Easy to choreograph.*

Geoff's information came up. He'd spent the summer working at the Carey Hotel in Chautauqua, New York. The hotel was centrally located on the grounds of the Chautauqua Institution. It was about as old as Rollins. A grand summer resort area lost in a time warp. A vibrant place of education, religion, arts, and culture. And entertainment.

When he wasn't working as a bellhop at the hotel, Geoff took advantage of the family's lakeside cottage. Hoisted at the dock was his family's Flying

Scot sailboat, *Misty*, and a Glastron ski boat floated nearby. Geoff honed his water-skiing skills on Chautauqua to prepare himself for the Rollins water-ski team.

He was a Phi Delta Theta fraternity member—Phi Delt for short. He, too, was well-liked. Very social. Easygoing.

I scored him with all plus marks as well. *This project is too simple.* Ironically, I felt nonplussed.

*Phillip will not be impressed with me—not with this couple. Not when they've scored all plus marks. I won't receive any credit or recognition. No awards. Not when they're already so secure and happy. I'm sure Phillip wants to see evidence that I've done something. Serious nudges. Obvious changes. Big improvement.*

*What is that requirement in the manual? Here it is.* I read.

"Blah, blah, blah," I murmured. *The relationship must self-sustain for at least three months.* I scrolled further.

"Okay, here," I muttered. "In order to acquire new relationships . . . blah, blah, blah . . . supervisor signs off . . . and only *then* are new projects assigned."

I looked up and let my thoughts wander across the lake, where mansions dotted the shoreline. *Phillip should sign off on Poppy and Geoff before the winter break. I'll add a new project then. If all goes well, I'll still be the top choreographer.*

A quick glance at Poppy and Geoff's schedules revealed that they shared only one class together. Not just any class, but a class with the beloved "Doc" Rivers. I unrolled the scroll further to read more information on the teacher. Doc, loved as a charismatic professor, was known for humorous and unfiltered comments. No student ever dozed off or looked out the window in his class. They were always engaged and entertained.

*When classes start next week, I'll waste no time getting them together. Here's how I see it: Arrange for them to meet. They'll hit it off. Give them three months and acquire Phillip's okay to add a new couple to my workload. One that's more of a challenge, to show my strengths. My expertise. So I'll really make a name for myself.*

One of the first things I'd need—possible points of intersection. The campus offered a lot of good places for overlap and chance meetings. Most obvious was the cafeteria, the Beanery. Beans for short. Another option was the Student Union. Below it was the Pub, where student bartenders legally served beer and wine to anyone 18 or over. There were also the cozy, intimate classrooms. Maybe they could meet at Sandspur, the soccer field. Or Mills Memorial Library. Any one of the tiled breezeways on campus would also work.

I glanced to my left at the pool—Alfond Pool. Another option. Or even Harper's Bar, just off campus.

I know I'm great at timing. Just have to find the right place. I thought back to my internship. My peers used to tell me, "Jesse, you're the best at finding perfect venues for couples to meet."

I intended to plan a detailed script for my couple to meet. I walked to Knowles Chapel, the place I'd call home while I choreograph at Rollins. Phillip had advised me to use the chapel as my home base.

Knowles Chapel sat diagonally across Mills lawn. The stone structure, which could be described as Mediterranean revival, offered high-vaulted ceilings and stained-glass windows. A pretty rose window. The pipe organ was a showpiece. But the most striking feature was the tower. At night, a rich blue light shined on it. Lapis blue.

~∂

On Monday, September 12, I implemented the first of my timing nudges for Geoff. He'd finished water-ski practice in the afternoon before heading back to the fraternity house.

I nudged him to pause at the pool. In the shade of a palm tree, Geoff leaned his ski against the fence. His light-brown hair, still damp, rested on his neck. It flipped up in the back. He searched the bleachers at Alfond Pool, a regular gathering spot for the co-eds. The cement seating ran the length of the twenty-five-yard pool, the concrete slabs the perfect size for the students to tan their bodies. From the bleachers, sunbathers saw Lake Virginia, and to the right, the ski team dock and jump ramp. Geoff's eyes locked on a girl in a yellow bikini.

Poppy, just out of the pool, stood on the bleachers, a few feet away from her towel and books. She combed the water out of her long brown hair. Her tanned body leaned to one side. Drops of water sprinkled on the steps of the bleachers. She straightened, and the ends of her hair just grazed the clasp of her bikini top. She tilted her head back, as if about to apply eye drops. Instead, she closed her eyes and squeezed a plastic lemon over her wet hair. The juice trickled down her head.

Geoff gawked at her. Transfixed. He watched her saunter down the cement steps. I'm sure the plentiful contents of her bikini top caught his attention.

I shook my head and grinned. *Guys are predictable.*

Geoff, still in a state of wonder when he returned to the frat house, burst into the frat living room. Two of his brothers, Desmond and Gavin, both redheads with blue eyes, stood up, startled.

"Guys! I gotta tell you about this." He began to gesture with his hands. He cupped the air in front of his chest and reenacted what he'd just witnessed at the pool.

"She was gorgeous. Her boobs, like, floated up and down when she walked. They didn't bounce all over the place like some girls' do. She put that lemon crap in her hair. And her mouth was open. God. She had this flat, tanned stomach. Gorgeous hips. Nice butt. Man! I have to meet her. She's a babe."

"Close your mouth, Spence. You're drooling," Desmond teased.

"What's her name?" Gavin laughed.

"I don't know. Did I mention her beautiful pair of . . . eyes?" Geoff grinned. He raised his eyebrows.

"Alright already. Go meet her, will ya? Jeez, Spence. Stop slobbering. Go find her," Desmond insisted.

Usually it took at least five or six nudges to get people together. I'd done it with one. I just needed to set up the ideal spot for Geoff to meet Poppy, before I asked Phillip for a new assignment, so I could get the recognition I deserved.

By the next morning, I'd found a place for them to notice each other but not actually *meet*. Doc Rivers' speech classroom, located downstairs in the back of Mills Library, proved just the spot.

I'd set it up beautifully. A tiny nudge for these two to glance at each other. Just a glance, nothing more. Priming the pump. I knew I wouldn't have enough time for them to meet between classes. With Gavin there, I nudged him to speak with Geoff as the class ended. Long enough for Poppy to leave. But not before she'd shared a smile with Geoff.

A mere three days into the fall semester, and I had them scripted. *Perfect so far.*

I chose the Pub as the place they'd meet. Just a few days into the first semester, students wouldn't have too much homework.

At ten p.m., I nudged Poppy and three of her sorority sisters to head to the Pub. Unlike many of the college students I saw, Poppy didn't wear jeans. She stood out in her white painter's pants, and her red-strapped wooden Dr. Scholl's clicked as she skipped down the staircase. She gently tugged at the cropped waistband of her hooded navy and red-striped velour top, as an inch of her tanned waist peeked out.

I felt confident Poppy and Geoff shared an appropriate mindset. Poppy appeared self-assured and comfortable with her courses of study. She'd already fulfilled her BA core prerequisites. After graduation in nine months, a fabulous dream job awaited her.

Geoff, always a positive guy, left one place of paradise at Chautauqua for another at Rollins College. Three days into the semester, this relationship appeared destined for soulmate success with just a glance. Even more incredible, their respective fraternity and sorority houses stood right next door to each other.

With my level of expertise, I'd expected a more complex couple to choreograph.

# CHAPTER 2

# Love at First Nudge

~

THE ROLLINS PUB FELT LIKE a rathskeller—a softly lit gathering spot in the cavernous basement of the Student Union. Amber lighting cast fuzzy shadows on the dozen or so steel-edged table tops with Formica surfaces. Even with stacks of matchbooks jammed under the legs over the years, the tables remained off-kilter.

In the week since I'd arrived at Rollins, I'd scrutinized the patterns of the pub-goers. They were predictable, with most students arriving after ten p.m. Nothing really happened before then. If anyone came before ten o'clock, they bartended. But just a half hour later, a crowd of three dozen or so students usually showed up, arriving in small clusters to avoid the young adult awkwardness of not locating a familiar face.

I'd already nudged Poppy to go to the Pub. With deep-brown eyes like warm fudge, the 5'4" brunette parted her hair a little off-center. The sunlit waves of her hair, the color of Italian roast coffee, fell like window curtains and framed her heart-shaped face. The frosted pink lipstick highlighted her big smile. She stuck her hands in her back pockets, a good resting place while waiting to hold a Schlitz beer.

She and four Theta sisters scanned the room for an empty table. Poppy stood closest to the bar, and as she turned her head toward the counter, she spotted Geoff a few feet away. Her face lit up.

*Good. She recognizes him.*

At 5'10", Geoff wore his handlebar moustache like a name tag. His eyes, also brown, were just two shades lighter than Poppy's. Auburn tones blended in his brown hair. Much like Poppy's, he parted his hair just left of center, and his hair also had a slight wave, gently tucked behind his ears. The back curled up on the white collar of his navy-and-green rugby shirt that was neatly tucked into khaki pants. His brown leather topsiders were lightly scuffed, no doubt from his summer in Chautauqua. With his left elbow on the counter—a guy's lookout point—the way men do to appear cool and casual, he talked with a sideways glance to the bartender, his frat brother.

Geoff spotted Poppy a few feet across from him. "Hi! I know you." He straightened, his elbow and the counter no longer on duty. The bartender grinned and shook his head, a guy understanding that any cute girl trumped a conversation with another guy.

"Aren't you in Doc's speech class with me?" Geoff stepped closer to Poppy.

"Hi. Yes." She tilted her head to the side. "Don't you just love Doc?"

"Yes, I do." Geoff imitated the husky, forceful voice of their professor.

"You sound just like him." Poppy's hand flew to her mouth in surprise. "I'm Poppy, by the way."

"Poppy? Really?" He continued to imitate their professor, Doc. "You don't hear that every day." Geoff smiled.

"You're *really* good at his voice." Poppy's face flushed and her eyes twinkled flirtatiously. "And because you'll probably ask, my real name *is* Poppy."

"I like that. It's different." A dimple appeared as he smiled. "I'm Geoff. Geoff Spencer."

"Oh!" Poppy giggled, and her smile faded into seriousness. "Bond. James Bond."

Geoff laughed. "I spell my name with a *G-E-O*, not *J-E-F-F.* I'm a Gee-off." His brown eyes sparkled.

"Like Geoffrey Beene? And Chaucer?" Poppy spoke louder as more clusters of students crowded into the Pub.

"Yes. Exactly." He leaned back on his elbow and assumed his lookout stance, although this time his eyes focused only on Poppy's face, particularly the focal point of her face—her smile. "I'm impressed. Most people don't know either of those two."

"A designer, and the author of *Canterbury Tales.*" Poppy enumerated on two fingers as if being quizzed. "Dickens. *Great Expectations.* With Pip, not Pop." Poppy grinned and pointed to herself.

Geoff's lips parted into a grin. "Can I get you a beer?" He gestured to his frat brother, who hid his smile behind his arm as he pulled down the tap, a look that suggested that he'd get the details on the girl later.

Poppy nodded and clasped her hands in front of her. "Thank you."

Geoff faced his bartending frat brother. "Hey, Benny, can you pour another?"

The two things I first noticed about Benny: huge dimples, like divots in his cheeks, and his thick black moustache—much bushier and straighter than Geoff's.

He pulled the Schlitz tap lever. "No problemo, bro." Benny cleared his voice as if ready to officiate a business meeting.

Geoff took the beers from Benny. "Thanks, man." He turned from Benny and handed the plastic cup to Poppy. "Cheers!" The plastic cups squished together, with the foam on Poppy's cup spilling over the side onto Geoff's hand.

"Oh, sorry." Poppy leaned down and sipped the foam off her cup. She licked her lips and straightened. "Does your moustache ever get all foamy?"

"All the time." He took a sip, deliberately coating his moustache with white suds.

Poppy's eyes twinkled. "How do you get it off?"

He stared directly into her eyes. "Sometimes, I ask a pretty girl like you to help." He flashed a flirty smile. "Would you like to sit down?"

Poppy ran her finger over the top of her lip as if she, too, had a foam moustache. "Umm, sure." She glanced out into the room, spotting her roommate at a full table. She turned back to Geoff. "That would be great. My roomie and my other pals have already found a spot—they're all set."

I wondered about her hesitation to join Geoff—the need to check on her friends. But the back of Geoff's fingers gently touched her elbow to prompt her toward a table.

"How about over here on the left?" Geoff nodded his chin toward an empty table.

Geoff pushed the chair leg out with his foot and set his beer on a small square table against the wall. A brown cord, like an electrical vine, hung from the neon Schlitz Beer sign above the table.

"D'you want some pretzels? Chips? Anything?" Geoff hovered above his chair.

"No, thanks." Poppy shimmied her chair closer to the table. "But you go ahead."

Geoff sat. "No, I'm fine, too." He folded his arms and rested them on the table, anchoring it so it no longer tilted or rocked.

"So do you . . .?" Poppy started to speak.

"D'you live . . .?" Geoff began at the same moment.

They both laughed and tilted their heads back simultaneously.

"You start." Poppy grinned.

"So, do you live around here?" Geoff teased.

"Yes, just a few doors down." Poppy gestured with a hitchhiker thumb. "I live in the Theta House. You?"

Geoff's eyebrows raised. "A Theta!" He leaned toward Poppy. "I'm right next door to you. Mayflower Hall. I'm a Phi Delt."

"I love the Phi Delts," Poppy said, as if she was talking about her favorite band. "I knew Hank from the golf team last year."

"So you play golf?" Geoff asked as he sipped his beer.

"Yes, but I decided not to be on the team this year. It takes too much time." Poppy turned around and pointed to students sitting at three tables shoved together, and where her sisters laughed with others. "And I love living in the house. Maybe you know my roommate, Catherine, over there?"

"Sure." Geoff followed Poppy's gaze. "She never wears shoes, right?"

"That's the one. No shoes." Poppy laughed, and leaned in toward Geoff and whispered, "Or bra, by the way."

Geoff widened his eyes in mock surprise. "Really?"

"Catherine—C-Bell—is great." Poppy smiled as if she was recalling a funny experience she'd shared with her roommate. "How about you? Do you have a roommate?"

"I room with Ernie." Geoff paused. "He's on the soccer team."

"Ernie!" Poppy squealed his name as a chant. "He's so cute. I love the way the whole school yells his name at the games." Do you play soccer, too?"

"I used to, and I still play intramurals. Now I'm on the water-ski team."

"I'm impressed." Poppy sat back and draped one arm across the back of the rounded wooden chair. "I'm embarrassed to say that I've never skied on snow or water." Her fingers twisted a strand of her wavy hair.

"Never?" Geoff shifted to the edge of his chair. "You've got to be kidding me."

"Nope." Poppy glanced up at Geoff with a sheepish grin and ran her hand across the speckled Formica tabletop. "It's sad, I know. Especially snow skiing. I mean, I live in the Midwest. I should've tried it at least once. And I never went to summer camp. But I did play a lot of golf and tennis. And I can throw a baseball like a guy." She stared directly into Geoff's eyes. "For real."

"That *is* impressive. I don't know any girls who throw like a guy." He studied her face with an intrigued look. "Where in the Midwest are you from?"

"Wisconsin. Milwaukee. Beer capital. Schlitz." She pointed to the humming sign above them. "PBR. Miller High Life."

Geoff's eyes followed her hand and rested on her face again, his dimple still exposed. "Yep, the beer mecca."

"I stopped saying I was from Milwaukee. I transferred from an all-girls college last year in Virginia. All the Southern girls used to say, 'You're from Wisconsin? Is that in Minnesota?'" Poppy batted her eyelashes as she feigned a South Carolina accent.

Geoff laughed. "I'm from the Midwest, too. Cleveland." He leaned forward, grinning. "That's in Ohio."

"Stop!" She smiled and swatted the air above his elbow.

As they sipped their drinks, they looked directly at each other. *Almost like a couple who drinks from the same wedding cup,* I thought.

I watched them gaze at each other, and I thought back to my internship. In many first meetings, couples have awkward pauses. They look around the room. Stare at torn posters and graffiti on the wall. Discomfort and distraction show themselves. There's fidgeting. Playing with the thin paper napkins.

Not these two. They showed an immediate ease, a natural flow of conversation. Intrigued with their eyes, I noticed they held each other's gaze when they spoke.

"You never went to camp? What'd you do in the summers?" Geoff asked, his dimple receding before he smiled again.

"Well, I played golf and tennis. Competed in tournaments." Poppy lowered her eyes ever so slightly and, pointing to his left cheek, said, "Oh my gosh." She paused, her lips parting. "I just noticed you have a dimple."

As if Geoff's dimple had a mind of its own, it grew more pronounced as his smile broadened. "They sell them in the bookstore."

Poppy laughed, her whole body shaking. "I've always wanted a dimple. A good one, like yours."

Geoff's eyes scanned her face. "So what else do you do in the summers?"

Poppy exhaled residual laughter. "Well, this past month I had a really neat experience. My grandfather, who's sixty years older than me, took me to Europe for two and a half weeks. We flew on the Concorde to Paris. We went to London, Rome, and Athens. That's France, England, Italy, and Greece." Poppy suppressed a smile.

"Haha." The dimple flashed. "That's cool. You flew on the Concorde?" Geoff's mouth formed an *O* as if she'd just said she'd walked on the moon with Neil Armstrong.

"Yes, and just to let you know how utterly *spoiled* I was"—Poppy lifted her chin with a mock air of Windsor royalty— "we sailed home on the *QEII.*"

"Holy cow. What a trip!" Geoff's arms fell limp at his sides.

"My grandfather is the best." Poppy crossed her arms on top of each other and leaned forward. "I had an amazing August."

Geoff stared at Poppy, the space between his eyebrows scrunched together. "The Concord. SST—Supersonic Transport." He blew out air. "I'd love to do that."

Poppy straightened in her chair. "What did you do this summer? Not like a teacher asking for a report in September." She chuckled.

"My childhood summers were spent on a lake in Michigan. And then, in my teens, at a place called Chautauqua, which is in western New York State. We had a cottage there on the lake. I worked all summer at a hotel. When I wasn't working, I skied and sailed. Summers there are a blast."

"Nice. I think it would be fun to be somewhere different all summer." Poppy stared at him; his brown eyebrows blended into his tanned face. "By the way, I've never sailed, either." She winced.

"What? Are you kidding me?" Geoff's forehead wrinkled into three straight lines.

Poppy nodded in agreement. "I know, I know. Pretty pathetic."

"I had an interesting experience a few summers ago with the sailboat." Geoff paused. "I died."

"Pardon?" Poppy leaned across the table. "I thought you—" She shook her head in a cobwebby way. "Did you just say you died?"

"Yep. I did," Geoff turned his left palm up and, like a palm reader, pointed to a line in the center. "See this line, across here? That scar is where I held the wire that holds the mast up. I was standing barefoot on the damp morning ground. And neither my dad nor I noticed the power line until it was too late." Geoff paused and looked up from his hand into Poppy's eyes.

Poppy's expression froze, the color drained from her face. Her hand quivered near her mouth. Her eyes grew round and big—floating orbs of shock.

"I took the hit for about five seconds until my father figured out what'd happened. He pushed the mast away from the power line. I was electrocuted. It seized up my heart and lungs. I was legally dead. Once I realized what had happened, my last thought before I went down was, *I guess I didn't make it.*"

"Oh no," Poppy whispered, shaking her head back and forth. She reached out and touched his right arm. "I'm so sorry. I feel so badly," she murmured.

"I'm fine. Really. Are you crying?" He dipped his head to see her eyes, as if he were looking under an awning. "I'm okay." He chuckled, patting his chest with both palms. "You can see I'm right here." He cocked his head to the side to see her eyes—big pools of water. "You're not really crying, are you?"

Poppy fanned her right hand in front of her face. "That must've been awful. Frightening." She wiped the corners of her eyes. "Then what happened?"

"Well, my dad is a doctor—"

"Oh thank God!" she said before he could continue.

"And he knew how to do CPR. He brought me back. He beat the shit out of my chest to revive me."

Poppy's hand went to her mouth again. This time, Geoff reached out his hand to cover her wrist.

"I'm fine. It's all right. I walked around like Frankenstein all day when it happened." Geoff hiked up his shoulders. "Stiff as a board from the electrocution."

"How long before you were really okay?" Poppy's elbows hugged her waist.

Geoff rested his fingertips on his chin and looked up. "Probably the next day."

"Really?" Poppy sat back, blinking.

Geoff leaned forward. "So tell me about you. You said you transferred here from an all-girls college?" He grasped his drink and made a crinkling sound with his ribbed plastic cup. "I went to an all-boys' prep school in Cleveland. University School."

"What did you say?" Poppy tilted her head. "What was your school called?"

"University School. An all-boys prep—"

"Oh!" She raised her hands. I went to University School. All my life." Her shoulders fell back against the rounded chair—a curved piece of wood inside of another—like an upside-down beaker shape. "It's pre-K through twelve."

"So was ours. Didn't know there was another University School." Geoff glanced at Poppy's near-empty cup. "Can I get you another beer?"

"Sure. Thank you." Poppy slid her plastic cup toward him. She studied Geoff as he walked to the bar.

The bartender, Benny, smirked as he filled the two cups. He tilted his head toward the table where Poppy sat. "Looks like that's going well." Both of his dimples the size of thimbles, indented.

"I'm keeping her away from you. She likes my dimple." Geoff snorted. "Thanks, Benny. See ya." He sipped the foam off one of the beers as he headed back to the table.

Geoff slid Poppy's beer in front of her. "Good group of Thetas here tonight," Geoff said as he gestured toward Poppy's sisters.

She smiled and sipped her Schlitz. "I always knew I wanted to be a Theta. My mom was a Theta here, too."

"Really? Is that why you came here?" Geoff's expression turned earnest.

"Sort of. I knew I wanted to be at a co-ed school after Mary Baldwin."

One of the Thetas at a nearby table raised her plastic cup in a salute.

Poppy cocked her head toward the celebratory group. "Speaking of birthdays, when's yours?"

"January sixteenth. Same as my dad." Geoff sucked in foam from his moustache.

"The same day? How cool. And another January birthday." Poppy shook her head. "I'm in July. My brother tormented me when I was eight years old. Both he and my parents have January birthdays. I was the only one in the family not born in January. He told me I was adopted." Poppy held up three fingers. "For three years, I thought that my parents didn't want me."

"That's awful. What a terrible thing to tell you." Geoff's jaw dropped. "God, older brothers can be such a pain in the ass."

"He was mean, but now we get along great." Poppy smiled. "So you have an older brother, too?"

"Yep. One brother. He's five years older. He's a third, so they gave him the nickname Twig. His real name is George, after my dad and grandfather."

Poppy's words came out in a rush. "My dad's named George, too."

Geoff raised his eyebrows. "I think that's why I'm a *G-E-O* Geoff. All of our camp underwear had *G. Spencer* on it."

Poppy's roommate appeared at the edge of their table. A barefoot Catherine rolled up the sleeves of her large white untucked shirt—a man's shirt. Long, tanned legs jutted out from under her cutoff jean shorts, and her shirttail brushed the fringe of her cutoffs.

Poppy turned to her. "C-bell!"

"Hi, you guys." She smiled at Geoff and turned to face Poppy, her eyes widening in an exaggerated way, as if it were some sort of code between roommates. "I'm heading back. See you in the room."

"Okay. You know Geoff, right?" Poppy nodded toward Geoff.

"Sure, of course. Hi, Geoff." From her eyes, she brushed back her light-brown bangs on a Dorothy Hamill wedge haircut.

"Hi, Catherine." He looked at her bare feet, a blue-and-gold-beaded ankle bracelet on one tanned leg. He smiled at Catherine. "How are you?"

"Good, good." Catherine nodded once. "Okay, guys. I have a test tomorrow. I'll see you back in the room, Pop, okay?" She winked at Poppy.

"I'll be there in a sec." Poppy grinned at Catherine.

Poppy watched Catherine walk away. More like sashay. Poppy turned back to Geoff, her eyelashes lowered, as if an unwanted memory had crept in. "Catherine was so nice to pick me for her roommate. You know . . ." She looked down at her fingers. "I was a new pledge this past January. Didn't know many people. Didn't really like my junior year until I joined the Thetas."

"Oh, right. You transferred in as a junior." Geoff rested his chin on his hand.

"Mm-hmm. She didn't have to pick me. When she realized I was the only rising senior pledge, she turned down a single room and asked if I wanted to live in the house as her roommate." Poppy's voice softened. "And you know what? Catherine and I have the same room my mom lived in when she was here . . ." She smiled, shifting back into playfulness. "A million years ago."

"The same room, really?" Geoff inched closer to Poppy. "Which one is it?"

"It's on the second floor, in the front. We face your house."

"Let's see." Geoff looked up at the ceiling—fluorescent lights surrounded by acoustic tile. "So your mom lived there, too. That's incredible."

"Yep. She went to school with Mister Rogers."

"*The* Mister Rogers? Fred Rogers?" Geoff leaned his chest against the table. "*Mister Rogers' Neighborhood?*"

"That's the one." Poppy leaned down and slipped off her sandal. "Won't you be"—she flipped it from one hand to another— "my neighbor."

Geoff laughed, his laugh bursting from his mouth.

"Last call!" Benny's voice echoed—a bellow.

"I suppose . . ."

"I guess we should . . ."

They both spoke at once.

"Yeah. I 'spose we should get going." Geoff glanced over his shoulder. "Benny's taking the taps off the kegs."

"I guess so." Poppy stood. She stacked her empty beer cup inside of his.

"C'mon, I'll walk you back." Geoff put his face close to hers and smiled. "All the way to the Theta House."

Poppy put on a dramatic, wide-eyed expression. "Are you sure it's not too far out of your way?"

"Well . . ." Geoff exhaled. "I suppose I can walk the extra hundred feet."

Their shoulders bumped each other several times as they strolled in the balmy Spanish tiled breezeway.

"This was so fun." Poppy gazed up at Geoff. "I had such a nice time talking with you—a fellow Midwesterner." She grinned.

Neither seemed to be in a hurry on the fifty-yard walk.

Geoff turned, walking almost sideways. "I had a great time talking with you, too, Poppy. Sorry if I upset you with my near-death story."

She shivered deliberately. "Don't even bring it up again. So frightening."

"I still can't believe you cried." Geoff shook his head, smiling, the moon catching his dimple. "Well, we're here." He stepped in front of her. "I'll see you tomorrow, right? In Doc's class?"

"For sure." Poppy cocked her head to the side. "By the way, does your dimple always show?" Poppy flirted.

"Just when I'm really happy." He breathed the words.

Under the loggia, the glow from the lighting the color of peach sorbet, he brushed her lips with his. A gentle whisper of a kiss.

"I've never been kissed by anyone with a moustache," she purred.

"Neither have I." Geoff tilted his head and gave her a second soft kiss. "Good night," he murmured, leaving an intimate echo in the breezeway.

"Good night," Poppy breathed back, her lips parted.

He held the door open and Poppy stepped through it backward, her eyes still fixed on his face. She leaned to the side to watch him as the door swung shut. When the click sounded, Poppy grabbed the wrought-iron railing and paused on the first step. With her finger, she touched the top of her lower lip. She stepped slowly up into the softly lit stairwell, a round window offering ambient light from a gibbous moon.

Geoff grinned as he paused in the living room of his frat house. Four guys watched the console TV—*The Tonight Show* with Johnny Carson trying to keep a straight face as Carnac the Magnificent. Desmond and Gavin's red heads bobbed in laughter.

"We saw you, Spence," Gavin said, a spirited accusation.

"You were talking to the Theta babe, Poppy. So . . . ?" Desmond stole a peek at Geoff before looking back to the TV.

"It went fine." Geoff grinned. "Oh, Carnac." He gestured to the console.

Desmond turned around on the couch 180 degrees to face Geoff. "That's it?"

"She's great. We had a fun time." A huge grin spread on his face, concealing his excitement by laughing a little too loudly at Johnny Carson.

Gavin also turned to look at Geoff. With an affirmative nod like a doctor giving a diagnosis, he said, "Oh yeah. You're totally hooked."

Poppy and Geoff quickly eased into a comfort zone with each other. They grinned and laughed in sync. In their speech class, they'd looked at each other when Doc Rivers had brought up famous people who'd attended Rollins. Poppy and Geoff had whispered, "Mr. Rogers" at the same time.

I was sure Phillip would ask to see the many steps I'd taken in getting these two together—plenty of well-timed nudges. Full documentation of many weeks of planning. *I've done none of this*, I thought. *One nudge and nothing else for me to do. Nothing award-worthy.*

Choreographers won awards for their excellent orchestration. Intervention.

I'd ask Phillip—demand—that I be given the choreography for a challenging couple that could showcase my talent and put me back at the top of my peer group. *I want proper recognition. I want to be the one remembered for groundbreaking discoveries. I want to be respected and known as the best relational choreographer.*

CHAPTER 3

# Hand in Hand

~⁓

POPPY AND GEOFF HAD SEEN each other every day for the past month. I knew Phillip expected me to review all aspects of my assignment, including a diary that Poppy kept. Even though she and Geoff jelled, it wouldn't hurt to double check.

I expected her diary to be a leather-bound book. With gold edges. Maybe even a lock. Yet, she used a green spiral notebook leftover from a math class. She'd removed all of the math pages, as well as the paper shreds that get caught in the spiral binding. I paged through and found the most current entry—like someone who reads the last page of a novel first. I wanted to have the most up-to-date information for Phillip.

On October 11, Poppy wrote:

> *All of my friends have done it and say it's no big deal. I knew when I made love for the first time, it'd be special. Really special. I didn't want to make love with other guys. Because something always felt off—missing. It never felt right.*
>
> *I knew I'd have to fully trust the man. Making love is sacred and special. Something with the one person I completely trust. Period.*
>
> *Yesterday afternoon felt amazing. We made love for the first time—my first time. It wasn't like Becky, who, so shitfaced, couldn't even remember even having sex. And yes, for her—just sex. And we were both completely sober—the middle of the afternoon. Ernie was at practice. Thank God!*
>
> *And I wasn't afraid. Before we made love, I didn't even think about planning it. Like when, where, why, or how we might do it. It just happened. Naturally. I thought I might've felt guilty or ashamed. But I don't. I feel great.*
>
> *We laugh all the time. He's really tender. I always have butterflies. I love the way he kisses me—his moustache tickles my upper lip. My stomach flip-flops every time. Finally, I'm not afraid to open up. To share. He tells me all the time that I'm beautiful. Even sexy. No guy has ever told me I'm beautiful. Or sexy for that matter. Ha!*
>
> *And he is it. I love him.*

~⁓

I set the dog-eared diary back where I'd found it, under a corn-silk ivory-colored mohair sweater on a shelf in her closet. Poppy seemed very certain in her intentions and feelings for Geoff. I wondered if Geoff felt the same about their shared intimacy.

Next door in the Phi Delt House, I paused in the doorway of Geoff's room—the one he shared with Ernie. Their skinny room was a former hallway that connected two sorority houses. It felt like an aisle in a train car. Tight and long with beds and desks that lined the walls. Only one person could pass through at a time.

"So how's it going with Poppy?" Ernie's question turned into a chuckle.

Ernie stood no more than 5'8," with a personality that screamed fun. Like Happy, one of the Seven Dwarfs, Ernie's infectious laugh echoed in their narrow room. His high-pitched chuckle skipped, like a 45 record with a scratch.

"I'm crazy about her, Ernie. She's so cute." Geoff ran his hand through his hair and hooked the longer front bang behind his right ear. "I'm glad you were at practice yesterday afternoon." Geoff grinned. "Because we were here."

"Really?" Ernie's Ringo Starr haircut flopped as he looked up from his three-ring binder notebook. His sandy brown bangs drifted past his eyebrows and covered his slate-blue eyes—mischievous eyes. "How was it?"

"It was, considering it was her first time, wonderful." Geoff looked past Ernie's desk to the open window. The soft breeze rustled the leaves on the Spanish oaks. "Everything with her is easy." Geoff spoke in a breathy tone. He looked at Ernie's mouth, which had suddenly spread into a wry grin. "No, I know what you're thinking, you dog." He waved a disgusted hand at him. "*She's* not easy. *Being* with her is easy."

Ernie's smile quickly faded, like he'd just been summoned to the principal's office after a school prank. "No, no. I know." He nodded as he tried to recover. "That's good. I'm happy for you. Poppy's a really nice girl."

~ゥ

Near the end of October, Poppy and Geoff already showed perfect symmetry. Soulmate stuff.

At ten thirty on a Saturday October evening, a petite brunette paused outside of Geoff's fraternity house and pulled out a compact mirror on the steps of Mayflower Hall.

She blotted her raspberry-colored lipstick, even though she'd just done it next door in the foyer of the Theta House. The sorority girl snapped the compact shut and dropped it into her wooden-handled pink-and-green monogrammed purse. A Bermuda bag with four plastic pearl buttons for interchangeable covers. She adjusted the loosely tied silk scarf around her neck—a Gucci, with vines, butterflies, and flowers—and exhaled as she lifted the door latch to the Phi Delt House. She looked like many of the co-eds who attended the college.

Around five feet tall, Poppy's Theta sister, who had hazel-green eyes, took in the noisy living room. She scrutinized the fraternity gathering and wrinkled her nose at the combined smell of cigarettes, beer, and lingering athletic sweat. She pursed her glossy lips, seemingly to prevent any unpleasant odors from getting in.

To the right of the front door, an arched alcove with ornate crown molding seemed out of place for a frat house. Much too fancy. A stereo with a 33 LP played Earth, Wind and Fire's "September." The Bose 501 floor speakers blasted the song. "Bah-dee-ah, say do you remember, bah-dee-ah, dancing in September, bah-dee-ah, dee-ah, dee-ah..."

The beige carpeting, new last year according to my scroll, now looked like a topographical map. Beer, Purple Jesus party stains, and Sunday morning brunch celebrations with Screwdrivers and Bloody Marys had all taken their toll.

The L-shaped beige couches—upholstered in leather-like vinyl—appeared filled to capacity. Like a sofa oasis, men and women sat or leaned everywhere but on the cushions—the arms, the back, even the front of the sofa, where students sat on the floor. The top of the couch, sticky in spots, didn't bother the dozen or so co-eds.

Still hand-in-hand after dancing the jitterbug, Poppy and Geoff walked to the couches. Geoff used the back of his hand to wipe his damp forehead.

With flushed cheeks and breathing hard, Poppy leaned up on her toes and kissed Geoff's dimple. "That was so much fun—thank you."

Poppy's petite Theta sister came up beside Poppy near the vinyl oasis. "Y'all are such great dancers." She put her hand at the side of her mouth, so her Texas accent reached Poppy's ear.

Geoff handed Poppy a beer in the same opaque plastic cups that were used in the Pub. "Hi, Maureen," Geoff said and gave her the other beer.

"Thank you, Geoff. That's so sweet." She held her purse out in front of her and looked right and left for a suitable resting spot. Her lips tightened into a disapproving line as she tucked it under her arm. Coral manicured fingers held the brimming cup with both hands, and Maureen took a sip as if it were boiling water instead of beer.

As I watched Poppy's friend move on to flirt-speak with a fraternity brother of Geoff's, I opened my scroll and reviewed what my supervisor had taught us about a couple's viability. I wondered about the petite Texas girl and the scruffy guy at whom she batted mascara-laced eyelashes. They seemed mismatched. I recalled that Phillip had said that sometimes couples force a relationship through rationalizations.

I looked at the six subcategories of rationalization:

1. *Convenience. Same age, same location. Looks good on paper.*
2. *Though not perfect, he or she is close enough. They believe they'll grow to love each other.*
3. *Family or outside influence. Do the parents or others like him or her?*
4. *Socioeconomic. Money. Social connections.*
5. *Society. Cultural norms. People get the idea that it's time to settle down.*
6. *And all too common: the belief that one can change the other.*

"People can't change each other," I murmured as I set down my scroll and made a note to watch for the red flags that people tended to ignore. I remembered learning about the ego. The defense mechanisms inherent in every human being. Part of human evolution. I read further on my scroll.

*Rationalization. Denial. And fear.*

I left the frat house and pondered the concept of fear. During my internship, Phillip had once mentioned something about fear and how it can sabotage a relationship. He'd said something about people who have a fear of vulnerability—who had no pretense, who were honest and authentic—although I hadn't really understood what he meant.

A sentence darted across my scroll: *Through complete vulnerability, we achieve absolute empowerment. Vulnerability goes hand in hand with courage and is at the intersection of humility and courage.*

CHAPTER 4

# Trick and Treat

~⁀

UNDER THE LEADERSHIP OF HAMILTON Holt, the eighth president of Rollins College, Presidents Roosevelt and Truman visited the Rollins campus and most likely marveled at the elegance and beautiful surroundings. As the architectural visionary responsible for the splendor of the campus, Hamilton Holt was also credited with the Spanish Mediterranean design—the stucco buildings and barrel-tiled roofs that, in various shades of paprika and basketball orange, resembled clay flower pots that'd been cut in half.

On the back side of what used to be Sorority Row—though it was no longer called this since the fraternity of Phi Delta Theta had landed smack dab between the Kappa Kappa Gammas and Kappa Alpha Thetas—the lush foliage, oaks, and palms almost reached to shade the roof, but not quite. The tiled rooftops of the loggia slanted at a perfect angle for students to sunbathe—their bodies slathered in Johnson's baby oil.

Several weeks after the fraternity party, three of Poppy's tanned sisters reclined on the Theta roof and enjoyed a great view of the tennis courts where co-eds and some future Wimbledon-bound athletes practiced for hours on end. Finding a comfortable spot to lie down on the terra cotta tiles was an art, and the girls proved resourceful in their use of full-size quilts and half a dozen beach towels to pad the sunning platform. A *Princess and the Pea* kind of layering.

Poppy and Geoff walked past the courts, hand in hand—each carrying a book, a tube of suntan lotion on top, and a towel around their necks. Poppy was in a white bikini, her MAC— Milwaukee Athletic Club—shorts over the bikini bottom. Geoff's athletic shorts—in standard navy—bore the college's name and doubled as swim trunks.

"Like you're really going to study!" Catherine yelled from the roof as she hugged her knees. She adjusted her Ray-Ban aviators, and the mirrored lenses reflected greenery and sky—a miniature Monet, like the Impressionist's painting *Harbour at Argenteuil*. "I'm so sure," she shouted and threw an acorn she'd wiggled out from the tiles.

"We might." Poppy dodged the playful ammunition. "You never know."

"Y'all are so cute!" Maureen shouted and shielded her eyes under a pink floppy-brimmed hat. The lavender-and-pink-flowered accent ribbon on her hat matched the print of her one-piece bathing suit—also identical to the bow on her straw tote.

The third Theta, in cut-off shorts and a T-shirt, stood barefoot on the rounded tiles. She inched her way closer to the edge to be sure they heard her. "You two going to get some nooky?" Her husky voice echoed throughout the rear courtyard.

Poppy lifted her towel and covered her head. "That Hannah. She's wild." Poppy picked up her pace—an attempt to outrun the bawdy comment.

Geoff turned to look at the three sun worshippers and gave them a thumbs-up. "Now that's a good idea," he muttered.

Poppy yanked Geoff's arm as if he were a little kid tardy for school. "Agh! Does everyone know?"

"Probably." Geoff grinned. "C'mon, Honch. Don't pay attention to her. We have some water-skiing to do." He peeled back the towel from her hair. "Hannah always says shit like that."

The first time Poppy had spent the night in Geoff's room, his roommate, Ernie, had stumbled in at two thirty in the morning. In Geoff's twin bed, Poppy squeezed between Geoff and the wall—they'd been asleep. She'd pulled the sheet up to her chin like the wolf in *Little Red Riding Hood*.

"Don't let Ernie see me," she'd whispered to Geoff, panicked.

"Hmm?" He'd mumbled. "Don't worry. He'll be lucky to find his own bed. He won't even know you're here. Promise."

Her mouth, an inch above the sheet, breathed, "You're sure?"

"Yes, Honch, I'm sure." Geoff pulled Poppy in tighter.

Like many young lovers, Poppy and Geoff had given each other pet names. She called him Chief. He called her Honch. Once when they'd been undecided about whether to go to the Pub or to Harper's Bar, Geoff had said, "You decide. You're the head honcho."

She'd said, "If I'm head honcho, you're the chief."

Honch and Chief it was.

In a yellow Neoprene ski vest that seemed to gobble her chin, Poppy buckled the last black strap. When it clicked, she exhaled dramatically. "Okay, ready." She wriggled on the bench anchored to the ski dock.

She teetered before she entered the water. Geoff caught her, and his fingers grazed the side of her breast underneath the jacket. "Excuse me," he murmured.

"Squeeze you? I barely know you," Poppy muttered in a nervous giggle. "Okay," she sighed. "I guess I'm ready. I hope." She plopped in and made the water rush around her. "You love me, right? I know I'll make a fool of myself."

On her fourth attempt, Poppy stayed up on the two skis. She criss-crossed the wakes and made it back to the dock with a big smile on her face. Breathless, she sputtered like a little kid who'd just taken a ride on Disney's Splash Mountain. "That was fun."

"You did really well, Honch." Geoff leaned over the back of the boat and gathered the ski rope. "Here, grab the rope and I'll pull you in. You did great." As she climbed out of the water, he kissed her cheek, still wet from the lake.

At the boathouse, Poppy leaned on the creaky wooden door and watched Geoff's movements as he coiled the rope and hung up her ski jacket. The wet suits and lake-water-drenched ropes maintained a unique aroma in-side—like water inside a vase where flowers have overstayed their welcome. Spartan on the inside, the boathouse felt bare-bones all the way. There were slots for skis and jackets, and a couple of hooks for hanging ropes with lopsided nails in the wood paneling. Yet the boathouse had an allure to it. A homey feel. A musty old lake cottage that someone's beloved grandfather had kept for years. And the legacy of all of the skiers that'd come before.

Poppy came up behind Geoff as he stowed an extra life vest. "You know your way around the boat and this boathouse like Mario Andretti at Indy." She hugged his waist and laid her cool cheek and damp hair on his back. "I love you, Chief."

～♪

As a choreographer, I at first felt concerned that I'd given so few of the recommended nudges expected of new choreographers. Yet when I saw the blossoming relationship between Poppy and Geoff, I realized they didn't need any interventions from me. They bobbed along, like two lovers in an idyllic rowboat, the current always with them. The wind always at their back.

*I know Phillip said this is what the organization desires, but I can't see how these two are going to advance my career. No fights. No divisive words between them.*

*No tension. And their eyes—always locked on each other. Trusting eyes. Vulnerable. Playful eyes that say, "I adore you."*

It'd been a week since Geoff had taught Poppy to ski. They'd been together every day and each night during the week. Last Friday, Catherine had offered to "find a spot for herself" if Geoff wanted to stay over. Ernie had done the same on Saturday night. Young lovers with friends who opened doors so that they could close them.

The Friday afternoon before the Saturday night Halloween party, Poppy sat bare-foot, cross-legged on the living room floor of the Theta House. Next to her, a rectangular wooden coffee table—the surface of which had its share of nicks, scratches, and beer can rings. In khaki shorts, a navy-blue-and yellow Kappa Alpha Theta T-shirt, and her Dr. Scholl's sandals, she held back a strand of hair that'd come loose from her ponytail with one hand, and with the other, she painted a large white *M* on green poster board that'd been cut into a circle and laid on top of five sheets of newspaper.

When Geoff walked into the living room, Poppy jumped up and blocked his view of the painting project. She extended her arm, a flat-tipped paintbrush in her outstretched hand, and leaned into Geoff. He wrapped his arms loosely at her waist. "Hi, Honch." His lips touched hers and he, too, brushed back the errant lock of hair from her face. "Ooh. That was nice." He grinned and leaned in again for another kiss.

From deep inside of her, Poppy uttered a throaty giggle. "Hi, Chief."

He peered over her shoulder. "What're you working on?"

Poppy stood on her tiptoes and swayed like a grandfather clock pendulum. "You can't see yet." She grinned. "I'm almost done with yours."

"Done with my what?" Geoff's eyebrows scrunched closer.

"Our costumes for the Halloween party." Poppy kissed the dimpled side of his face. "Well, you'll probably figure it out anyway." She stepped sideways and revealed the crafts on the floor.

He bent over and rested his hands on his knees. The light from the courtyard doors reflected on the still glossy wet paint. "So . . ." He lifted his face to Poppy's, one skeptical eyebrow up, the other down.

She spread her arms wide, *ta-da* style. "We're M&M's, Chief." She beamed and kneeled down. "You're green and I'm orange."

He checked his navy Phi Delta Theta T-shirt and khaki shorts for white paint before he kicked off his topsiders—the white soles swallowed up in the rust-colored shag carpeting. He kneeled slowly and sat back on his heels. "M&M's . . . okay." He stared at the two-and-a-half-foot-wide circles. His tone sounded uncertain, as if he'd just been introduced to a column of the periodic table.

Poppy picked up four orange ribbons and four green ones. "We'll tie one on each side of us, and we'll wear them like sandwich boards." Her face tilted as she smiled.

"Yes, but these circle boards will only come to my thighs. What will I wear underneath?" Geoff's eyes bored into hers, yet his dimple reappeared.

"Well, I thought you'd wear these." Poppy held up a plastic bag with something green inside. "They're tights." She winced.

"Green tights? You've gotta be kidding me." He ran his hand through his hair. "I'm going to catch so much shit for wearing these." His knees collapsed to one side as he rested on his elbow.

"I thought we'd dress in one solid color from head to toe." She scooted on the floor and sat next to him, thigh to thigh. Still holding the paintbrush away, she turned and put her arms around his neck. She kissed his earlobe. "Please? It's just a costume," she murmured, "C'mon, Chief, it'll be fun."

His smile returned and he nodded. "When you look at me that way . . ." He pulled her waist into him and squeezed. He slid his hand up the back of her shirt. "Just checking to see what you'll be wearing under your M&M board," he murmured.

Poppy giggled and tugged her T-shirt down. "Geoffrey, not in the living room."

He breathed in her ear. "Oh, I'm sorry. I thought that was part of the costume."

Poppy closed her eyes and tittered, "It's only part of the costume for you."

"Oh, I see." He grinned. "Okay, I'll do it, but only if I get to tell everyone that I'm the peanut M&M—the one with the nuts."

With the paintbrush behind her, Poppy stroked his arm. "Thank you, Chief, for being such a good sport." Freehand, she finished the lettering. "I need one more favor."

He watched her arm move in fluid motions as she curled over the poster, her rhythmic strokes hypnotic. "You're not going to ask me to shave my legs, are you?"

"No, no." She laughed. "I think you'll like this favor. I have to turn in my next photography assignment by Wednesday. I have to have action shots. I thought it'd be neat if I took pics of you skiing. What d'you think?"

His fingers gently kneaded the shag rug. "*That* favor I like. I'd love to get some good action shots."

Poppy grinned—her eyes and hands on the poster. "You want some action shots or just some action?"

Geoff wiggled his eyebrows up and down and smiled. "Both."

~ ෨

In the darkroom, Poppy lifted the prints from the first tray, the developer. She eased them into the second, the stop bath. Under the red glow of the photo lamp—like a Gulf of Mexico sunset—Poppy stood in front of the second of four liquid-filled trays and checked her watch. Beneath the solution, the paper gently ebbed against the sides of the enamel tray.

"Oh my gosh. Look at him," she gasped as she used the rubber tongs to lift the image from the second tray. The black-and-white photo dripped as the tongs held the upper-right corner of the glossy paper. "And there's his dimple—he looks so good. These actually turned out," she whispered.

As she gently rocked the dark photo paper side to side in the tray, pale shades began to appear. Murky images took shape and morphed into identifiable forms.

In the slick still-wet photo, Geoff skied backward as he looked over his shoulder at Poppy in the boat. He balanced one foot on a single trick ski and the other in a toehold foot grip on the trick ski handle.

Yet his expression—that was the real trick she'd captured. His eyes glistened, even in the photo. The photo—still processing—revealed Geoff's arms out, palms up. It gave the viewer the idea that backward, no-hands skiing was a piece of cake. His smile, however, innocent and spirited, caused Poppy's face to flush—his smile, just for her. The tongs gripped the photo and quivered in Poppy's hands. She seemed reluctant to let go of it, to put it in the fixer. As if she wanted to memorize it.

"There you are," she breathed.

# CHAPTER 5

# The Emotional Clock

~

IN EARLY NOVEMBER, I RECEIVED my supervisor's update on my scroll. Phillip wanted us to integrate our assessments with the organization's new device, the Emotional Clock, a guide and tool that I'm supposed to use to measure how and why people make—or don't make—emotional decisions.

Seated in my haven in the Rollins chapel, I gazed at the screen of my scroll. The image was blurry at first, then morphed into clarity. A clockface with twelve numbers appeared; each number with a different human emotion beneath it. The numbers one through six indicated the right side of the clock as the discouraged side. The left side—empowerment.

> *One O'clock: Confusion. Something feels off. A few see this as a gift, if they allow vulnerability and courage to lead the way.*
>
> *Two O'clock: Anxiety. People may feel something like an elevator lurch. They often do not pay attention to this sensation. Here, some avoid conflict or care what others think, so they put on a mask. And some—familiar with this feeling—will accept this because in its familiarity, it is comfortable.*

I set down the scroll and tsked. "So something's better than nothing—better than being alone." I stared at the middle of the right side of the screen.

> *Three O'clock: Despair. Often, people can't see a way to make things better, and they lapse into hopelessness. This setting can last for minutes or years.*
>
> *Four O'clock: Shame and Guilt. A feeling of unworthiness. People have poor coping strategies—low self-concept. They may think they're unlovable. Unacceptable to others.*
>
> *Five O'clock: Anger. Everyone feels Anger. Women with Anger sometimes express it in a passive way. Men are often at home with more directness in their expression of Anger. Although counterintuitive, some feel empowered when angry because there is movement in Anger. The human ego's need to "be right" feels good to some, although it is one of the giant barriers to conflict resolution.*

I stared at the Six O'clock setting. *What is it I heard the fraternity guys say? "Shit or get off the pot?"*

> *Six O'clock: Fight or flight. Decision time—face-the-music time. Some will experience a desire to feel better, because they believe they have something more to gain by letting go of the Anger, or not. They will either summon the courage to advance clockwise or settle back into the familiarity of Anger. Or Shame and Guilt. Or Despair. Six O'clock is the junction of fear and courage.*

I sighed and laid the scroll on my lap. I reflected on what Phillip had said once about courage. "Many people can't summon the courage to take action because they don't know how, *and* they don't know where they're going. Often, going backward is the only thing they know how to do. It's familiar. They want all of the moments of their lives to be scripted. To know everything will be okay."

"But there *is* no script," I muttered. "No one's future is certain." I stared at the window. The lead panes outlined neat squares where nothing at this moment felt neat. *Trusting when the end is unknown?* I thought. "People are afraid to move forward unless they know what'll happen next," I murmured and glanced again at the image of the Emotional Clock.

> *Seven O'clock: Relief. It's a leap of faith to advance clockwise. No leap at all to backpedal to the familiar. With courage, people arrive at this setting. People find Relief because they've taken action.*
>
> *Eight O'clock: Forgiveness. Without the ability to forgive the self or another, people can't move forward. It's about letting go.*
>
> *Nine O'clock: Hopefulness. Once here, the door is open for an existing relationship to blossom, or to find a new one. The relationship with the self is whole. A person is at peace. Nine O'clock offers a chance for fulfillment—for people to build emotional momentum.*
>
> *Ten O'clock: Confidence. People feel good about themselves and aren't afraid to move forward. There's a surefootedness. A belief in themselves.*

I stared at the remaining two clock settings.

> *Eleven O'clock: Joy. The ability to experience pure happiness. Authentic glee.*

I thought of Poppy and Geoff—what Joy looked like with them. They always smiled and held hands. Exchanged intimate looks. They were playful. They enjoyed being together—all the time.

> *Twelve O'clock: Love. Love is about trust. And a willingness to be completely vulnerable. To fully open one's heart. Love is a joyous union of pure connection.*

"Definitely in love," I whispered as I reflected on Poppy and Geoff's passion; how they made each other laugh. Their comfort with each other, even when intimate. "They completely trust each other," I mused. "Although, it doesn't seem logical that vulnerability and love are connected."

I scrolled further down the page on my device. *Many get caught in an endless loop between Three and Six O'clock. When they can't get past Six, they fall back to Despair, Shame and Guilt, or Anger. And the cycle repeats. It takes courage to be encouraged or to be in the heart.*

"Emotional Clocks are meant to run clockwise," I murmured. "It's up to me to choreograph people to find courage, to keep them moving forward on the clock. Courage is the spring—the energy source of the clock. Without it, they can't advance past Six."

I set my scroll on the chair and stood. My head began to spin.

I felt overwhelmed. In a no-win scenario. *I have this great couple that doesn't need my help, because there's nothing for me to do. I'll never get recognition for the hard work it takes for a choreographer to keep couples together. And it's only through their success that I'll attain success.*

In my update from Phillip, he'd said all college couples are not created equal. Many are immature and have weak communication skills. He'd advised me to read their nonverbals—their body language. Facial expressions. Couples need constant reassurance. Daily affirmations—they need to cherish one another, not take each other for granted.

*My couple is fine. They don't need anything from me,* I thought, feeling a little disillusioned about my career.

When I left Knowles Chapel, it was dark out. The lighting around the campus offered spotty illumination for the errant student. I scoffed at the concretized words on the front of the chapel entrance—*Fiat Lux.* The school's motto, "Let there be light," seemed to be a sarcastic warning about the clarity and wisdom I lacked right now. The cicadas droned from the trees, adding to the cacophony of jumbled thoughts in my head. I turned and went back inside.

CHAPTER 6

# Big Eyes and
# Crooked Noses

~⁓

*I'M STILL IN A SLUMP—NO doubt about it.*

In the eight days since I'd studied my scroll's training material about the topic of the Emotional Clock, I found that my couple hadn't landed on the discouraged side of the clock. *How will I prove I'm great at getting results if I can't show my supervisor the step-by-step progression of their relationship?*

I found them in Poppy's room. She stood at her dresser, where the late-afternoon sun streamed in from the second-floor window. Poppy cleared off her jewelry box, hairbrush, and Rollins mug, an Ebony pencil and an 11x14 Strathmore drawing pad. She looked at the paper and stared at her face in the mirror. She chewed her lower lip and held the pad up for Geoff to see.

"That looks really good, Honch." Geoff leaned back on her bed—his elbows sunken in the navy comforter. His topsiders dangled off the side. "You've got that beautiful face just right." Poppy turned back to the mirror, her eyes wide-open—focused. "I think I have my eyes too close together. Throw me that eraser, please, will you?" She held out her arm behind her.

Geoff straightened, looking around the room. "Where is it?"

Her lower lip dropped open the way many women's mouths do when they apply mascara. Into the mirror, she mumbled, "On my nightstand. It's that gray thing."

"This?" He held up a gray ball of putty. "What the hell kind of an eraser is this?"

Poppy looked over and laughed. "It's a kneaded eraser." She smirked. "I *need* it."

Geoff tossed it, like a shortstop to first base.

"Thanks, Chief." She breathed out. "I can't believe this takes so long. I've done self-portraits before . . ." She turned and grimaced. "I feel badly making you wait for dinner." She glanced at the clock on her nightstand. "I'll be ready in a few minutes."

"I'm fine, Honch." He came up behind her. "It's fun to watch you."

Poppy squinted at the drawing and stared into the mirror again. "There. Now they're the proper distance apart, right?"

"I think so." He leaned back and forward again. "Are you talking about the eyes on the paper or on your face?" Geoff grinned.

Poppy swatted his tanned arm.

He rested his cheek on the side of her face. "Your eyes are perfect," he murmured. "So why are you spending so much time on this if it's not for an art class? You said it's for your relational studies class?"

"Mm-hmm. I'm the only art major in my group. The rest are English or political science majors." Poppy balled up the putty eraser and stretched a piece of it into a thin point. She dabbed at her drawing and extracted a dark edge from the corner of her hand-drawn eyes.

She looked at his reflection in the mirror. "This course has four segments: literature, history, science, and art. I'm horrible at the science part," she mumbled and cocked her head at the drawing. She used the side of her baby finger to blend the blackened pencil marks on her drawing, and smudged just above the eyelids.

"Your drawing is excellent. Your class will be blown away." His lips grazed the top of her head.

The next afternoon, Poppy sat on the steps outside of Orlando Hall. She tugged at a weed in between the cement cracks. Her hair fell forward and veiled her face.

In painter's pants and a rugby shirt, Geoff came up from behind her. He quietly set down his textbook, bent down, and gently poked his fingers into her waist. "Hi, Honch." He sat next to her and pulled back her hair. He kissed her cheek. "How'd they like your self-portrait in class this morning?"

Poppy turned away and faced Mills Lawn. Her eyes filled. "Awful."

"What?" Geoff's jaw dropped and he pivoted around to see her face. "What're you talking about?"

"I went there all excited. I knew I'd done a really good job. I mean, you know it took me *forever*." She turned to him, her cheeks already wet. "I put shading and value study and good contrast in there. Everybody else had smiley faces, two dots for eyes. A curve for a mouth. I mean theirs were pathetic." Her words limped out in a soggy tirade.

"What happened?" Geoff caressed her back.

"Mrs. Edwards, the art teacher," she spewed, "she held up each one and made positive comments, like, 'This picture is well balanced and centered.' Geoffrey, the eyes consisted of teeny black circles—no shading. Nothing." She wiped her nose with the back of her hand, and took a breath. "She tacks mine on the board, and the very first thing—the *very* first thing she says is, 'Okay. What's wrong with this picture?'" Poppy's bottom lip trembled.

Geoff gasped. "What?"

"Yeah. Everyone else did just that. They gasped. Before class, they said, 'Yours is so good. You're so amazing. That's totally an *A*.' They loved it. And she ignored them. Kept looking for stuff wrong with my picture."

"I don't understand. Why did she pick on you?" Geoff leaned forward, his elbows on his knees. "This is relational studies, right?"

"Yes. We have a different teacher for each segment." She straightened and sniffled. "So on our art rotation this week, we got the art department chair. I thought she liked me. Not!" She spat out and shook her head at Geoff. "I can't believe she embarrassed me in front of everyone." She bristled. "Said I drew my eyes *too big*."

"C'mon, let's walk back." Geoff lifted her elbow and leaned back to grab his books. "You've had her for other art classes, right?"

Poppy shuffled, her wooden sandals making a clomp, clomp sound. "Yeah. Art history and my studio class. She's always been so nice to me." Poppy turned to face him and started walking backward. "And I know why my eyes were so big. I was, like, bug-eyed staring in the mirror for a hundred hours. Of course they're going to be big. I had to concentrate." She snapped at the ground.

"And you're the only art major in this course, right?"

"Right, but . . ." She turned to walk by his side.

"Honch, don't you see?" Geoff stopped them on the walkway near Ward Hall, and held her wrist. "You're a ringer."

"What d'you mean? She totally humiliated me." Poppy searched his face. "I feel so stupid." Fresh tears formed in her eyes.

"Don't you see? It'd be like if I showed up for an intro to water-skiing class. Of course I'd be the best one there. And the coach would be all over me." Geoff opened up his arms. "He'd use me to set an example of what to do and *what not* to do."

"He wouldn't embarrass you in front of twenty people." Poppy crossed her arms over her stomach.

"Yeah, he might. If I acted like a hotshot—expected to impress everyone."

"I didn't draw it to impress everyone," she scoffed. "I wanted to do well for me."

"I know that," Geoff said gently, as his hand caressed her shoulder.

"It wasn't just you, by the way, who watched me draw it. C-Bell said she wasn't even going to go to class when she saw mine. Some students drew a line like an *L* for their nose. I mean, c'mon." Her voice pitched up.

"Come up to my room for a little bit. I'll show you what I can draw." He grinned.

"The blinds?" She smirked and took his hand in hers.

"How'd you know?" He wiggled his eyebrows twice.

When they got upstairs to his room, Poppy plopped down on Geoff's bed and sighed. "Thanks for listening. I'm too sensitive, I guess." She patted his comforter for him to sit. "You're wonderful."

"I don't care what that silly teacher said." Geoff sat next to her. "I think your eyes and face are perfect." He kissed the corner of her left eye.

"Even though I have flaws?" She lay her cheek on his, and her eyelashes caressed his face with butterfly kisses. "Like my crooked nose?" She murmured.

"What!" Geoff bolted upright. He stood above the bed and stared at her with mock seriousness. "You never told me you had a crooked nose." He ran his hands through his hair. "This changes everything."

Poppy's body shook with silent laughter as she clamped a hand around her waist. "Oh God. Stop!" She gasped. "I can't breathe!"

"See, Honch?" Geoff traced his finger along the slightly curved bridge of his nose. "Mine's a little off center, too." He wrapped his arms around her. "I still think you're perfect. Crooked nose and all."

The circular staircase that led to the bell tower of Knowles Chapel—off limits to the students—proved to be a good thinking spot for me. The winding metal stairs and wrought-iron gate gave me a sense of solidness, as if nothing could fall apart. I found the solitude perfect to evaluate the progress of my assignment.

Concerned at first by Poppy's distress, I monitored them and noticed her at Three O'Clock. Despair. Not Despair about them as a couple, but about the perceived betrayal from her teacher. But—without my intervention—Geoff had returned her to the left side of the clock.

I thought about what Phillip had cautioned, that couples may take each other for granted. *I won't let that happen with Poppy and Geoff. Not that it ever would anyway.*

Poppy lay on her stomach in the center of Geoff's bed, and the thin white piping on the navy-blue comforter made an impression on her forearm. With her knees bent and ankles crossed above her back, she absentmindedly straightened a wrinkle. Geoff, cross-legged, leaned against the wall. His macroeconomics textbook rested on his lap. With one hand on a page of the book, and the other twiddling the corner of his moustache, Geoff glanced at Poppy and smiled.

With a psychology textbook just below her chin—sheets of paper that said *Exam Review* tucked inside the pages—Poppy twirled a strand of hair into what looked like a Pepperidge Farm Pirouette cookie. Her dark lashes grazed the top of her cheekbones, and when she looked up, she caught Geoff's smile. "Oh, hi," she giggled. "Why aren't you studying?"

He wriggled his eyebrows. "I *am* studying." His lips curved into a lopsided grin.

Poppy sat up and scooched to face Geoff. "Are you excited to go home for Christmas? Can you believe it's only two weeks away?" She raised her eyelids.

I tried to do what my supervisor wanted—focus on facial expressions. Poppy had a curious look—a look like several different thoughts were occurring at once. Like voice bubbles that all talked at the same time.

Her fingers smoothed the corners of her textbook, and she looked down. "It would be great if you could visit after Christmas. And stay for New Year's Eve." Poppy said it fast, as if she knew it was a long shot.

Geoff's mouth spread out wide. "That'd be great! I'd love to come." Inches from her face, he tilted and kissed her mouth. "I'll check with my parents on Sunday night."

"Really?" She propped herself up on her knees, as her textbook flopped closed. "You think they might actually let you come? Visit during the break?"

"Yes, they'd let me come." His forehead scrunched into wavy lines, and he smiled. "They might let me visit as well."

"Geofffreeeyyy." Poppy laughed.

~⁀

I headed back to Knowles and immediately got out my scroll. I was sure there'd be something in it about meeting family. Phillip warned that sometimes when couples see each other outside of the bubble of their college world, things can change. *What if Poppy's parents don't like him?* I wondered. *And factor in friends who sometimes stir things up. Have I done all I can to make sure that these two are on solid footing?*

I reviewed all of the times they'd been together in the past month. They'd gone to Beef and Bottle restaurant, sat in a booth, both on the same side. They went to the Melting Pot for fondue, to Park Avenue for ice cream. Harper's for drinks. Rosie O'Grady's in a big group for nickel beer night. The Park Plaza for a romantic dinner. And every day on campus.

I wanted to achieve my objective to be at the top—above all other choreographers.

# CHAPTER 7

# Welcome Aboard

~

ON THURSDAY, DECEMBER 29, WITH Poppy at Milwaukee's Mitchell Field, I watched as she stood at the window. Her excited breath fogged the glass and her hands framed her face as she attempted to see her college lover in the teeny airplane window. The runway, chalky white from salt, welcomed United flight 793—Geoff's plane from Cleveland. The bright sun, blinding from a fresh overnight snowfall, caused Poppy's eyes to water.

She wore a wool cape—all creamy white except for black trim on the edges—one of the gifts she'd received from her grandfather on their European junket last summer. Just before she'd met Geoff. Before she'd discovered love.

When the plane parked behind the Jetway, Poppy joined a pack of greeters and jockeyed herself around the small crowd at the gate. She craned her neck and danced on her tiptoes, as she tried to see around large navy and green ski parkas that obscured her view. Finally, she saw him—his familiar walk. He spotted her, too. Poppy jumped up and down, excited. The kind of excitement only young lovers feel. Geoff beamed.

"There's my Honch." Geoff's forest-green parka swished when he hugged her.

"I missed you so much." Poppy buried her face in the collar of his puffy jacket.

Geoff snuggled his hands inside her cape. "Ooh, I like this." His eyes twinkled. "I can find all kinds of nice things in here."

"Geoffrey." She giggled. "Not in front of everyone." She grinned and removed his hands with prissy reluctance.

They made their way down the concourse and folded their hands together just as they'd done every day on campus.

They both shivered with the seven-degree blast as they stepped outside, the wind chill minus 18. As they drove north on Highway 43, Geoff rubbed his hands together, his still-tanned fingers hovering in front of the heat vents as if at a campfire.

"Cedarburg is about a half hour north of Milwaukee." Poppy glanced in her rearview mirror before she looked at Geoff. "It's kind of in the boonies." She winced.

After fifteen more miles in light traffic, where Poppy pointed out numerous landmarks—the Allen Bradley Clock, the Schlitz Brewery, and her University School—the heater finally provided warmth in the vehicle. Geoff looked out the passenger window and squinted at the expanse of farmlands, covered in a marshmallow-like coating of snow and separated by the occasional farmhouse, barn, and silo.

The Buick's tires crunched on the snow and ice as they pulled into the driveway. With the untouched snow on the large front lawn, the home—painted the color of parchment and accented by dark-green shutters and a burgundy front door—looked like a hand-painted Christmas card. Poppy angled the Buick into the first spot of the carport, sixty feet off to the right of the main house.

From the covered carport, Geoff stood at the trunk of the Buick and looked at the other four cars—a gold four-door Cadillac, a navy BMW coupe, another four-door Cadillac, this one black. And a marine-blue MG Midget.

"Oh, you have a little MG. That looks fun." Geoff walked over to it.

"It's a riot to drive." Poppy ran her gloved hand over the convertible top. "My dad has it as his *extra* car."

Geoff peered into the car window. "And you know how to shift this?"

"I do." Poppy lifted her chin. "I'm not just another pretty face, you know."

"I *do* know." He grinned. "I'm impressed." He grabbed his suitcase from the trunk of the Buick, and his eyes wandered to the vertical-board barn a few feet away, the north end of which featured an off-center wagon entry, and six-paned stanchion windows above. "Is that the barn with the chickens?"

"Yep." Poppy tugged her cape tightly under her chin and shivered. "Fresh eggs, and my mom makes yummy soufflés. C'mon Chief, let's go inside. You'll stay in the guesthouse." Poppy pointed to their right. "Beyond that is the other barn." Poppy shielded her eyes from the sun's reflection off the snow and gestured to her right. "And of course, that's the pool."

Geoff paused at the bottom of the steps to the main house, his leather glove resting on the wrought-iron railing. "This is a cool place, Honch."

"Okay, before we go in." Poppy paused. "I'll just warn you that my brother might say something off-color. Some reference to sex." She whispered the last word as if nice girls weren't even allowed to say it. "He teases me all the time. Even though he's three and a half years older, he's *so* immature." Poppy scoffed and swung open the storm door. "We're here!" Poppy sang out.

At about six feet tall, with brown hair the color of his sister's, Stacy greeted Geoff. "Welcome aboard!" He gave Geoff a hearty handshake and grinned. His dark-brown eyes flashed, and his face revealed his authentic five o'clock shadow.

As they entered through the back hallway into the kitchen, Poppy hung up Geoff's jacket and her cape. "I can't believe my bro remembered you're a sailor." She smirked. "Usually, he doesn't pay attention to *anything* I say."

Stacy held his hands up in a mock surrender. "What're you talking about? Geoff's a skier. Lives in Cleveland. His dad's a doctor. He has an older brother about my age."

"You're so bad." Poppy swatted her gloves at her brother, who dodged the leather attack and headed into the kitchen. "Stop showing off."

From a swinging door in the dining room, Valerie Terris joined them in the kitchen. Her wide and welcoming smile filled the room. With short brown hair with natural curls streaked blond, Valerie appeared to be an older replica of Poppy. Her eye shadow, robin's egg blue, accented the whites of her dark-brown eyes.

"Hi, Geoff!" Valerie extended the first three manicured fingers on her right hand—a ladylike handshake that drooped into his hand. "I'm so happy to meet you. Pops has told us so much about you." She gently shook his hand, and the ruffles on the cuffs of her burgundy blouse slightly fluttered.

"Good to meet you as well, Mrs. Terris. Thanks for having me." Geoff smiled and held her fingers, not sure if he should continue to lightly shake them or not.

"Please, call me Valerie." Her eyes twinkled as she released Geoff's hand. "All the kids do."

"They do." Poppy rocked on her tiptoes, her palms on the counter.

From the large cutting board on the counter, Valerie removed cellophane from a plate of cheese and crackers. "Come and sit." Valerie gestured to the oval wooden table by the bay window that overlooked the carport and chicken barn. "Was your flight on time, Geoff?"

"Yes, right on time." Geoff smiled and looked down. "And who's this?" Geoff scooped up a purring gray cat that weaved around his legs.

"The Gray Maggot." Stacy said and slid out one of the six oak chairs. He plopped down as the antique wood groaned. "Dumb cat," he scoffed. "Not allowed in the house."

"Isn't that a terrible name, Geoffrey?" Poppy lamented as she sat next to Geoff. "My dad insisted we get a cat to keep the mice out of the chicken coop. He didn't want us to get attached, so Stacy gave him that awful name." Poppy glared at her brother. "But I love him. I sneak him inside in the winter—put him under my blanket." She leaned over and put her hand to Geoff's ear. "But don't tell my dad," she half-whispered.

"What a horrible name for such a sweet little cat." Geoff stroked the still-purring cat. The Gray Maggot closed his green eyes—content. As if the cat knew a cat lover when it saw one. "I love your home," Geoff said, as he glanced around. The nineteenth-century wall clock chimed six times, its ring out of tune.

"Thank you. It's so far from everything, but I love it." Valerie slid the cheese plate in front of Geoff. "Would you like a cheese and cracker?"

"Thank you." As though the cat were fluid, he poured the animal from his hands to the floor.

"It's Brie. A staple in our house." Poppy took a round cracker and plopped the room-temperature cheese on top. It oozed to the edge of the cracker.

Valerie smiled and scooted the plate in front of Stacy. "George and I like all things French."

"Where's Dad?" Poppy hopped up and peered around the eggshell-painted cupboards. "In the library?"

From the other side of the front hall, a television, on a low volume, broadcasted Walter Cronkite's voice.

Poppy touched Geoff's arm. "Let's say hi to my dad."

The foyer, with dark wooden floors and a large oriental carpet, led to a curved staircase that flowed into the cozy family room. Hand in hand, Poppy and Geoff walked into the room and near two oversized sofas at right angles to each other. A square wooden coffee table faced the television in the corner, a built-in bookcase on either side of the wide entry. Across from the doorway, the wall of windows looked east and revealed seventy acres of cornfields.

To the left of the door, a fire with embers that rumbled and separated from the logs within the marble hearth warmed the room.

Just beyond—in a small alcove in the room—sat an ornate mahogany desk. At the top of the desk, five brass candlesticks with rustic ginger-colored candles stood ready to cast candlelight on the polished desk. The candlesticks, neatly arranged between a pair of blue-and-white antique vases, appeared to be sentinels of work, play, and family. The room, scenic and well-orchestrated, looked as if it had jumped off a page of *Better Homes and Gardens*.

A tie—wine-colored claret with tiny beige fleur-de-lis—was neatly folded and draped at the edge of the mahogany desk.

A dark-haired man with graying temples leaned back in a burnt orange leather chair, the creaky springs objecting. He leaned over the leather-edge blotter on his desk, finger-checking a ledger.

Poppy led Geoff into the room. "Hi, Dad!" Poppy grinned and kissed her father's cheek when he leapt up. "This is Geoff Spencer."

"Hi, honey. Good to meet you, Geoff," he said, and gripped Geoff's hand with a tugging handshake so strong that Geoff almost lost his balance.

"Daaad," Poppy sang in a nervous giggle.

In brown Allen Edmonds laced shoes, charcoal trousers, a tan-and-gray blended tweed sport-coat with brown leather buttons, George Terris stood about six feet. His oval face had a strong jaw and hazel eyes that appeared as though they'd seen a lot of life. Poppy's father looked Geoff smack dab in his eyes.

"Hi, Mr. Terris." Geoff rebalanced himself. "Thank you for having me here."

George Terris swiveled his chair around and backed into it. He motioned for his daughter and Geoff to sit on the couch. He looked at Geoff. "So you're from Cleveland," he said, as he cut to the chase. "Too bad about the Browns. Lost their last four games." He rested his elbows on the arms of his chair.

Geoff nodded and quickly dove into the familiar topic. "Yes, that was too bad. They had a decent season initially."

George Terris swatted the air. "At least the Browns did better than the Packers."

"Dad took me to the Packer games. We froze." Poppy hugged herself. "But I didn't care."

Geoff looked from Poppy to her father. "I used to go to all the games with *my* dad." Geoff popped his head up in an a-ha way. "His name is George as well."

"Ha," George said and smiled. "I understand your dad's a doctor?"

"Yes, chief of orthopedics at Saint Luke's Hospital." Geoff sat sideways on the couch and folded his hands over one knee.

"Oh. Chief of orthopedics." George rocked forward, his tone impressed. "You guys go on. Get Geoff settled over there in the guesthouse. Tomorrow, you kids can take the snowmobile on the trails." George spun his chair by walking his feet back to his desk. "Let us know if you need anything. Glad you're here, Geoff."

"Thanks, Mr. Terris." Geoff smiled at Poppy. "I'm glad I'm here, too."

Poppy's father leaned back in the noisy chair and called out as they left the room, "Pops, I swept the pathway when I got home. It might still be slippery, so be careful."

"Thanks, Dad." Poppy squeezed Geoff's hand. "We will." She skipped a few steps and spun in front of Geoff. "They love you," she whispered. "I can tell." She stuck her head in the kitchen doorway. "I'm taking Geoff over, Mom. Be back in a few."

Geoff, with suitcase in hand, followed Poppy on the curved path to his quarters, the round stepping stones dusted with snow. The fieldstone and wood structure looked nothing like the clapboard colonial—more like it belonged to the era of *Little House on the Prairie*. It was in the back of the house, which stood on eighty acres.

With her hand on the black iron thumb latch, Poppy turned around and winked at Geoff. "I wish you could stay in the main house, but we'll snuggle over here, too."

Geoff grinned and looked above the door, as a rooster weather vane creaked on the roof in protest to the icy wind. "Wow, this is cool. How old is this place?" Geoff ducked his head as he went in.

"Umm, 1850, I think. It's the original farmhouse." Poppy reached under an ecru lampshade and flicked on the light, a bulbous brass table lamp. Timber beams in the ceiling and in between the stone on all four walls gave it a rustic feel. A great-grandfatherly appeal.

They dipped their heads under the open-riser staircase and stepped down into an addition to the original saltbox home. The hallway groaned under their passage.

"How cool." Geoff's eyes surveyed the ten-foot-long fieldstone hearth. Black log skeletons remained in the grate.

"The fire should keep you warm after I leave." She nibbled his earlobe.

Geoff ginned and dropped his luggage on the wooden floor near the blue-and-white-checkered fold-out sofa.

"Don't you love this bar?" She ran her hand along the varnished top. The maple bar-top's curve measured close to twelve feet. "We keep the stereo back here," she said as she walked behind the counter. "What may I get for you, sir?" she purred.

Geoff followed her and kissed the side of her head. "What a great place to throw a party." His eyes took in the liquor bottles, wine, and 33 LP albums—all intermingled. As if everyone knew you had to pour a drink and change a record as part of the predictable etiquette.

Geoff's eyes widened at the furry floor covering in front of the fireplace and couch. "A bearskin rug." He grinned. "I'd like to get your bare skin on that rug."

Poppy tittered. "That'd be nice." She nuzzled her nose into his neck.

On Saturday morning, the day after Poppy and Geoff's invigorating snowmobile outing, they headed downtown. Geoff adjusted the heater vent in front of him. "I'm glad I'll meet your grandfather, Honch. From what you've shared about your trip with him from last summer, he sounds like a remarkable man."

Poppy briefly rested her bare hand on Geoff's arm. "He *is* wonderful." Her eyelids fluttered in a lazy blink. "He's eighty-two years old, going on forty. He calls me 'Poochie.'" Poppy grinned. "He lives downtown at the MAC—the Milwaukee Athletic Club." She held an imaginary cigar to her mouth. "He always has a cigar. Sometimes lit, sometimes not."

"Poochie?" Geoff chuckled at the name.

"Yep, that's it." Poppy smiled. "He's one of the top five tobacco and sundries distributors in the country. He always gives to others—he's adored by everyone in the Milwaukee community. He's really good at gin rummy—plays all the time." Poppy's bottom lip rolled into a pretend pout. "He definitely wins every time we play."

Geoff raised his eyebrows. "And you forgot to mention that he spoils you rotten."

"He does." Poppy grinned. "And just with me, he calls you, 'Sailor Boy.'"

Poppy's grandfather stood and dabbed the tip of his cigar into the ashtray—smoke lingered above the table. At six feet tall, Stanley Stacy, with neatly combed thinning silver hair, looked sharp in a gray suit with a light-blue shirt. Poppy's grandfather smiled at Geoff, his coffee-brown eyes warm and engaging like his daughter Valerie's. Stanley seemed archetypal to me—the wise man.

After they'd finished lunch, Stanley leaned back in his ivory-and-gold armchair, an unlit cigar in his fingers. "It has come to my attention . . ." Stanley rolled the cigar in between his thumb and two fingers. "That my granddaughter has taken a fancy to you." His sage eyes gleamed.

"Well, Stanley, I've taken a fancy to her, too." Geoff smiled at him and rested his hand on top of Poppy's.

The three of them continued with easy conversation. Poppy prompted her grandfather to share highlights of their trip to Europe. Geoff leaned forward on his elbows, his eyes wide, eager to hear from the sage octogenarian.

As I watched him, it occurred to me that Stanley's eyes gave people the immediate understanding that he understood them. They were eyes that said they're already one step ahead of you. They knew what you were going to say before you even thought it.

When Geoff had excused himself to the restroom, Poppy leaned close to her grandfather. "Well, what d'you think?" Poppy put her hand on his, her face eager.

"Sailor Boy?" With his relit cigar raised off to his side, Stanley paused to study her face. "He seems like a nice young man." He smiled through a veil of Partagás smoke.

"I love him." With her finger, she touched the gold signet ring on her grandfather's hand. She met his eyes and whispered. "He's so good to me."

"Poochie." Stanley smiled and glanced down. He looked at Poppy, and his eyes glistened from the reflection of the chandeliers. "If he's good enough for my precious granddaughter, he's good enough for me."

In the foyer of her home, Valerie slipped on her three-quarter-length mink coat. "We should be home by twelve thirty." She wiggled her fingers into black leather gloves with mink cuffs. "So you kids aren't going out? No New Year's Eve's parties?"

"No." Poppy crossed her arms and rubbed them. "We're going to get things ready for tomorrow. Set things up for our Poppy Bowl party." She grinned at Geoff.

"You'll meet Cecelia. And Jack and Jenny, whom I introduced a few years ago. Remember Jenny's the one who corrupted me?"

Geoff grinned.

"So a dozen kids tomorrow." Valerie nodded. "We'll have plenty of food."

The front door opened, and a blast of frigid air filled the foyer. With one hand on the door knob, George Terris reached out for his wife's hand. "Car's all warmed up, honey." He glanced at Poppy and Geoff. "You guys have fun. I wish *we* could stay in and be warm." He chuckled as he eased his wife's elbow down the four steps at the front door. "And keep that fire going in the library, Geoff. Please throw some more logs on."

"Sure will. Have fun." Geoff leaned above Poppy and pushed the door shut. "Finally." He grinned. "Alone."

"Do you want to see my room?" she murmured.

"Sure do." He kissed her as she walked up the stairs backward. He untucked her cream-colored turtleneck from her black wool slacks.

"Wait," she giggled, tugging. "Wait 'til we get to my room." Poppy flicked off the light switch in her room and approached the dormer window over the front door.

Geoff stood behind her. "They're gone," he murmured, as he unbuttoned his shirt.

She sat on the edge of the bed, her eyes darting from Geoff to the window.

"A twin bed?" Geoff sighed. "Couldn't you have something bigger?"

"Doesn't this bed make you feel like we're still at school?" Poppy rested on one elbow, languid. And suddenly, as if she'd slept through an alarm, she bolted up. "What if they come back? Like if they forgot something?" She searched Geoff's face. "You know my mother thinks I'm still pure as the driven snow."

"Poppy . . ." Geoff rested his hands on her waist. He kissed her neck, her cheek, and the corners of her lips. "They're gone," he whispered, as he lowered them to the bed.

Her concerns slipped away, as did her clothes. "Welcome aboard," she purred.

# CHAPTER 8

# Happiest Birthday

~⁹

I SAT BY LAKE VIRGINIA and reviewed my notes. Even though I hadn't nudged my couple much, I hoped Phillip would be impressed with their Emotional Clock location.

I opened the scroll and reviewed the past few weeks. The nudge for Geoff to visit Poppy in Wisconsin had worked like a charm. Geoff had fit right in with Poppy's family—aware of the same social customs and lifestyles, right down to the same bright patchwork corduroy pants—red, navy, and green squares—that both George Terris and Geoff sported.

With her Rose Bowl party, Poppy seemed comforted that their two University Schools—and worlds—appeared interchangeable, as were their college-aged peers. Whether they'd reminisced about frat keg parties, high school glee clubs, soccer, or summers at the lake, their common ground proved unmistakable.

~⁹

"C-Bell, I'm surprising Geoff tonight." Poppy opened her closet door so quickly it almost dislodged from the hinges. She slid each hanger fast, as though in a race. On the metal rod, the hangers sounded off: *shwick, schwick, schwick.* "I need something nice to wear. Pretty."

"Where are you going?" Cross-legged, in faded and frayed cut-off jean shorts with a gold Theta T-shirt, Catherine sat on her bed and folded her laundry.

"We're going to celebrate his birthday *early*. It's on Monday." Poppy inspected a white-and-navy skirt. "And C-Bell," she whispered, "I booked us a room at the Park Plaza."

"Wow!" Her sky-blue eyes widened and her hands dropped in mid fold. "That's nice." She grinned, as she shook out a wrinkly denim shirt. "When do you leave?"

"In a few minutes. He'll come here first." Poppy returned to her closet and hung up the skirt. After several *schwick, schwick, schwicks* of the hangers, she held out a halter-top dress with a small black-and-white floral print. "Do you like this one?"

Catherine nodded. "Geoff will *really* like that. Your cleavage will show."

Poppy shook her head. "Oh, and I wonder if I can borrow your nightie?" Poppy grinned, zipped up her duffle bag, and set it at the floor of the closet.

"My nightie?" Catherine's puzzled expression shifted when she noticed Geoff in the doorway. Poppy hadn't noticed him yet. "Ohhh, my *nightie.*'" She smiled, her head nodding. "The nightie I don't wear, or *even own*? I get it."

With her bag packed, Poppy continued to inventory her clothes. I pulled up the scroll and questioned this activity. The report mentioned this behavior—the second-guessing of original decisions—so common to women. Poppy's arms, tangled in with the plastic and fabric hangers, worked faster than a drycleaner's rotary chain.

"You didn't tell me to pack a nightie." His arms crossed, Geoff, dressed in his light-blue oxford shirt and dress khakis, leaned in the open doorway.

"Oh!" Poppy peered around the closet door. "You're here."

Geoff walked in. "I still don't know what's going on."

"You'll see." Catherine's cheeks pinked. "You're gonna like it." Her voice sang out the words "like it."

"Thanks, C-Bell." Poppy leaned over the plastic laundry basket and gave her roommate a loose hug. "I'll see you tomorrow." She winked.

Geoff took Poppy's bag, a quilted French print design. Pierre Deux. "Okay, Honch. Where are we off to?"

"You'll see." She grinned as they walked.

Geoff pulled at his mustache, a gesture I'd come to know as both eager and thoughtful. He watched her halter straps as they moved silently on her tanned back.

"We'll walk there." Poppy pointed down Park Avenue where pedestrians strolled, cardigan sweaters thrown over the shoulders of a few women, and Shetland wool sleeves tied around necks in floppy knots on the men.

Geoff glanced in as they passed the East India Emporium and then, turning back to the street, squinted into the setting sun.

In a grand gesture, Poppy held out her arm at a pair of double glass doors with dark cherry frames. "Voila." She smiled.

Geoff looked up at dozens of ferns that fluttered over balconies above the front-entrance awning. He stared at Poppy, and his jaw fell.

"Welcome to the Park Plaza Hotel." Poppy bowed and held the door open for him. "Right this way, sir."

Above the entrance, where the only natural light shined, six vertical windows, like dominos, lined the doorway. The all-wood walls in the foyer made the lobby dark, in spite of two inset fan-shaped windows that served more as a display on either side of the front doors.

Spanish antique tiles on the floor peeked out from an oriental rug that looked to be twenty by thirty feet. A mirror ran the length of one wall, where an oversized camel-colored leather couch and matching chairs— deeply tufted—welcomed guests who'd become enchanted by green palms, pale pink hydrangea, and a pair of Tiffany lamps. An enormous ceramic planter, painted in the trompe l'oeil style to look like a wicker basket, held an enormous variety of green sprigs. Plush and inviting.

Just two feet from the all-cherry front desk, a wooden staircase with an oriental runner and large brass handrails led guests upstairs under an ivory-painted tray ceiling.

Geoff blinked his way inside as he took in his surroundings. He looked back at Poppy, a dazed expression on his face. "How can we *do* this?"

"Well, we *are* twenty-one." Poppy looped her elbow in his.

Geoff spoke to their reflection in the mirror. "You made a reservation?" Poppy grinned a nod.

"You got us a room here?" Still astonished, yet grinning with uncon- ditional joy, he rephrased his earlier question. As if asking it in a new way would convince him he wasn't in a dream. Not tangible. Not part of every male college student's reverie.

Geoff lowered their bags slowly. "How will you—or we—pay for this?"

"I have my ways." A coy smile. "Stay right here," she whispered in his ear. "I'll get the key."

A young man in a white dress shirt and navy slacks checked Poppy in. He handed her a gold key on a ring, an oval brass disc etched with *Park Plaza Hotel Room 220.*

The stairway's soft lighting caused both of their eyelids to flicker. Geoff set down their bags and turned the key. "Wow Honch, look at this," he said and burst into the room, leaving their suitcases in the hall. "And a bal- cony." He turned sideways, and his dimple flashed at Poppy. He ceremoni- ously opened the French veranda doors that overlooked Park Avenue. He squeezed past the two wicker chairs and table, and leaned his elbows on the wrought-iron railing like an excited tourist on Bourbon Street in the French Quarter during Mardi Gras.

Poppy stood behind him and softly clapped her hands together, a silent acknowledgement to herself that she'd done it. She'd surprised him.

Geoff turned, his expression pure delight. "I can't believe we're actually *staying* here." His gaze drifted past Poppy and fell on the brass bed. He rushed over and sat on the edge. "Oh my God, a king-size bed!" He jiggled up and down and patted the downy pink-green-and-white floral spread—an invitation for Poppy. He wiggled his eyebrows. "I can't wait to check *this* out with you."

Poppy kissed his dimple. "So you like your birthday present so far?"

"Are you kidding?" He leapt up and opened the hand-painted doors of the armoire, the glossy mahogany shelves an offer to make hotel guests at home. "This is great." He spun back to look around the room. His eyes fell on the open door where their luggage remained—dumped in the excitement. "Oh shit. I forgot our stuff."

At the balcony entrance, Geoff turned his head toward the room. He waved her over. "C'mere Honch."

She ducked under his arm, and his hand rested on her shoulder. "I love that I surprised you." She lifted her chin. "Do you know where we'll have dinner?"

"No, where?" He gazed at her face as if it held the answers to all life's mysteries.

Poppy steered Geoff inside. "Downstairs, at the Park Plaza Gardens."

"That's easy." He laid his hands on her waist and steered her backward. "Afterward, we can come right upstairs and explore this," he whispered and guided her to sit on the edge of the bed.

"Okay." She grinned and straightened. She folded her hands on her lap and, with a soft voice, said, "I need to ask a favor of you."

His hand on her back, he faced her, his expression earnest. "Sure, Honch."

"After dinner, you know, when we head back up here." Her words stumbled. "I'm just wondering . . ." She searched his face for something.

"What is it, Honch?" Geoff shifted sideways, his knee resting on the bed.

"Well, do you mind doing me a favor? I know it's silly..." Poppy looked down at her fingers.

Geoff lowered his head to see her eyes. "What is it, Honch? Just tell me."

Poppy took a breath and hurriedly exhaled her request. "Would you come up to our room here a few minutes before me? And then I'll follow."

The corners of Geoff's mouth drifted inward. "Okaaaaay." He leaned back. "And *why* am I doing this?" His forehead creased in curious confusion.

"Don't be mad. It's just that . . ." She braved a glance at his face and lowered her eyes once more. "Well, I don't want to seem promiscuous. You know, a slut."

"And *who* would think that?" His eyes widened. "Who'd *see* us? The desk clerk?"

"Well, you never know," she whined. "And yes, maybe the desk clerk."

Geoff tsked. "The desk clerk that you'll probably never see again?"

Poppy shifted to face him, her knee matching his. "Well, what if my parents stay here and the desk clerk says to me, 'Oh nice to see you again. Are you and your *husband* also staying with us? Do you want the same room as last time?'" Poppy shuddered.

"Agh! God, Honch—you're too funny!" Geoff laughed. "You're kidding, right?" He cocked his head, and grinned. "Why was it okay when we just checked in, and after dinner it won't be okay?"

"Well, we're going right back down now." She bounced slightly, as if that gave her rationale some momentum. "So maybe he'll think just *one of us* will stay here."

"Sure, I'll do it." He shook his head. "You're something else." He caressed her shoulder.

Poppy turned her head away from him and faced the armoire.

"What's the matter?" He pulled back a veil of hair that shielded her cheek. "Are you crying?"

She sniffled.

"You're not upset because I laughed, are you?" He pushed back her hair again.

She shook her head. "No, it's because you're so good to me." She stared at him, as splotches of red began to appear on her face. "You're not angry with me because I act like such a squirrel?" she asked.

She smoothed the bedspread with her hands. "It's just that I was raised to be proper. And now I'm *clearly fallen*." She exaggerated the words. "My mother used to tell me that she'd put me in a convent if I had sex before marriage." Poppy wagged her finger. "Sex is a big no-no." She stood and dabbed under her eyes. "My parents gave me that message loud and clear. Girls who have sex are floozies. *Hussies*." She spat out the word.

Geoff stood. "Okay." He steadied his hands on top of her shoulders. "Poppy, we'll come up separately."

"You're wonderful." She circled her arms around his waist and rested her head on his chest. "Most guys would be angry about this. They wouldn't care what the girl wanted." She sniffled and wiped her cheek on her bicep.

"Yeah, you're probably right." He grinned. "Most guys would *want* the desk person to know he's getting laid."

She gurgled a laugh. "That's why I cry—because you're not like that. You don't mind my prudish thoughts."

"Besides, it doesn't matter if the desk clerk knows." He chuckled. "I know *I'm* getting laid."

"Stoppppp! You know what I mean." Poppy swatted her hand in the air.

"Yes, Honch. I know what you mean. I just want to see that beautiful smile again." He brushed his lips on her mouth. "Let's go have that birthday dinner, okay?"

After dinner, a grinning Geoff went upstairs—first, as he'd promised. Playing the role of an intrigued tourist, Poppy stood in front of the brochure stand. She lifted a few flyers: Disney World, Cypress Gardens, and Rosie O'Grady's Good Time Emporium. The desk clerk, his back to Poppy the entire time, never saw Geoff head upstairs.

With her back against the brass railing, Poppy faced the front desk and sidestepped up the stairs, her sandals hooked on her fingers. At their room, with one knuckle, she softly tapped on the door.

Geoff cracked the door open—only his mustache peeked out. "Who's there?" he asked like the Big Bad Wolf.

Poppy pushed the door. "Stop it," she giggled.

"You made it!" Geoff threw his arms wide.

With her fingertips, Poppy quietly closed the door and latched the chain. "Phew!" She exhaled. "I don't think the desk clerk saw me. I tiptoed up here." She rolled her eyes, mocking herself.

Geoff slipped off his loafers and gently took Poppy's hand. "Now, what about this king-size bed?" He pulled back the comforter and lowered her onto her back. "This is the first time we get to share a *real* bed."

"What if I can't find you?" Poppy giggled.

"Don't worry." His fingers untied the top of her halter dress. "I'll find you."

CHAPTER 9

# Tea for Two

~~~⌒~~~

A MONTH LATER, MY COUPLE was still sailing along without any more nudges from me. The hands on the Emotional Clock appeared to float between Eleven and Twelve, Joy and Love.

On the drive to Cocoa Beach, Poppy and Geoff exited the Bee Line Highway in a mint green 1975 Mercury Capri.

"It's great I can take you to the family condo, and it'll be just you and me. They won't be coming 'til next month." Geoff rubbed Poppy's shoulder.

"I feel a little guilty being so sneaky." Poppy sighed.

"It's fine, Honch. Oh, and remind me to top it off before we return Fred's car to him."

"You want me to take my top off? Now? Here?" Poppy feigned indignation.

"If you insist . . ." Geoff laughed, his dimple rocking in the corner of his smile. He patted Poppy's knee. "When you see this place . . .," he said as if in a trance. "The views are fantastic." He grinned at her. "And you'll be the best part of the view."

From their car, they stole glimpses. The ocean winked at them between buildings. As if it knew the secrets of listening to hearts in love—a staccato rhythm. Low-rise buildings, a flash of bright aqua water. Building. Ocean. Building. Ocean. Heartbeats. Geoff slowed the car into a numbered spot in front of the Conquistador Condominiums.

"We're here, Honch." He leaned over the bucket seat, and his excited kiss made a loud smacking sound as his lips met hers. He swung open the car door and raced to Poppy's door. When she got out, he grabbed her hand in midwalk, like track runners on a relay team who pass the baton while still moving. "I can't wait to show this to you. Just you and me. Alone."

Poppy giggled, her feet in a skip-step to keep up with him. "I've never seen you this excited."

Next to the ground-floor unit's front door, Geoff tilted a stone garden statue, an angel holding a lyre, and removed a key. He jiggled the key into the lock and turned to face Poppy. "I can't believe we get to share this." He grinned and flattened his arm against the open door to allow Poppy to walk in first.

Without a glance, he dropped the key to his left—on a counter that opened to the galley kitchen. In quick strides, he whisked Poppy through the aqua and beige-toned condo living room and into the master bedroom on the right. He tugged on the drawstring of the green linen curtains, like an acolyte who'd just been given the honor of ringing the church bells in the bell tower. He slid open the green sheers beneath. "Honch." His eyes danced. "Look at this great view."

The Atlantic Ocean swooshed—the tide out—just fifty yards away.

"Ooooh," Poppy cooed, and she nuzzled her head into the crook of his neck. "It's beautiful, Chief." Her voice dropped off to a whisper.

"C'mon." He pulled open the sliders. "Let's go check out the water."

A natural barrier blocked their path to the beach. They took a cut-through—past the sand spurs, sea oats, and grasses—their bare feet stepping carefully over the broken shells. The waves just big enough to make some noise, but not big enough for the last few surfers to enjoy a decent ride in. The beach appeared empty except for a woman a few hundred feet away in white pants whose cuffs were sloppily rolled up. Her stooped figure examined the shells.

"This is so pretty." Poppy linked her arm in Geoff's. "It's perfect here," she said as the water foamed around their feet. The seventy-five-degree breeze behind them blew wisps of her hair in her face.

"It is perfect." He smiled at Poppy and slid his finger across her brow to push the hair from her eyes.

Poppy's toes kneaded the sand, and with one hand, she held back her hair. She bent down and retrieved an opaque white shell. "See this one, Chief? This is a baby's ear." She held the specimen like a gemologist. "They're really hard to find."

He pointed at the inch-long shell. "So you want to keep this one, right?"

"Yes, for sure." She used her baby finger to wipe the wet sand from the shell. "It'll always remind me of being here with you." She closed her hands around it.

I watched my couple now over dinner, their smiles animated. They sat in the plush burgundy leather booths of Bernard's Surf, the color designed for intimate escapes—people lose track of time in the presence of red. The subdued lighting and saxophone player added to the romantic ambiance, to say nothing of the photos on the wall of legendary astronauts who reinforced the feeling that lovers could be over the moon.

Poppy and Geoff leaned into each other, their hands rolling and caressing together. Their hearts melted together. Sensual lips exchanged soft kisses, along with easy conversation that slid into satiny words. The words poets write to caress young souls. The words lovers share.

~~~

Still languishing from their romantic dinner, Geoff parked the car next to the condo. "Let's go check out the nighttime beach, Honch."

The hibiscus trees landscaping the condo—now veiled with what seemed like a magical violet shadow from the night sky—guided them down the path to the beach. The sea grasses swayed like violin bows leading a gentle concerto. Even though the sand appeared uneven, their bodies made their way to the foamy surf, their arms around each other's waist. A synchronized ballet.

*A nudge from me would be as useless as a pair of high-heeled shoes on the sand,* I thought.

"Look at the sky, Geoffrey." Poppy pointed to the full moon, a round magnet for lovers. They both kicked off their shoes, sandals and topsiders sideways in the sand, like abandoned boats on the shore. She tugged on Geoff's arm and pulled him toward the water's edge, as the moon's lavender spotlight illuminated the quiet beach.

"Doesn't look like there's anyone else out here." Geoff rolled up his cuffs. "Maybe we should take off more than just our shoes." He slipped his hand inside of her red lace halter top and grazed his fingers across her left breast.

"Geoffrey." A gurgled laugh escaped her mouth, yet she pressed her body into his. "What if someone comes?"

He wiggled his eyebrows. "Isn't that the idea?" He explored the inside of the lace halter.

She crossed her arms around his neck. "I love you, Chief." She slipped her lips inside his shirt collar and whispered, "How about we take a short moonlit stroll and go inside and see what comes up?"

"Sure." He breathed. "I especially like the second part."

Outside the sliding doors to the master bedroom, they clapped their shoes together, and sand sprinkled down on the cement porch like fairy dust. He slid open the door and closed it along with the drapes.

"Let me help you with that top," he murmured, as he glided her backward into the master suite. He unfastened the three buttons in the back of her halter—and her top slipped down to her waist.

She began to unbutton his pink shirt, her eyes fixed on the slow movements of her fingers as they lingered on each button. "What's fair is fair," she whispered.

"Absolutely." He inserted his upper lip in between her parted lips.

The shag carpet soon held what looked like a small fabric sculpture: Geoff's khaki pants and boxers, his pink shirt over Poppy's white slacks and red halter. The two lovers made their way to the queen-sized bed.

Geoff re-opened the drapes, leaving the sheers to filter the moonlight. He turned off the bedside lamp and slid next to her. "It's just you and me."

Propped up on one elbow, Geoff gazed over at Poppy, still asleep on her back, her profile silhouetted by the pale-green sheers. Like the moon had done the night before, the sun filtered a greenish-yellow shimmer into the room—the color of buds in spring.

His caramel eyes blinked as they studied her. A look of wonderment.

A few moments later, she stirred. "Mmm," she sighed as her black eyelashes fluttered open. She turned toward him and stretched a lazy arm over her head. "Hi." Her lips curled into a sleepy smile.

He smiled, yet said nothing—just continued to drink her in.

"Chief?" She also sat up on one elbow. "You okay?"

A small tear slid down his right cheek. "I've never seen anything so beautiful."

She turned behind her and looked through the pale sheers as the sun danced across the water.

She smiled and turned back to him. "It is beautiful here, isn't it?"

"No, Honch." His breath caught. "You." He steadied his gaze at her. "I've never seen anything more beautiful than you. The light behind you, the glow, your beautiful profile." He choked through the words. "You're breathtaking. Like an angel."

Poppy leaned over him, and her finger smoothed away the teardrop from his cheek. "You make me feel beautiful." She laid her head on his chest, her hair falling on his shoulder. "I've never felt this kind of love. Your love." A tear slid out and ran from her cheek to his chest.

Twenty minutes later, she tiptoed out of the bedroom, after she'd thrown on his pink shirt from the pile. She buttoned the shirt as she left the room.

"Would you like some tea?" She shouted with a proper British accent from the kitchen as she folded the cuff up on her forearm.

"No thanks." Geoff lay in bed, his arms behind his head—eyes closed—with a *died and gone to heaven* smile.

With little running steps back to the bedroom, like Nadia Comaneci, Poppy pounced on the bed and landed on her knees—a minx. "Where were we?" She purred.

Geoff seemed to enjoy the vision of her tanned legs sticking out from the tails of his shirt. She saw his arousal from beneath the sheet. Playfully, she unbuttoned the shirt.

I realized when she'd returned that she'd buttoned all but the top two buttons on her way into the kitchen. *Still trying to maintain some semblance of propriety?* I'd have to ask my scroll later why some young people believe that "what others might think" is important. *What is considered to be proper and respectable today, and why, when it's just the two of them, does Poppy feel the need to be proper?*

In the living room, I stared out the sliders, where the aqua sheers cast a blue tint on everything. On my scroll, Phillip had one sentence where he mentioned that he'd introduce a challenge for all of the choreographers. *I can't imagine what it is, but I know I want to be the one who wins the challenge.* As I wondered if Phillip would make a grand announcement of the winner on the scroll, I heard a sound. *What's that noise?* I turned from the window and traced the sound back to the kitchen. *Oh. Just the teakettle.*

From the kitchen, the whistling got louder. *It's been going for almost ten minutes. And they haven't come out yet. Maybe they hadn't heard it. This is bad.* Just then, the whistling stopped.

I made my way into the kitchen, the small pass-through window nearly obliterated in smoke. The teakettle should've still been vibrating on the electric burner. Instead, it had collapsed onto the surface of the stove. I nudged the smoke from the kitchen toward the two lovers. Acrid metallic smoke wafted to the bedroom and permeated the opening under the door.

I still heard nothing. *Oh c'mon. That was a perfect nudge. How can they not smell this?* The burner had melted off the entire bottom of the teakettle. *Shit. Shit. Shit.*

I listened again for footsteps. *Nothing. Nice, Jesse. Your couple is about to go up in flames. Literally.* I paced outside their room. *What's the protocol for something like this? I can't let them die.*

I fanned the smoke again into the bedroom doorway. *Come on, you two. Pay attention to all of your senses.*

Geoff's fingers played with Poppy's hair. "Honch? Do you smell something?"

*Finally.*

"Hmm?" Her fingers made little circles on his chest. She sat up. "Oh shit!" Her feet kicked at the tangled sheets. "The tea!"

"Oh shit!" Geoff ran naked into the kitchen.

I nudged Geoff to open a drawer for a hot pad. *Don't burn yourself.* He grabbed a kitchen towel off the counter.

The entire teakettle—what remained of it—glowed crimson red.

Geoff dropped the charred kettle into the stainless-steel sink and turned on the faucet. A giant sizzle erupted along with a cloud of steam.

He turned off the molten lava burner. The coil element revealed a few smoldering remains of the ill-fated teakettle. The kitchen towel—charred—was now striped with black burn marks. Branded with illicit evidence.

Poppy, in Geoff's unbuttoned pink shirt, looked horrified.

"OhGodohGod!" She said as one word. "I almost burned the place down!" Poppy gasped as her hands covered her mouth.

"Holy cow. This could've been really bad." Geoff held out his arm like a traffic cop. "Don't come too close, Honch. It's still really hot over here."

"I'm so sorry, Geoffrey." Her pupils swam. "I feel terrible," she wailed.

"It's not a big deal. Don't worry about it." He shrugged, and opened the kitchen window. "C'mon, let's get dressed. We can go the beach again."

She stared at him open-jawed. "No!" She shriek-whispered. "Not until we get a new kettle. And towel." She fanned the smoke toward the open window.

"Honch." He threw the charred towel into the trash under the sink. "It's over. It's really no big deal."

"Are you crazy?" Poppy's face contorted into disbelief. "We can't go to the beach! We have to buy a new teakettle." She grabbed a folded napkin, snapped it open, and frantically fanned the air. "They're going to know I burned it up. Wonder why we didn't hear the teakettle. Know that we were *doing it*. That I'm a slut." She grabbed the pleats on the pink shirt, her fingers fumbling at the buttons, the holes and buttons misaligned.

"Oh, stop it." He laughed. "How could they possibly come to that conclusion?"

"They'll just *know*." Tears fell on the uneven shirttails in her hands.

"Okay." He turned around, removed the twisted metal from the sink, and dropped it into the garbage. He wiped his hands on a dishcloth and steered her out of the kitchen. "We'll get a new teakettle first."

"And a towel, too," she said, and turned to face him. "I hope you're not upset with me." She sniffled and chewed the inside of her lip.

Geoff smiled and shook his head. "Of course not, Honch." He reached in his duffle and yanked out a pair of shorts. He stepped into them. "I'm just as much to blame as you. I distracted you from the tea."

Poppy rummaged through her luggage, her eyes red from either the smoke or crying. Or both. She wadded up her sundress and stepped into the bathroom. "I'm sorry I ruined everything."

"You didn't ruin anything." He stood in the bathroom's doorway and circled his arms around her. "I adore you, Honch." He smiled as he looked at his crooked shirt. "You didn't button my shirt properly, but we can fix that." He grinned.

Two hours later, alone in the sauna room near the pool—and after buying the replacement items for the kitchen—they breathed in the steamy air.

Poppy dangled her legs over the cedar bench. "I wish we could've found that same gross avocado green." She searched Geoff's face. "What if your mom notices that there's a new color?" Poppy shivered. "My mom would *totally* know."

"Poppy, the stainless-steel one is fine." He took a jug of water and poured it on the hot stones and made a loud *tssshhh*. Steam filled the small room. "You have nothing to worry about," he said, as he tiptoed his fingers up her leg to the edge of the bath towel.

· She looked at his hand and then his face. "You're sure?" She cupped her palm over his roving fingers.

"I'm positive," he whispered, and peeled back Poppy's towel.

I realized two things: *One, the sauna is a public place—anyone could enter. Poppy seemed more concerned about the color of a teakettle than about a stranger walking in on them. Two, they'd both abandoned their bathing suits—willingly— even Poppy, with her prudish ways.*

## CHAPTER 10

# Brownie Points

~⁀

FIVE FRATERNITY BROTHERS, WITH GEOFF and Poppy squeezed in next to them, sat on the lumpy leather couch in the Phi Delt living room—Mayflower Hall—where a piece of the Mayflower proudly stood on a bronze plaque on the wall to the right of the fireplace.

A collection of used cups and bottles littered the floor. Pretzels, month-old bread crusts, and McDonald's fries were lodged beneath seat cushions. An unopened Trojan condom—a hopeful vestige from one of the optimistic men who lived in the house, curled up as if it were keeping one eye open for another opportunity. It was Saturday night.

As they watched an episode of *Delta House*—a spinoff of National Lampoon's *Animal House*—they chuckled.

In the kitchen, Geoff's former roommate, Fred, inserted a toothpick into a chocolate-filled pan and slid the pan back into the oven.

*That's a generous name—kitchen,* I thought. It seemed like a condemned zone, really. No one cooked. The *Edmund Fitzgerald* of frat kitchens.

"I'm making some brownies for everyone." Fred's deep-set brown eyes twinkled under an Eddie Munster-like widow's peak. His dark head of wavy black hair poked up from the oven door as he pulled out a pan of chocolate from the heat.

"Great." Desmond's cornflower-blue eyes widened. "Are they magic brownies?" Desmond's fingers rested just beneath a ketchup dribble on the doorframe.

Geoff laughed and pulled his eyes away from Desmond. He rubbed his hand up and down the sleeve of Poppy's striped velour top.

Poppy looked at Geoff over the top of her vodka and grapefruit drink. "Magic?" She took a sip. "What? A special recipe?"

"A family recipe." Fred peered out from the open archway. He turned back to the stovetop and continued to slice the brownies into large squares.

When Fred walked into the living room, he looked like a juggler as he balanced the pan on top of the hot pad. "And here they are."

"Yum." Poppy licked her lips, as she chewed the oozing chocolate.

"Great brownies, Fred." Gavin chewed and, mid-grin, gave Fred a thumbs-up.

Poppy set her drink on the beat-up coffee table, and with the napkin in her palm, she took another bite. "Who was the baker in your family, Fred?" Poppy dabbed at the corner of her mouth. "Your mom? Grandma?"

The five guys laughed, as did Geoff. Fred offered the pan of brownies to Poppy again. She reached in and took another. "Thanks. These are so good."

Fred puckered his mouth, fish-like, to avoid a snicker, while the other guys—Geoff included—laughed.

"What?" Poppy turned to Geoff with a *what's going on* expression.

With his thumb and forefinger beneath his moustache, he pressed on the corners of his mouth—mostly to prevent his lips from curling into a smile.

"What?" She shifted sideways to face Geoff. "What's so funny?" Poppy turned from Geoff to the others, who immediately averted their eyes.

His face flushed, Geoff hid his eyes from Poppy, as his shoulders began to shake. The other guys slapped their thighs, and laughter burst from them.

Poppy stood up and looked at her white linen pants and turned her head to scan her backside, as if she had just sat in dog poop. "C'mon, you guys!" she said, her voice now shrill. "Stop laughing." She glowered at Geoff, her betrayed face revealing a scathing look.

The noise in the living room became a small roar. The brothers doubled over and held their stomachs.

"You guys are so . . ." Poppy reached for her red-and-white cotton purse on the back of the couch and spun around. Her arms flailed as she gripped the air to support her teetering body. Her mouth fell open as she collapsed backward onto the sofa. "Wha..." she blinked. "I'm like . . . "—she put the back of her hand on her forehead—"out of it here."

The guys wiped tears of laughter from the corners of their eyes.

Poppy turned to Geoff, who'd wound down his laughter into a chuckle. "Is there pot in these brownies?"

Geoff nodded, and a blurted "Yeah" escaped from his mouth.

"You *knew* this?" Her lips quivered, shivering in disbelief.

"Oh, c'mon, Honch." He straightened, and rested his forearms on his knees. "It's no big deal. We all ate them." He smiled at his brothers. "I just . . ."

"You *knew?*" She stood and this time held the back of the sofa. "I can't believe you did this." She walked her hands down the sticky vinyl sofa, pawing her way to the end of the couch. Her feet wove side to side, as if on a rocky boat, as she neared the door.

"Honch! C'mere." Geoff stood and walked sideways between the couch and coffee table. "Where are you going?" he called out as he stepped over Gavin's outstretched legs on the floor. "C'mon. I'm sorry I laughed." He chuckled when he said "laughed"—unable to prevent himself from reliving the humorous moment. He caught up with her and linked his elbow inside hers.

She shook her elbow as if she'd been stung by a wasp. "Don't," she spat.

Geoff wheeled in front of her, blocking the doorway. "Honch, Poppy, I'm sorry." He held her upper arms. "I had no idea you'd be this upset."

Her shoulders stiffened. "I feel so weird—it's scary." She looked down. "And I already had the vodka?" She glared up at him in the shadowy foyer. "How could you be in on this? You know how I feel about that shit."

Geoff gently rubbed her arms. "I really didn't think you'd mind. I mean . . ."

Poppy turned and grabbed the door handle. She opened it and groped for the railing. "Don't follow me. I'm going back to my house." She eased down the three steps. "All of you; a bunch of dickheads."

On the sidewalk, Poppy staggered, like she'd just come to a sudden stop after a pirouette. Her feet trudged on, serpentine.

Geoff hurried up behind her. "Wait, Honch. I'll come with you." He took her elbow. "Hold on."

They took little steps as if they were walking on ice with street shoes. Shuffle. Shuffle. Sway. Shuffle.

"I can't believe you knew what was going on." She took a deep breath. "I've never tried weed. Never been high," she said, her tone fragile.

"Aw, Honch. I didn't think . . ."

Poppy cut him off. "I know what happens when I drink too much. But pot? C'mon, Geoff. You knew I didn't want to touch the stuff." Her voice got higher. She stopped at the front walkway to her house. "Just go back with those assholes, okay?"

He wrapped his arms around her. "If I'd known, I wouldn't have let you eat one."

"Just . . ." She shook her head and jerked away. The streetlights on Holt Avenue revealed Poppy's frightened and on the brink of tears.

"Please forgive me." He jockeyed his face in front of hers. "I know it feels weird," he said, trying to quell her rising fear.

She stumbled into the foyer, groped for the bannister. "I can't even find the stairs."

He curled one arm around her waist. "It'll wear off soon, Honch. I promise."

Catherine, blackened feet in an oversized light-blue man's denim shirt—the same color as her eyes—looked up, startled as they entered the room. "What's the matter?"

Poppy used the dresser to guide herself into the room, walked slowly, and lowered herself onto her bed. "That asshole, Fred. He put pot in the brownies. I ate *two* of them," Poppy blurted. "I'm all dizzy."

"Oh." Catherine turned her gaze back to the small eight-inch TV. She uncrossed her legs and recrossed them, switching which leg was on top. "You'll be fine in half an hour," she said to the television screen.

"That's what I told her, too," Geoff whined, eager to have an ally.

Poppy's fists gripped her comforter, as she inhaled and blinked a few more times.

Geoff stroked her back. "You feeling any better yet, Honch?"

"Maybe," she said in a pathetic tone. "Just go back and watch your stupid show. So you and those assholes can continue to laugh at me."

"I don't want to go back with those guys. I'm staying." Geoff put a tentative arm around her shoulder. They sat still for a few minutes, as Poppy drew in deep breaths and exhaled, as if a doctor were checking her lungs with a stethoscope. Catherine gave an occasional peek at her roommate, her expression nonplussed.

Poppy turned her face to Geoff. "I'm sorry I got so mad. I just freaked." She lowered her head onto his shoulder.

Catherine swung her legs to the front of her bed. "Do you guys want me to get a Coke from the machine?" She grinned. "Score some brownie points here?"

Geoff shook his head side to side, rapid fire. "Too soon, C-Bell." Geoff bolted up and jammed his fingers in his front pocket, unable to get the coin out fast enough. "Thanks Catherine." He strode across the room quickly. "Here's a quarter."

"Thanks, C-Bell," Poppy muttered.

Geoff hurried back to sit next to Poppy, as if afraid someone might take his place. She scooched backward and slowly lowered herself against her white eyelet pillow rest.

Geoff inched back next to her, his feet dangling off the edge of the bed. "I love you, Poppy. I'd never want you to feel badly." He rubbed her knee.

"I was just so taken off guard." She shook her head. "And that you were *in* on it. Well, I felt so . . . so . . ." She began to cry.

"I know. I know." Geoff stroked her hair. "I'm sorry."

A first conflict between the two of them, Poppy was on the right side of the Emotional Clock. She'd gone from Confusion and Anxiety to Despair, and straight to Five O'Clock, Anger.

An hour later, the Coke can unopened on Poppy's nightstand reflected shadowy light from the street lamp. Geoff stroked her hair as she lay asleep against his chest.

*Geoff's right about one thing. This is not a big deal. From start to finish, their misunderstanding lasted less than two hours. Poppy and Geoff are now back in double digits on the left side of the clock.*

~)

A week later, thirteen people showed up to Geoff's frat house, a popular party spot. By five, Geoff and his brothers had already tapped the keg—the centerpiece—in the arched alcove of Mayflower Hall.

Although Poppy had forgiven Geoff, I wasn't sure if his friend, Fred, was out of the doghouse. In a group of women across the room from Geoff, and in a red-and-black skirt with a black top, Poppy laughed when her sorority president, Meredith, told a joke.

Poppy and Geoff, comfortable in a group, didn't have to be the focus of everyone's attention, nor did they have to be together. And they both shared a more-the-merrier attitude to welcome others into the fold. Poppy, in a group of women, stepped to the right to open a space for a mousy-looking girl to join the gathering. The girl's face brightened, her face opening like a beautiful oriental fan.

By ten p.m., the lack of the keg's handle indicated an empty tank. The crowd had dwindled. Near a corner of the couch, Poppy—the only girl left—snuggled with Geoff. A couple of his brothers were draped in chairs, their bodies like articles of damp clothing that needed to dry.

Poppy glanced at the two carrot-topped guys, Gavin and Desmond, their Gumby-like limbs drooped over the other end of the sofa. "I think I'll go."

Geoff watched Desmond unfold himself from the chair. "We're just hanging out." Geoff yawned his words.

She glanced at Fred, who, like a sly cat ready to pounce, eyed her empty place on the sunken couch. "I know. Just stay here with the guys." Her lips blinked a smile.

"Spence." Gavin gave an exaggerated belch and scrunched his beer can. "You like the Hulk, right? He's such a fucking badass."

Geoff grinned at the carrot-topped brother. "Sure," he said and turned his attention back to Poppy.

She'd already gone.

# CHAPTER 11

# Late at Lighthouse Point

~)

IN MY HAVEN AT KNOWLES Chapel, I sat in the petit point chair and reviewed my weekly updates to my supervisor. I'd documented the brownie incident and touched on Poppy's somewhat hasty departure from Geoff's frat house. I threw it in there because my documentation was otherwise sparse.

In Phillip's one-sentence response, he'd simply stated, *Remember, Jesse, most challenges begin at One O'Clock, Confusion, that point where you can't put a finger on any one thing.*

I reread Phillip's words. *Does Phillip think that Geoff has eroded some of Poppy's trust?*

"I would've intervened with a nudge if they'd needed one," I grunted.

*I can see it in their eyes and their faces. They both light up when they see each other. Poppy's smile radiates off her face. And when Geoff sees her, it's as if the entire campus melts away. His gaze locks on Poppy, as though he hasn't seen her in years. Poppy exudes great energy—always bubbly and happy, a natural buoyancy in her step. They're like two magnets—positive to positive, being pulled into each other.*

*And even though Geoff is kind and thoughtful of Poppy, it's easy for him to get caught up with guys and their boisterous behavior.*

My scroll illuminated a few words: *It's the little things that whittle away at relationships and make couples take each other for granted.*

As I headed out the front door of the chapel, Phillip's sentence had planted a tiny seed of concern about Poppy and Geoff, who today were headed to Lighthouse Point on the east coast of Florida to visit Geoff's aunt and uncle for the day.

~)

I wasn't sure if it was Phillip's words that hung over me like a fog or Poppy and Geoff's exchange in the car on the way back to Rollins, but something felt off. Even though she'd been pleasant and cordial with Geoff's relatives, now in the car Poppy seemed, in a word, subdued.

"Everything okay, Honch?" Geoff glanced at her, a smile still on his face.

Poppy stared at the solid stripes on his rugby shirt, as if she could find answers within the crisp green and white lines. "I didn't want to tell you this—bother you," she blurted. Her whole frame shook with staccato gasps, and tears began a steady descent onto her red blouse.

"Honch, what is it?" Geoff reached his right hand toward her arm.

She shook her head side to side. "My period," she whispered. "I've never been late. I don't know what to do." She exhaled a sob.

"Oh, Honch." He rubbed her arm. "We've been really careful," he said casually. "I'm sure you're not pregnant." He nodded once, and his lips formed a consoling smile. "You'll probably get it tomorrow."

"I tried to keep it to myself, but these past four days have been hard. I even wrote in my diary before we left this morning. I've been terrified." She gulped air. "You know." She looked up, her face damp with tears. "If I am . . ."

"Hey, don't cry." He rubbed her shoulder to subdue her body tremors. "I love you, Poppy." He clenched his hands at ten and two on the steering wheel. "Honch, can you talk about this with Catherine?" He unclenched his grip, and his hand dusted her knee. He regripped the wheel. "Anyone?"

She rubbed her arms. "Maybe Cecelia, who's at Bowdoin. You met her when you visited me at the farm. I've known her forever. She'd be great to talk to. But that would mean an expensive long-distance phone call that could last for hours." She wiped her face with the back of her hand.

Poppy shuddered. "What if I *am* pregnant?" She whispered, mouthing the last word. Her eyes flew open in a Norman Bates kind of terror.

"If you're pregnant, we'll just get married," he said casually, as if they'd just discussed a quick trip to the grocery. "We'll deal with whatever we have to, Poppy." He patted her leg.

Her eyes swollen from fear, she nodded. "Okay," she whimpered. With a blank stare, as Poppy looked out the car window, her hands wiped tears from her eyes, intermittent wipers.

"I promise everything will be all right." Geoff's words tiptoed out.

From beneath her tanned skin, Poppy's face revealed areas of splotchy scarlet distress. "I *know* I'm pregnant. I've never even been a *half* day late, Geoffrey. I'm *five* days late." Her terse words hovered above her jutted chin. "I know my own body."

"Well, let's go to the Health Center on Monday." The car slowed in his preoccupation. "Get it checked out."

As though she hadn't heard his last comment, Poppy spun in the seat, and her words tumbled out in an avalanche of fear. "I could *never* have an abortion." Her eyelids shut out the word. "I'm so scared, Geoffrey. My mother will kill me." Fresh tears of disgrace pooled in her reddened eyes. "My parents will be so . . ." She shook her head in self-admonishment. "So ashamed. What if . . . ?" Soft brown bangs fanned forward around her face. Poppy's shadowy eyes were cast downward, and the edges of her eyes looked like a road map of Florida, with red lines that pointed in many directions.

"Stop." Geoff shook her knee. "We'll get married. You won't have an abortion."

Poppy straightened and pushed her hands on the seat. "You'd really do that for me?" Her eyes widened. "You're not just saying that?"

"Of course I would." He nodded.

I checked my scroll again. *Shit. Nothing on how to nudge in a situation like this.* Perhaps Poppy's diary could shed some light.

> *Saturday, March 25:*
> *I'm so scared. I've never been late before. Late at Lighthouse Point, (like a bad Nancy Drew title). And I'm afraid to tell Geoff. It IS my problem. Mom will kill me. I'll totally disappoint Dad and Granddaddy. Should I get an abortion? Ugh. Can't even imagine doing that. AWFUL. I'd never get an abortion!*
>
> *I have no idea what to do—whom to trust. Catherine might understand, yet I don't want the word to get out. And it IS my problem. I don't want Geoff burdened with this, even though he's the only person I CAN trust! I have to handle this on my own.*

And suddenly her thoughts came back in a sudden wave. "Geoffrey?" She pivoted her left shoulder into the seat back. "I'm sure your parents will think I'm a slut if I'm pregnant."

"Poppy." Geoff shook his head. "That word isn't even *in* my mother's vocabulary."

Poppy's head nodded like a bobble head.

There was no sunset to watch as light rain fell on Rollins College. The nighttime clouds seemed to reflect the mood of the day. A few passing students held blue or black umbrellas that bobbed up and down like musical fermatas punctuating the dark sky, attempting to hold the raindrops at bay.

Geoff pulled into the parking lot across from their houses.

"I'm going to stay in my room tonight," Poppy murmured. "I need to sort some things out."

"I don't like leaving you." He cocked his head. "Do you want to stay with me?"

Poppy met his eyes, and her lips pursed into an expression of contemplation. She straightened the collar of her blouse, the flattened pinpoints now upright. As if she lived in a Jane Austen world, Poppy lifted her chin like Elizabeth Bennet and set a token smile on her face. "I'll be okay."

She lifted her face to his, as she'd done seven months ago when they'd first kissed under the arched loggia. Back in September. When they hadn't had a care in the world.

# CHAPTER 12

# Emotional Flotsam

~~

ON SUNDAY AFTERNOON, ROLLINS FELT unlike any other time for Poppy and Geoff. The customary banter between them, stalled by cumbersome thoughts of an uncertain future, subdued their usual buoyant energy. Palpable destinies hung like an offshore fog or a pending storm that causes barometric pressure to drop. Just last week, a zestful Poppy had taken some more photos of Geoff as he skied. At a happier, unencumbered time.

I quickly made notes to update my report. This new dynamic could derail my couple, but I'd give myself some time to prepare a nudge.

*Should my nudge move them toward marriage if she's pregnant? Would they have to leave school early? Before graduation? If they married, would my choreography results still be considered successful?*

I opened my scroll and updated the clock placements for Poppy and Geoff. *Definitely an unfamiliar clock location for them.* Like flotsam, both floated in transitional space. The unknown area. The in-between place of no-man's land. Stagnant. An endless fear-filled waiting game.

With Geoff at two, Anxiety, and Poppy at three thirty—wavering between Despair, and Shame and Guilt—I had good reason for concern.

As I wrote, I recalled my first correspondence with Phillip, who had described transitional space as not knowing what would happen next, a kind of limbo.

*Transitional space is mercurial. Slippery.* He wrote. *Uncharted seas.* He shared the best strategy for transitional space: *meet the challenge head on— calm and steady.*

*I can't let them flounder.* I studied Geoff, his eyes and body language. I wondered if I'd have to employ emotional paddles—defibrillators.

In my notes, I included more details about their personal history. Both had been raised in a world of unconditional love, and they shared predictable strengths. That level and potency of love prevailed over almost any obstacle.

With a note in the strategy section of the update, I decided to think of a specific and effective nudge. *Yet what if she decides to jump ship and ultimately capsize their relationship?* I imagined Phillip's prize from the yet-to-be-introduced challenge—the one he would award to me for my success, now evaporating. *If their ship sinks, so do I.*

~~~

Monday morning signaled a difference in the breezeway. A shift from the moon, which had gone off duty. The sun now cast shadows on the tiles, the color of goldenrod.

"C'mon, Geoffrey. Hurry," a pacing Poppy whispered to herself. Her eyes scanned the length of the tiled loggia, a tunnel, with Mills Lawn as the vanishing point.

She walked to the front steps of Mayflower Hall and spun around. Poppy looked up and down the sidewalk and strode back to the covered walkway. And paced.

When a group of six students turned into the Student Union, she spotted him—his distinctive walk she knew so well.

In sandals and black-and-white-checked shorts that looked more like culottes, she ran to Geoff and grabbed his arm, her wide smile immediate at the sight of him.

"What? What is it?" Geoff stumbled and picked up his pace to match hers.

At the back entrance to his house, she pulled him inside. The carved wooden door involuntarily slammed against the doorstop. She led him up two stairs at a time.

"Poppy!" He grabbed the railing as he hauled himself up after her. "Wait. Slow down. What's going on?"

She jerked his hand inside the room—like crack-the-whip on an ice rink, his arm and body followed in a snake-like manner. Poppy shoved the door shut. "I got it! I got my period!" She threw her arms around his neck.

"You did?" He lifted his head to the ceiling and exhaled. "I knew we'd be okay." He stepped back and held her with his arms out straight, as if admiring a rare painting.

"I feel so silly, Chief! Oh, I was such a *wreck*!" She pushed a strand of golden-brown hair from her eyes.

"Yes, I know." He grinned.

"I've never been late before." She stepped farther into the room and spun on her heels. "And six days!" She blew out the words and made them sound like a bellows. "Geoffrey, thank God you were right."

"What a relief." He wiped his brow in exaggeration. "And your beautiful smile is back." He folded her in his arms. "That's the best part."

"And your dimple." She lifted her mouth to kiss it. "I'm so relieved."

"Me, too." Geoff tucked a cinnamon strand of hair behind his ear.

"I'm sorry. I wasn't any fun." She flounced on the bed. "But, oh, Chief. I feel *so* much better." She reached her arms out to him and beckoned him to join her. "This is the first time I've ever been *thrilled* to, you know . . . " Her lips turned into a lopsided smile.

He sat and stroked her hand. "So, no fooling around for a couple of days?"

"You have a one-track mind, don't you?" Poppy's lips met his.

"Yep." He smiled. "I'm still crazy about you."

She swallowed, her eyes searching the floor for words. "I love you so much, Chief," she said, as she looked up at him. "Thank you for being so, so . . ."

"Now I'm just so-so?" He cocked his head in feigned surprise.

"No," she sputtered. "So wonderful, so patient. So good to me."

The outgoing tide had swept the flotsam to sea.

# CHAPTER 13

# What's Not to Love

I WALKED ON HOLT AVENUE toward the Greek houses, content with Poppy and Geoff's current status: back on the encouraged left side of the Emotional Clock.

Next to Sandspur Field—Rollins' singular athletic field—I noticed something blurry under the bleachers and realized after a moment it was a raven foraging for food. I gave a second look at the black bird, now closer to me. It eyed me suspiciously, its blue-black head cocked to the side as if to give me the stink-eye.

I opened my scroll. I wanted to know if Edgar Allan Poe's raven was some sort of messenger of doom.

As my scroll rolled shut, I peered at the bleachers and Sandspur Field, the crow no longer in sight. *I hope its presence is a harbinger of good news to come,* I thought, as I focused my attention on several voices across the street.

I stepped off the cracked and worn curb onto the pinkish-red bricks paving Holt Avenue and walked to where Poppy and Geoff and three others appeared to be in the middle of some sort of photo shoot—with Poppy as the photographer.

Poppy's roommate, Catherine, and their sorority sister, Maggie—the editor of the Rollins yearbook, the *Tomokan*—along with Geoff and a blond-haired guy, took turns with meringue pies smushed on their faces. Poppy clicked away with her Canon 35-millimeter camera. Action shots with humor.

I left as Poppy kissed off the sugary sweetness from Geoff's lips. *Too bad that this moment wasn't captured. The full spectrum of their loving relationship, something they can look back on years from now, as nostalgic and arthritic fingers turn the pages of the 1978* Tomokan. That was thee magic of black-and-white images—to prompt a living-color memory.

I strolled on Holt Avenue toward Knowles Chapel. I felt confident. *That crow—definitely a good sign.* It gave me the knowledge that Poppy and Geoff had returned to their authentic selves.

*I feel upbeat, confident, about Poppy and Geoff.* It'd been a couple of days since the photo shoot, and both of them seemed in a good groove.

I expected high levels of recognition for my stellar work. *No bugs in this plan,* I reflected, and thought of the next observation opportunity with Poppy and Geoff: meeting the parents.

The one and only thing wrong with Florida in early April was the invasion of black orange-headed insects with an oxymoronic name—Lovebugs. Like tandem skydivers, they floated down from the heavens and ended up plastered on the grill, hood, and windshield of every car on the Bee Line Expressway and A1A. The unfamiliar tourist, whose instinct was to clear the windshield and use washer fluid and wipers, discovered too late it only made things worse. Like a coating of grease, all visibility was lost with the smeared remains.

Eager to see how my own lovebugs managed on their day-trip to Cocoa Beach, I traveled along with them. Curious, certainly, to meet Geoff's parents. Poppy and Geoff borrowed Catherine's car, a cream-colored Fiat Spyder, a two-seater sports car with an extended hood, and also not immune to the connected ebony pests that dive-bombed and wildly splattered the vehicle. It made the car look as if Rorschach had personally created ink blot tests on the sleek hood.

Geoff pulled onto A1A and merged Catherine's car—New Jersey tags on both bumpers—in with the other snowbirds, many from Connecticut, New York, and Massachusetts.

"I'm excited you finally get to meet my folks." Geoff rubbed her knee, and his fingers slipped just under the hem of her red golf skirt.

"Me too, it's just that . . ." Poppy dipped her head under the visor and searched the sky for something.

"Ooh, this is fun." He grinned and moved his hand up her thigh.

"Wait, stop." She gently halted his fingers from wandering. "I'm serious. What if they're watching?"

Geoff snorted out a laugh. "Like they're on the roof scanning the city with a telescope?"

"You know what I mean." She touched his arm as he downshifted into the parking lot. "I want to make a good impression—want them to like me."

"Honch, what's not to love?" He moved his head side to side as he searched for a parking spot. He easily slid the tiny sports car into a spot between two cars that'd parked on the lines—a Cadillac Sedan de Ville and a Lincoln Town Car. "Besides"—he faced her and turned the ignition— "I'm crazy about you, and they'll be, too."

Poppy winced and swiveled the rearview mirror. "Okay," she mumbled as she applied her Clinique lipstick, a frosted pink.

Geoff smiled as she puckered her lips to put on the color. "Now remember," he started.

"I know, I know," she said without moving her lips. Poppy smooshed her lips together once and tapped on the silver cover of the tube. "This is my *first* visit to the condo," she said. She raised her eyes in the same manner that an arrested villain who searched for answers did, and she blurted, "I hope they don't say anything." She swallowed air as if it were her last breath. "The teakettle."

Geoff opened his car door and got out. He dipped his head into the opening to face Poppy. "Don't worry, they won't notice."

Poppy leaned toward Geoff and rested her hand on the driver's seat. "I'm so afraid she'll find out that you and I are, you know . . ."

"Doing it?" He began to close the door. "I doubt it. Don't worry."

"Wait." Poppy reached out and put her hand up. Poppy opened her door and got out. She hurried around to Geoff. "What if she asks me if I've ever been in your room? And what if . . ."

"Oh God, listen to you." He guffawed. "Getting all worked up. What if she asks you if you're shacking up with her son? Honch, she's *not* going to ask you." He reached behind his seat and grabbed their pool bag. He smiled at her. "But my dad will."

Geoff dodged Poppy's effort to swat him. "Stop making fun of me. I'm serious."

"I'm serious, too." He took her hand and walked toward the back entrance to the condo. "Back where we made wild, passionate love."

"Geoffrey—stop!" Poppy giggled.

As they strolled to the condo, I couldn't help but think of Poppy as if she were a little kid who'd had a bad experience in third grade—where the eight-year-old has all afternoon and evening to spill the story, but waits until after all the lights are off and she's been in bed for twenty minutes before she calls for her mother in a sniffling whine. Geoff and Poppy drove for more than an hour. Plenty of time for Poppy to shed her fears, yet she waited until they'd parked and sat, baking on the sun-drenched black asphalt, to bring up her nagging concerns.

Geoff waved to his mother through the screen of the kitchen window. "We're here."

"George, they're here!" A petite woman, just over five feet, called out as she came from the kitchen. Jean Spencer's dark-brown eyes twinkled on her delicate oval face, her coral lipstick the same shade as her skirt. The crisp white blouse—pressed just so—made her tanned olive skin appear even darker. The gold highlights, evenly placed in her caramel-colored hair, curled into soft swirls, like icing on a homemade cake.

"Hi, Mom." Geoff leaned over to kiss his mother's cheek.

"I'm so glad to see you," she said, and rested her hand on his wrist. "And you must be Poppy. I've heard so much about you." Jean extended both her hands, which were manicured with a salmon-pink polish.

"Hi, Mrs. Spencer." Poppy smiled. She tilted her head with sweetness and genuine interest. "It's wonderful to meet you."

Geoff's father, a man with a full head of thick, silvery-white hair, came up behind Jean and thrust out his hand to greet his son.

"Hello, Geoffrey!" George Spencer's hazel-brown eyes sparkled beneath his glasses. His summer shorts, blue, white, and yellow plaid—paired flawlessly with a short-sleeve white shirt—gave him a nautical captain's bearing. In charge, ready to sail to any shore. George smiled as he turned to Poppy. "Hello, Poppy," he said, his tone upbeat and chirpy—optimistic.

"You can leave your pool things in here, Poppy," Jean pointed to the guest room. "And Geoff"—she pointed to the master suite— "you can change later in our room."

"Thank you," Poppy said, and looked at Geoff, who smirked and wiggled his eyebrows at his mother's instructions.

After they'd stowed their things, Poppy and Geoff joined Jean in the kitchen.

"May I help with anything?" Poppy asked. She stared at the stovetop, the new teakettle probably unused. She overcompensated, adding, "Where do you keep your water glasses?" She knew they already were on the table, but nerves prompted her to augment her politeness.

"Oh, no, thank you. I have everything ready." Jean smiled and reached into the oven. She removed a tin of cornbread muffins and made room on the stovetop. She slid the teakettle back. The shiny metal clanked as it awkwardly tilted against the dark green enamel. "Geoff?" She turned, the oven mitt still on her hand. "Do you know what happened to the green teakettle? The one that matches the rest of the pots and pans?"

Poppy's face reddened, and the color rose up from her neck. She stared at Geoff, her pupils dilated in a *help me* message.

Before I could nudge Geoff, he righted the teakettle on the unused burner. "Mom, you know how easily these tea pots rust out. Maybe Uncle Paul got a stainless-steel one."

Jean opened the refrigerator. "I made chicken salad sandwiches for lunch." She turned to Poppy, her eyebrows raised in hopefulness. "Poppy, do you like that?"

"Yes, I love chicken salad sandwiches." Her words burst out—overly enthusiastic. "Are you sure I can't help you with anything?"

"No, thank you." Jean's delicate fingers placed the muffins into a wicker basket, a crisp linen napkin lining it. "Everything's ready. Please come and sit."

"My mom *always* has everything ready." Geoff came up behind Poppy. "She's not good about accepting help," he said, and gave his mother a loving admonishment. "And Mom's the queen of hospitality."

"I'm so glad you could get over here today." Jean's face brightened. "I couldn't wait to get out of the Cleveland weather." She smiled at Poppy and lowered her voice, as if she didn't want to offend the city of Cleveland.

"You sound like my mom. Milwaukee has the same nasty weather." Poppy wrinkled her nose.

They shared similar stories of Cleveland and Milwaukee—of golf, curling, and football. They talked about their commonalities—Valerie and Jean's love of antiques, warm weather, and gracious hospitality.

"No, no." Jean gently touched Poppy's shoulder, as she stood to help clear. "You're our guest. I'll clean up. You two go on out to the pool. We'll join you in a bit."

Poppy and Geoff walked out the front sliding-glass door that faced the ocean on the same path they'd taken six weeks earlier. Near the entrance to the pool, Geoff raised his eyebrows. He tilted his head down the hallway. "Hey Honch, wanna grab a sauna?"

She puckered her mouth to contain a smile and waved her arm in mock protest.

Poppy spread out her towel, aqua blue on the yellow-and-beige lounge chair, the rubbery slats catching her towel. She pulled off her cover-up, a red, gauzy maxi dress.

"No bikini today?" He stared at her navy-blue and white one-piece Speedo.

"I don't want my *boobs* to hang out." She looked at him as if a bikini were a ridiculous idea. "Have your mother think of me as *loose,* which she probably *already* does," she scoffed. "A one-piece is more proper." She tugged her straps up.

"She wouldn't care." Geoff tsked and laid his towel on the chaise longue.

"By the way, what *did* you tell them about me?" Poppy asked as she walked to the side of the pool. She dipped her foot in to test the water and, at the same time, tested Geoff's predisposition for family gossip. "What did your mom mean when she said she'd heard 'so much' about me?"

"I told her you were great." He smiled as he stood next to her. His tone turned serious. "That even though we sleep together all the time, we only have sex on the weekends."

Poppy shoved him in the pool, and his laugh bubbled up under water.

The early evening sun, blocked by the condo, reflected Gauguin's light off windows and patio doors. Shimmering. It'd cooled, although the temperature still hovered in the mid-eighties.

Jean stood partially on the cooler grass where it bordered the hot asphalt. Her leather sandals, half on the grass, half on the white line next to the Fiat, softened from the ambient heat of the sun. She ignored it. I imagined each moment with her son, Geoff, and his Poppy, felt essential. She began her wave, as if she was bidding a quiet bon voyage to British royals, and gracefully shifted as if the wave were a metronome that kept time and slowed the minutes—*adagio, adagio*—as they put their pool clothing in the car.

"Have fun seeing Twig and Cathy when they visit next week, Geoff. And call us when you get back to Rollins," Jean said, adding, "Will the dining hall still be open?" She shielded her eyes from the setting sun. "Or should I pack you some sandwiches?"

"We'll be okay, Mom. Thanks for everything." Geoff kissed her bronzed cheek. "I wish we could stay longer. But Poppy reads in Knowles Chapel on Sundays." Geoff put his arm on her lower back. "She has to be there early tomorrow morning."

"Thank you so much for having me, Dr. and Mrs. Spencer." Poppy leaned in and hugged the top of Jean's shoulders—polite but not overdoing it. "It was so nice to finally meet you. And your chicken salad tasted delicious."

"Well, we loved having you, Poppy." Jean smiled, gracious.

"Do you have enough gas in the car, Geoffrey? Here." George reached in his pocket and pulled out a ten-dollar bill, as if it'd been waiting for this moment. "Here's some gas money."

"Thanks, Dad." Geoff slipped the bill in the pocket of his khaki shorts.

Geoff and Poppy—in the car—waved one last time at his parents, who waved and didn't stop until the Fiat's taillights were out of sight. Jean's wave: *Adagio, my son.* George's wave, a proud father's wave, exclaimed, *There goes my son with his wonderful girl.*

"See, Honch? I told you they'd love you." He shook her leg as if to reassure her.

"You think? They weren't just being polite?" Poppy flipped in her seat, and her words poured out. "Oh God, I thought I'd *die* when she asked about the teakettle!"

Geoff laughed and nodded. "Did you like the way I just sort of brushed it aside?"

"You totally saved me." She shook her head and fingered the zipper pull on the pocket of her golf skirt. "How can you tell they liked me?"

"Will you stop it? I just know. I knew you'd fit right in. Mom and Dad smiled the whole time. They adore you," he said like it was obvious. "Besides"—he glanced at her and caressed her thigh— "what's not to love?"

It'd been six days since Poppy and Geoff returned from the visit with Geoff's parents at the beach. They hadn't seen much of each other—just an occasional dinner at Beans. But as seniors, I knew they both had a lot of work to complete before graduation.

Outside of the Phi Delt fraternity house, Geoff spoke with a man and woman. *Oh, of course. Geoff's brother and sister-in-law.*

I scanned the background information. Twig, five and a half years older than Geoff, had graduated from Trinity College in Hartford, Connecticut. He worked at a bank in California, where he'd met his wife, Cathy. They married a year and a half ago, and were expecting their first child.

A little shorter than Geoff at 5' 9," Twig had wavy brown hair, the color of roast coffee, that covered his ears. With coloring similar to his father, the doctor, Twig's eyes shined light brown, with a green hue. He leaned in closer to Geoff, and in a typical older brother gesture gave a jovial slap on his younger brother's back. The scroll popped up with an evaluation of the behavior: *Big brothers do this often to reassert their firstborn status.*

Except for her stomach, Cathy appeared lithe. At seven months pregnant, her swollen belly revealed an obvious contrast. The light-blue maternity dress floated on her. I couldn't help but notice her warm brown eyes and gentle manner. Her hickory-brown hair, just past her shoulders, flipped up to reveal honey-tipped curls.

"It's so neat that you guys are here. Cathy, you look great!" Geoff leaned over slowly to give Cathy a careful hug. "Let me run next door to get Poppy."

A moment later, Poppy and Geoff came out from the Theta House—Poppy's knee-length white skirt drifting behind her. The blouse, a colorful pattern with marine-blue, red, and pale-blue geometric shapes, looked like the artist, Mondrian, might've painted it.

"Hi, Cathy and Twig!" Poppy hugged both of them as if she already knew them well. "I'm so excited to meet you. Finally, I've met the whole family." Poppy touched Cathy's arm. "You look wonderful, Cathy. You feeling okay?"

"Yes, I feel fine." Cathy's voice sounded diminutive, delicate and gentle. "This little one kicks like crazy. I think he or she's a soccer player." Cathy smoothed her palm over her belly.

With small steps, Twig began to walk back and forth as his eyes took in everything. "This is a beautiful school. Cath and I walked around campus while we waited for Geoff to get out of his class," he said to Poppy.

"We have it made in the shade." Geoff hugged Poppy with one arm and smiled at her as if she were in charge of the beautiful setting. "You guys ready to head out for lunch?"

"I am!" Cathy chuckled, her laugh like a trickling stream. "I'm always ready."

"We'll just head right up Park Avenue." Geoff gestured across Holt Avenue to the entrance to the college.

"This is gorgeous. Beautiful." Cathy breathed, as though the outdoors were a museum. "The campus begins right here? At these two matching archways?" Cathy looked up at one of two identical stone pillars. Majestic entry points, with *Rollins College* etched in the stone header.

"Yeah, they're like miniatures of the Arc de Triomphe." Poppy walked underneath and through the west opening. "And just like that we're on Park Avenue."

As they made their way up Park Avenue, Twig turned to talk and continued to walk backward, making grand gestures when he spoke. Animated and energetic, it seemed as though he played charades as they walked.

Outside the front door of the restaurant, Geoff pointed up to his left. "See that balcony up there?" Geoff grinned. "That's the Park Plaza Hotel."

"It's charming." Cathy smiled, her soft-pink lipstick the color of her cheeks.

"Oh God," Poppy mumbled, her pupils wide with alarm.

Geoff glanced at Poppy. "I've *stayed* there. For my birthday, my college sweetheart booked a room. Actually *we* stayed there." Geoff squeezed Poppy's shoulder.

"No kidding." Twig looked at Poppy, who blushed. He turned back to his brother, and his expression implied, *A hotel? Adult fooling around? Not the back seat of the GTO?* For a moment, Twig studied Geoff like he'd become more of a peer than a younger brother, before resuming his older brother status and gesturing for all of them to enter.

The open-air East India Emporium felt breezy, and enormous palms waved to the sounds of Jimmy Buffet beneath the wicker fans on the ceiling. The negligible lighting was a sharp contrast to the Florida sun. All four of them blinked as they walked in. They found seats at a round table. East India—more of an ice cream shop that also served lunch—featured a massive twenty-foot wooden counter.

After they'd ordered, Geoff smoothed his placemat and readied himself with a smile. "So. Twig, did I tell you what happened to the teakettle at the condo?"

"No-o-o-o," Poppy shrieked, and unsuccessfully tried to cover Geoff's mouth.

"What teakettle?" Twig looked from Poppy back to Geoff.

"It's okay, Honch. I'm sure Twig has tons more wild stories than this." He lowered her hand from his face and held it. "He won't tell our mother."

"Agh." Poppy stared at the table, its glossy veneer reflecting her embarrassment.

"So she puts on the tea, okay? And we got, umm, distracted. In the bedroom. The next thing I knew, I smelled burnt metal. All the water—gone from the teapot. We almost burned down the fucking condo!"

Twig thumped his palm on the wooden lacquer tabletop. "Are you *kidding* me?" He stared at Geoff, his laughter caught in between his words.

With her hand as a shield at the side of her face, Poppy whispered to Cathy, "The worst, though . . . Last week, Mrs. Spencer asked Geoff if he knew what'd *happened* to the ugly old green teakettle that matched all of the other stuff." Poppy exhaled, a close-call sigh. "I almost died." She grimaced and shook her head.

"Oh, I know." Cathy's eyes grew wide, and her eyelash tips grazed the top of her eyebrows. "Jean's very sharp. She doesn't miss *a thing*."

Twig shook his head, still laughing. "I can just hear Mom say in her worry voice," Twig began, and raised his voice to a chirp, "'What happened to the teakettle?'"

~❧

For another hour, the brothers, Poppy, and Cathy lingered at the table, the smell of a new batch of freshly baked sugar cones wafting in the open court-yard just as they said their good-byes. I'm not sure of the nature of Geoff and Twig's relationship before, yet from my observation today, they seemed more like friends than siblings. The four of them chatted easily, laughed, and shared stories.

Around five o'clock, I returned to campus and headed straight to Knowles Chapel, uplifted from the afternoon.

I felt confident in my choreography with Poppy and Geoff. Certain that I'd receive some recognition in the form of a plaque for my work with my couple during the school year. I stared at the wooden shelf in my haven in Knowles Chapel and even cleared off a space to place the yet-to-be-determined award.

With Rollins graduation about six weeks away, I could relax with Poppy and Geoff. *Things are going superbly.*

# CHAPTER 14

# Two Words

~⌒~

I REVIEWED MY NOTES AND realized I hadn't updated my scroll on Poppy and Geoff since his brother visited a few weeks ago. Nothing noteworthy to add. Phillip teased me with the unannounced challenge—little hints. Something about the highest level of connection a couple could achieve. *How could any couple have a higher level of connection than Poppy and Geoff?* I thought, as I made my way across campus.

At dusk, the balmy weather and light breeze swirled around Poppy as she returned from the art room. With graduation a few weeks away, she seemed focused on completing her final projects. She paused outside of Geoff's fraternity and chewed her lip as if she weren't sure about going in. *A propriety thing, no doubt.*

I followed Poppy as she climbed the stairs to the second floor, her large sketchbook in hand, with an army-green book bag that slipped off her shoulder. She was unsteady as she clambered. Rather than monitor her, I paused to observe a crow eyeing me on the courtyard wall between the Phi Delt House and the Theta House.

~⌒~

Several minutes later, I found the two of them alone in Geoff's room. They sat on his bed—Geoff semi-leaned on a pillow against the wall, hands clasped behind his head. Poppy lay on her side, her elbow on the comforter, while her hand propped up her head. *They seem to be in the middle of a conversation,* I thought.

"Hmm. I don't know." Geoff looked up to his right. "I know I'll be captain of the water-ski team."

Poppy silently looked at her fingernails, seemingly fixated on some oil paint on her cuticles. "I better go." Poppy swung her legs to the floor. "I have a lot of work to do," she mumbled, as she flattened her hands on the spread.

As if hydraulically powered, Geoff unfolded his hands as his arms slowly drifted to his chest. "What do you mean? You just got here." He sat up on one elbow.

"I know." She glanced over at him and stood. "I have stuff to do." She kissed him and, from the doorway, flashed a disappearing smile. "See you tomorrow."

Geoff's fingers gripped the edge of the bed, his brow wrinkled. He muttered, "What was *that* about?"

I followed Poppy back to her room. She dropped her bag and pad on her bed, and went downstairs. In the first-floor living room, she waved a silent greeting to four of her Theta sisters who were watching *Welcome Back, Kotter*. She picked a spot and sat cross-legged on the carpet, her chin in her hands.

*There's something different,* I thought. Not the usual behavior for these two. I replayed the last half hour in my mind. *They hadn't argued, yet she'd had a short visit. Really short. She'd said she had some work to do, but she came downstairs without her books. Didn't talk to anyone. And Geoff hadn't walked her back as he typically did. Although she never even gave him the chance.*

I went back to the frat house. A subdued Geoff sat at the end of the couch in the living room with four guys, watching *CHiPs*.

*What was that I'd read in the scroll?* I curled it open and found what I'd been looking for. *Social solitude. The behavior of people who're physically present with others, but not engaged.* My scroll rolled up in my hand, limp and dangling like a loose thread.

I shrugged it off. *This couple always finds a way to self-correct. I'm not concerned. I felt more focused on what Phillip's challenge might be, than anything else.*

On Friday, April 21, after her classes, Poppy visited her parents at their condo on Longboat Key. Before she left, I looked at Poppy's journal entries. As I flipped through the days into the third week of April, I immediately stopped when I saw her entry dated just yesterday. I quickly skimmed her notes.

> *April 20.*
> *I feel so stupid. When I asked Geoff what will happen next year, he said he'd be captain of the water-ski team. It's not like I could say, "So, are we going to be together at all after graduation? Have you given any thought to what we'll do this summer and next year? Will we see each other? Write? Talk on the phone?" I didn't want to be TOO forward, so I simply asked,*

*"What do you think will happen next year?" He went right into what HE'D planned for next year. I'm not even an afterthought. Obviously, I don't mean that much to him. Have I been used this whole year??? I'm kinda scared. Going back to Milwaukee soon, living at home, working.*

*I've never loved anyone like I love Geoff. Never trusted anyone like I do Geoff. But clearly, the feeling is NOT mutual. He didn't even consider me for next year. Or for that matter, this summer! I know he goes to Chautauqua, but still . . .*

A slight miscommunication between them. *That must be what I encountered last night in Geoff's room. She just wants Geoff to reassure her that after they both graduate next month, they'll still be together.* My mind was still occupied with what Phillip would propose to us with his challenge.

*I'm not worried. I'll review my scroll this weekend. And when Poppy returns on Sunday, I'll nudge Geoff to communicate some plans to visit Poppy this summer. Maybe plan another visit at the holidays. And he'll have to make plans soon.* He'll need to prepare for what he'll do for work, where he'll live after he graduates. And graduation's only a month away.

I spent the weekend in Knowles. I crafted three different scripts for them. They all involved Geoff, who'd start a conversation about their future. The script I thought sounded best was for Geoff to look for jobs in Milwaukee. In my scroll, I saw ten job options for him. Six of them sought new grads. As a business major, all of them would be a good fit for him. I would nudge Geoff to ask Poppy about her hometown connections.

~~

Early on Sunday night, Poppy and Geoff still hadn't seen each other after Poppy's return from Longboat Key. Alone in her room, Poppy unpacked in total silence—unusual for any college student. Typically, songs from the Four Tops, Marvin Gaye, or the Temptations—"Ain't Too Proud to Beg" was a favorite—regularly blasted from her Bose speakers. Poppy shoved her suitcase under the bed and stood at the mirror. She scrutinized herself as if her reflection were an old photo she couldn't identify. She stared at her image, eyes hollow, shoulders slumped.

Always giddy and bubbly, Poppy didn't even look like Poppy.

*Why does she look like this? Whatever occurred over the weekend, perhaps Geoff could raise her spirits. This is the perfect time for a gentle nudge. And the ideal time to nudge Geoff to get the conversation rolling about their future together. A double nudge.*

Within minutes of my nudge, Geoff appeared in Poppy's doorway. She stood at her desk, her hands gripping the back of the chair.

"Hey, Honch." He walked in and slid his hands around her waist. "How was your weekend with your mom and dad?"

"Fine," Poppy said, her eyes locked on his laced topsiders.

"Did your mom make egg salad for you again like she did when we went to Longboat on our day-trip a couple of weeks ago?" Geoff tilted his head and grinned.

Poppy's mouth curled into a brief smile, as though she had never been taught how to smile correctly. "Uh-huh."

Geoff took her hand and guided her to sit on the bed. "Is something the matter, Honch?" He brushed back her hair.

Poppy exhaled, her stare straight ahead toward her roommate's bed. "I've been thinking a lot." She watched as her polished nails aimlessly rubbed her palms. Her voice continued, low and soft. "Since I'm graduating, and you have one more year here . . ."

*What did she say? One more year? Who has one more year? Geoff?*

My head began to spin. *What does she mean he has another year here?* I opened my scroll. My hands fumbled with my little-used device, as I re-checked Geoff's profile.

*And there it is. Geoff's a junior. Not a senior like Poppy. He's not graduating next month. This can't be. Shit. How did I overlook this?*

Poppy's monotone voice droned on. "And we won't be together, right? We'll probably break up. So, maybe we should just break up now." Her dull, muffled tone, even with the gentle delivery, did not come close to softening the crushing impact of her words, which included the dreaded phrase "break up."

"What?!" Geoff's jaw fell open and his body jerked sideways on the bed to look at Poppy. "What're you talking about?"

"Well, we're not going to be together anyway," she said, her words a resigned whine. "We may as well break—"

"You're *breaking* us up?" Geoff's face contorted in wild confusion. He braced himself on the edge of the bed. "Why are you doing this?" His raspy voice gave way to tears.

"I don't know," she started to sob and finally looked up at him, her expression also confused. "It's just that," she sputtered. "Well, we aren't going to be together, right?" Poppy's eyes brimmed, the salty water tipping on her lower lids—her face now a mosaic of microexpressions. She searched his face for answers to questions she didn't even know she could or *should* ask.

"Don't you still love me?" Geoff's urgent tone seemed to break through her emotional paralysis.

"Yes!" She heaved a gasp, dazed and nodding as if in shock. "Yes, I do."

"Then why are you doing this?" he wailed, now panting. Teardrops sprang from his eyes.

"I don't know," she cried out. "I don't know," she repeated in a hypnotic moan as tears bounced off her cheeks onto Geoff's sleeve. "I thought you . . .," she began, just as Geoff stood, his hands on either side of his head, as if he tried to hold the spinning thoughts in place.

"You thought *what?*" Geoff spun around, his expression demanding a reasonable explanation, his words reflecting stunned anger.

Poppy reached out to touch the sleeve of his red-and-white-striped rugby shirt. "Wait, I thought that you didn't . . ." She gasped and her eyes darted from her hand on his moving sleeve to his wet, anguished face.

"Didn't *what?*" He spat out, and moved closer to Poppy—a confrontational lunge. "Didn't think I'd be upset? Like you want to be *friends* now?" he sneered, and his mouth uncontrollably twisted in a scornful rebuke.

"No I didn't think you'd be . . .," she stammered and grabbed for his arm. "No, wait, that's not what I meant. I thought that you . . ." Her voice broke as her words dissolved into sobs.

*This is a nightmare.*

*How many times have I observed them? And I didn't see this coming? It's right here in the damn scroll. Been here the whole damn time. Since Phillip first gave me the assignment. I can't believe I missed this. I may as well resign right now from choreography.*

Both Poppy and Geoff huddled into themselves and held their stomachs. A physiological breakdown from the emotional upheaval. They kept repeating the same fatal dance—the death cycle of words.

"Why are you doing this?"

"I don't know."

"Don't you still love me?"

"Yes, I love you!"

"Then why are you doing this?!"

"I just thought that you didn't care that . . . wait! Don't leave," she whimpered. He shook his arm and rid his sleeve of her hand, as if it were a venomous black widow spider. He turned his back to her, as his shell-shocked gait staggered from her room.

"Please, Geoff. Come back," she cried, her words riddled with apocalyptic despair.

Already down the stairs, Geoff wiped his face with the back of his hand.

I felt like I'd just stumbled onto some horrific emotional crime scene. Pieces of spattered dreams—everywhere. Limp and lifeless on the ground.

*This is more than devastating. Not only for them, but for me as well.*

And my career? *Over.*

*Things can't get any worse.*

*I can't tell my supervisor about this. Not yet. Before he discovers anything about this colossal blunder, I'm going to read every damn word in that scroll about this couple. I can't believe I've been so blind. That I didn't catch this. I'll have to figure out something. Watch them every second. Look for the right moment to fix this.*

Monday morning, the day after the breakup, Poppy and Geoff went separate ways. None of their friends seemed to notice. I felt sure that their friends would've heard by now, yet Geoff had shared the news only with Ernie and Fred. Poppy told only Catherine and Cecelia—her Milwaukee friend—on the phone. Poppy merely said that she and Geoff had broken up and she didn't want to talk about it. No details. *Unfortunately for me, no chance for someone else's point of view.* No consoling conversations to unwrap the misery she was experiencing.

Not that I had answers, I realized, and I faced certain truths about my ability to choreograph. What had I learned? Nothing, evidently, except that with people, one thing remained elusive. Human emotions. *It's nearly impossible for me to have quantified, measured, predicted, or anticipated these elements in any meaningful way—to have prevented this fiasco.* Not that I excused my part in this breakup, but I felt the need to explain it, to examine my competence. To assess my—and this is difficult—my potential failure as a choreographer.

In three days, I saw a change in Poppy that I never would've imagined. She'd sequestered herself in the art studio, where her tears made intermittent plops in the turpentine and on her oil paint palette. The studio was a perfect hideaway for her, the building remote. Stuck in what seemed like the armpit of the physical plant, as if placed there as an afterthought.

It was safe to say that no one would find her there. In fact, most students didn't even know the location of the art building, or that Rollins even *had* an art department.

She took some comfort from her art friends, most of them introverted guys—the male art students not the norm for Rollins. I think Poppy found some relief in their gentle manner. They accepted her. They didn't judge her or her work.

All week, she clung to the art room as her sanctuary, a secret place to hide her obvious sadness. She didn't laugh, her sparkle now gone, Poppy's entire demeanor unfamiliar. After Sunday night, she didn't talk about Geoff anymore. Not even to her roommate.

My only source of information came from her diary, where her despair was evident.

> *Monday, April 24:*
> *I can hardly write; my hand is shaking so much. I'm shocked at how badly Geoff took the breakup last night—that he was SO upset. I was stunned when he cried. I never dreamed he'd be so undone. I thought I was just filler this year. That he could take me or leave me. Like Mom always says, "Boys just want ONE thing." And after we had sex, well, he probably didn't think I was that important anymore. That I'm just like one of his frat brothers, someone he could hang out with. And lately, Fred and Geoff seemed to spend more time together anyway. So it just goes to show that I'm not very special.*
>
> *But after last night and how sad he seemed, I think I might be wrong. But there's nothing I can do to fix it.*
>
> *I wish I could take back the words, but he stunned me by being upset. I couldn't even think straight. I didn't realize until after I'd said that we should break up that he cared more about me than I thought he had.*
>
> *I wish he'd stayed, so I could get through what I wanted to say. But I couldn't speak. No words came out. I felt desperate to shout out what I wanted to hear HIM say. That HE would be the one to love me all next year. Make plans for us to stay together. But I couldn't say it. I didn't feel I had the RIGHT to say it. And all I heard was Mom's voice in my head, saying,*

*"Girls don't chase boys,"* and *"Don't be too forward,"* and I clammed up. My feelings and thoughts got all twisted up and muddled. And he left and oh God . . . it was AWFUL.

*I called Cecelia at Bowdoin last night. She said I should talk to him. Try to explain. She said he is a good man. She'd never seen me like I am . . .or WAS . . . with Geoff. She's even upset that we broke up for what sounded to her, too, like a dumb reason. But I'm too ashamed and he's too angry at me.*

*I'm pretty sure I broke his heart. But my heart feels broken, too. I want to take it all back, to have him make everything better just like he always does. Or, anyway, like he did. I wish he'd said that I was the most important thing in the world to him. Like he used to. But it's too late. I lost the only man I've ever loved and the only person I completely trusted. I feel worthless and hate myself for hurting him."*

*Tuesday, April 25:*
*I saw Geoff from far away today and waited until he passed before I made my way to Beans with Catherine. I feel like there's a hole where my entire midsection used to be. How can I hurt this badly? Staying in the art room for nine hours today helped. It's dark. No one bothers me. I don't deserve to have anyone be nice to me anyway. I hurt this wonderful, kind person and can't even BEGIN to consider if he'll ever forgive me. Besides, he's not coming after me. He probably hates me anyway. I can't wait to get out of here. To LEAVE Rollins.*

*Wednesday, April 26:*
*It will be good to get away next weekend to go home. I feel so empty. Worthless. I don't deserve to be with someone like Geoff anyway.*

I put her diary aside and found myself stuck on what to do. *Could* I do anything? Was there any possible way to salvage this?

*I'm not sure if it's my imagination or not, but it seems like a pall has been cast over the second-floor hallway of Mayflower Hall.* Usually, soccer balls or Frisbees ricocheted off the walls and often knocked the receiver off the holder of the public wall phone. Usually, the percussion of collegiate spirits resounded through the building.

*Tonight it's quiet. Maybe exam prep, but I don't think so.*

Geoff came out of his room, without saying good-bye to his roommate, Ernie, who—deep into writing a paper—pecked away on the Smith Corona typewriter.

With the palm of his hand against the wall, as if he required a counterbalance for his movements, Geoff walked with his head down. He knocked on the open door of his frat brother's room. "Hey, Paul," he said, and noticed a foldout couch and coffee table in place of a bed and the typical beat-up frat boy trunk. "May I borrow your phone?"

Paul, with blue eyes and fine blond hair, ushered Geoff in as if he'd been expecting a dignitary. "Hey, Mr. I'm-in-the-greatest-campus-relationship! C'mon in."

Geoff winced as if he'd just witnessed a wreck on the side of the road and had been instructed not to discuss it. "Thanks, Paul," he murmured.

Paul looked at Geoff, and his expression registered the sadness on his friend's face. His eyes went to the floor, the courteous way, so as not to intrude. The same height as Geoff, Paul wore khaki pants—dress pants with pleats—and a button-down shirt with the sleeves rolled down, not rolled up as many of the other men did. "I'll just grab my books and go downstairs," he said and lifted his notebook and business management textbook from his desk. "Take all the time you need," Paul said. "I know you won't have any privacy with that hall phone."

Geoff sat on the kiwi-green couch, leaned over, and lifted the rotary phone from the nightstand. He took the receiver out of the cradle, laid it on his shoulder, and dialed. "Hi Mom, hi Dad," he breathed the words out. "I know it's Wednesday and I just called on Sunday." He blinked. "But I have some sad news." His voice cracked when he said "news." "Poppy and I broke up."

He squeezed his eyes shut. As he listened to the voices of his parents, he nodded to what I thought might be the voices of reason. Commiseration—a human balsam that caressed all the impairments of the heart—communicated in the voices of his parents.

Geoff opened his eyes and looked at a framed wall hanging above Paul's desk, a signed poster of a football player from the Kansas City Chiefs, Willie Lanier. "I really don't know what happened." He looked away from the red-and-white poster and stared into his lap. "We talked Sunday night, and she said that since she's graduating, we should break up." He choked out a sob and began to nod, and his tears spilled over his eyelids. "I am, too," he blubbered. His arm at his stomach, he rocked. "I know, I know, Mom. I'm shocked, too." He straightened and wiped his cheek on his sleeve. "Yeah, I thought we were great, too." He nodded again and wiped a tear from his cheek.

Geoff stood and hooked his fingers under the cradle of the phone. He unwound the tangled cord from the arm of the sofa. "I better go. I just wanted to tell you," he said, his voice low, as if he'd just told his parents his best friend had died. "I love you, too."

When he hung up the phone, Geoff's feet wobbled, as if they could no longer support his trim body. His shoulders collapsed into a heap as he put the phone back.

I felt something I'd never felt before. I, too, felt wounded. Hurt. *Have I been so focused on my own success and recognition that I haven't cared about the people I'm working with? Have I not given a damn about their lives? Their futures?*

Here's this couple. They were *great*. And now they had broken hearts.

I thought back to the art room earlier that week. I realize now what I'd witnessed—Poppy's feelings of loss and despair. She hadn't known how to ask Geoff for reassurance. It seemed as if she needed some sort of permission to ask him if she mattered—if they'd remain a couple after she graduated.

I could've prevented the whole breakup.

Hubris was something Phillip warned me about during my internship. He cautioned me not to let hubris get in the way of my work. I'd pretty much dismissed the comment. It seemed irrelevant at the time.

Mesmerized by the Poppy and Geoff show, I'd done nothing. I went through the motions, quick to get on with a new project. Why hadn't I paid attention to the nuances?

*Hubris, Jesse. Hubris.*

If I'd just stayed with them last Thursday night. When Poppy had asked Geoff about next year, when he had talked about being captain of the ski team—why hadn't I picked up on that? That he'd been talking about being back at Rollins? If I hadn't taken the time to stare at that mocking crow, I would've heard Poppy ask her vague question. I could've nudged her *right then and there* to have the courage to add two little words.

"What will happen next year . . . *to us?*"

If I'd nudged Poppy to add those two words—and nudged Geoff to pay attention—he would've thought about his response. I hadn't paid attention when Geoff said he'd be captain of the water-ski team next year. I'd even *seen* it written in her diary.

I'd focused on my future. My awards, *me*. From day one, I'd thought Geoff was a senior. But he wasn't. He was one year behind Poppy. How had I not realized that? My oversight loomed, huge and inexcusable.

If I'd known that all year, I could've helped them to plan. To discuss a future. But I was so caught up in what a perfect fit they were—what a *great* job I was doing. I was more concerned with how their success made *me* look good. *I now understand the unworthiness that Poppy feels. I feel it, too. And I'm culpable—the biggest reason for their breakup. I feel like there's an air-raid siren blaring in my head.*

# CHAPTER 15

# Candlelight

FOR TWO WEEKS, I CONFINED myself to Knowles Chapel. Poppy and Geoff remained on the right side of the clock, at the Three O'clock designation—Despair.

I felt intense guilt and shame. I sat alone in the third pew. I wasn't sure why at first. Maybe to get a fresh perspective. I didn't let my eyes linger on the stained-glass windows and stunning altar.

I couldn't shake the vision of Geoff, after he'd left Poppy's room that Sunday night, lying on his bed as he listened to a song with heart-wrenching lyrics on his stereo.

No one deserved to be stuck in that desolated landscape, but there they still were a week later.

I stared at the pulpit where Poppy had inspired the Rollins community with readings during the Sunday morning worship. Poppy had traveled home to Milwaukee for Mother's Day weekend. Her eyes had appeared lackluster on Friday. Her eyes would no doubt look the same when she returned later that afternoon.

Ashamed, and in despair, Poppy had wallowed for the past two weeks in her own sense of unworthiness. I gripped the edge of the pew, the well-worn veneer still shiny and smooth to my touch. Something solid in my world.

*Maybe somewhere down the road*, my scroll displayed in the middle of the screen. I stood and stared at the solitary candle that flickered on the side of the altar. A changeable light that revealed the uneven tiles in the chapel, the variations in the walls and ceiling. The inconsistencies.

I arrived at Geoff's fraternity house, a shred of hope in me that a nudge would present itself: *Maybe there's something I can do.*

I stood in the hallway and watched as Fred poked his head in Geoff's door and jingled his car keys. "Hey man, wanna to go to Steak 'n Shake?"

Geoff sprang up from his bed as if eager for the interruption. "Sure. I'm sick of Beans. Tired of seeing people." At his dresser, he tapped the lever on his Pioneer turntable and cut off Justin Hayward's lyrics— "Oh I dreamed last night I was hearing, hearing your voice . . ."—as the needle lifted from the album.

After dinner, the two brothers arrived back at Rollins and parked in the shared lot across from the Phi Delt and Theta Houses. Fred slurped the remains of his chocolate shake as he and Geoff walked across Holt Avenue. With an elbow to Geoff's ribs, he gestured with his head to the second-floor balcony of their frat house. The balcony, where four of their brothers crammed together, overlooked the Theta courtyard. Beers in hand, the Phi Delts laughed and jeered as they leaned on the wrought-iron railing.

"What's going on?" Fred bellowed, paying more attention to his Styrofoam cup than to the answer from the balcony. He held the straw and plastic cover in his hand and sucked the last dredges of chocolate syrup from the bottom.

Gavin formed his hands like a megaphone around his mouth and leaned over the railing. His fire-red hair caught the setting sun. "Theta Candlelight," he shouted down to the sidewalk.

"Really?" Fred quickly finished the remaining dregs of his drink and yelled up, "Who do we think it is?"

The four men on the balcony lifted their shoulders in a group shrug.

I went inside the Theta House to check it out. From my scroll, I already knew of Candlelights: *A Candlelight is a formal ceremony, a ritual that celebrates a woman in the sorority house who announces her engagement. A secret. Only the engaged woman and the president of the sorority know her identity. The candle is passed around in a circle from sister to sister. The first time it goes around, no one reveals the name of the bride-to-be. On the second pass, the engaged woman extinguishes the candle.*

The lights turned off in the Theta living room, the sorority sisters in white dresses quietly gathered in a circle, hushing the ones who giggled, giddy from the excitement of the announcement. When the room grew quiet, they began to sing the Theta anthem. Meredith, the president, lit the candle and passed it to her right—from one hand to another.

As I backtracked to the foyer of the house, I heard the *whoosh* of the extinguished candle flame, followed by squeals of delight. I turned back to look. Just curious.

Poppy held the smoldering candle.

Girls hugged her, their arms bouncing on her shoulders, their high-pitched voices shrieking their glee. "I'm so happy for you!" several shouted at once.

"When did this happen?" Catherine whispered to Poppy. Her room-mate's forehead and eyebrows crinkled together. "I didn't know you guys got back together."

"I just . . .," Poppy began, yet her half-smile faded. She caught sight of two sisters as they opened the courtyard doors. Poppy tried to pull herself away from the gaggle of women who barraged her with questions: "When's the wedding? How did he propose?"

As some of the Thetas spilled out into the courtyard, one of the Phi Delts on the balcony cupped his hands over his mouth and yelled, "Who is it?"

Poppy, distraught, hung her head like she'd just killed the beloved family pet.

Eyes wide, I stared at Poppy and surveyed the women in the courtyard as I tried to take it all in. *Have I missed this? They've self-corrected? They're back together?* I'd been in the chapel for almost two weeks, after all. *This miracle can save me!*

I walked through the courtyard and heard the excited chatter of the Phi Delts.

"It's Poppy!" They shouted to each other. Desmond, one hand still on the railing, leaned back into the room. "Yo, Spence, where are you?"

In the Theta living room, I heard whispers, then silence, followed by horrified gasps.

Poppy tugged at her roommate's arm and drew Catherine's ear to her lips.

"What?" Catherine's head jerked back. "It's *not* Geoff?" Her mouth fell—her mermaid blue eyes searched Poppy's face.

Poppy shrunk into herself and shook her head. She stared at the balcony where the Phi Delts stood.

Catherine saw Poppy's distress and suddenly felt the swell of Thetas closing in. She put a protective arm around Poppy, like a lawyer who shields her high-profile client from the onslaught of the press.

"What?" Many of the women gasped whispers among themselves. "Not Geoff?"

One of the Theta women, Hannah, garrulous and argumentative on her best days, burst through the polite group and barked, "So, who is it?" With a demanding face almost the color of her faded ecru dress, and one size too small for her straight-hipped body, she puckered her plain lips. She barked again, this time at a decibel level heard by bats and dogs. "Who is it?" Impatient, she adjusted her black-rimmed glasses and pushed them down her nose. All she needed was the sound of chalk on a blackboard. Her large teeth chomped on a stick of Juicy Fruit gum, and its syrupy scent drifted into Poppy's face.

"Someone I went out with in high school," Poppy muttered, and her words tumbled out in a single breath. Her eyes darted to the open courtyard doors, and Poppy shifted her shoulders, trying to angle her way out of the circle of sisters. "Please don't go into the courtyard." Her hand groped the air in a panicked grasp. "Please, don't—don't tell the Phi Delts," she begged, in a feeble attempt to free herself from the women. "It's not . . . Geoff," she sighed, her tone low, as if her words had fallen off a cliff. Poppy held her neck, her hand acting as a brace, her now vacant stare locked on the floor.

Even *I* knew it was too late to stop the spread of the news. The declaration, shouted by the excited Theta women, floated up to the now-empty balcony. *As far as the guys know, Poppy is engaged. To Geoff.* They ducked inside to share the announcement, to find him, and to celebrate.

*How can this be? How can she be engaged to someone else?*

Clinging to Catherine's arm, Poppy certainly imagined the gossip, the devastation when her Theta sisters finally understood—and worse, when the Phi Delts corralled Geoff and broke it to him. "He needs to hear it from me," Poppy whispered to Catherine, choking on her words.

As I arrived on the second-floor hall just outside Geoff's room, two of his brothers slapped a baffled Geoff on his shoulder as he stood silhouetted in his doorway.

Geoff stuck two fingers in between the pages of a text and lowered the book. "What's going on?" He looked from Gavin to the other tall, blond-haired frat brother.

"The Theta Candlelight man. Didn't you hear?" Gavin's light-blue eyes twinkled like one of Santa's elves. "It's Poppy. Congrats, man!"

"What?" Geoff staggered back as if the words had punched him in his groin. He lost his balance, and his hip slammed against the doorjamb. "Are you *shitting* me?" Geoff stared at Gavin, and his wounded eyes searched the redhead's face for the truth.

From the expression on Geoff's face, Gavin's laughter stopped, as though someone had suddenly turned a dial. Gavin looked at the other brother as if he, too, might've heard the wrong story. "Well, we *thought* it was Poppy." Gavin pointed in the direction of the Theta House.

Down the hall near the front stairwell, three brothers waved. "Hey, Spence. Way to go, man," they shouted before they disappeared into a room.

"It *is* Poppy, right?" Gavin said, his voice subdued, looking at Geoff's face—whose expression quivered from shock to anger and back.

"Yeah, but it's not fucking *me.*" He jabbed his finger at his chest and hurled his book to the floor. Gavin and the other frat brother jumped back as if splashed with cold water and gently ushered Geoff into his room.

"Are you kidding?" The blond guy slammed his fist on Geoff's desk, a physical display of camaraderie. "Man, that just sucks." He shook his head.

"Who's the guy?" Gavin mirrored Geoff's posture on the side of the bed, head down, elbows resting on his knees. "Do you know who it is, Spence?"

His eyes flicked a quick glance at Gavin. "Yeah, I think it's a guy she dated in high school," Geoff mumbled.

The door opened and Ernie strode in—a cowboy walk, as if spurs were poking out from his heels. "Oh, hey!" Ernie grinned, as if now the party could really get started. His smile faded, too, as he looked from Gavin to Geoff. "What's going on? What's the matter?" He stared at the two brothers, who stood in the middle of the room, their postures like seventh-grade boys at a cotillion.

Without looking up, Geoff turned his head. "Poppy just got engaged to some guy. I think it's the one she knew from high school."

"What? When?" Ernie looked at the other two, his mouth open in shock.

"Just a few minutes ago at the Theta House. You know, a Candlelight." Gavin fixed his gaze on Ernie, and his eyes widened as if wondering what to do next.

"Are you fucking kidding me?" Ernie bellowed, and collapsed next to Geoff on the edge of the bed.

"Nope," Geoff said, dragging out the *n.* "I wish I were kidding—that this is just some bad dream and I'll wake up and everything will be okay." Geoff fell silent.

Like the flame of the candle in Poppy's hand at the Candlelight ceremony, the perfect love of this couple drifted away, into the air. Extinguished.

CHAPTER 16

# Engaged Minds

~

*Two days after the Candlelight and I'm still shocked. It just doesn't make any sense at all. Poppy engaged to someone else? When did she see this other person?* I asked myself these questions as I sat on the step in the dark recess of the Beal-Maltbie Shell Museum. The museum, seemingly invisible to Rollins students, housed thousands of precious shells a short distance from Mayflower Hall, Geoff's fraternity. On the sidewalk in front of me, on Holt Avenue, two women paused, and I realized with a jolt, *It's Poppy and her roommate, Catherine.*

"Let's not cut through today. You know, near the Pub," Poppy said, as her eyes darted up and down Holt Avenue like a wanted fugitive. "I want to stay away from Orlando Hall." She leaned into Catherine, her hand cupped to her roommate's ear. "He's in there—he has English now," she said, and in two anxious moves, she tucked the back of her Theta shirt into her white golf skirt.

"Good idea," Catherine said, as her honeyed brown hair bobbed in agreement.

"Poppy," a voice commanded from behind them, its tone urging her to stop.

"Oh God," Poppy whispered, not turning around. "It's Fred. Geoff's friend." She froze in place. Fred caught up to them. He shifted a pile of three books from one hip to the other, as if he'd positioned his good side for a fight. An oversized textbook slid from his pile, and loose papers floated down like paper cradles. Fred picked up the slick cover and jammed the loose papers back into the middle of the book. He straightened his slight frame and puffed his chest out, the way birds and cats do. A primal display of physicality to appear bigger to a perceived threat.

He positioned himself in front of Poppy. "I can't believe how *cruel* you are." He spat out his verbal assault as his finger punctuated the air with short jabs—inches from her face.

Poppy's eyes blinked, not only from each of Fred's jabs but also to contain her oncoming tears.

Geoff's friend stepped closer. As the buttons on his denim shirt appeared ready to explode from his rapid breathing, he grabbed his chest and dug at the rough fabric. "I mean, it isn't bad enough to hurt the guy. But to get *engaged* right away?" He stared at her like she'd just run over a kitten in the street. "That's just coldhearted. You're a mean—"

"Just stop, Fred!" Catherine's arm shot out like a turnstile between Fred and Poppy. She slid in front of the silent Poppy and planted her feet like a sentry.

Poppy didn't seem to notice. Instead, she nodded her droopy head and looked like a puppy who'd just been scolded for peeing on the carpet.

Fred bobbed and weaved around Catherine, as his words came out like a left hook. "I can't believe—you broke his heart." Fred drew out the word "heart" and made it sound broken.

Poppy's eyes blurred with tears. "I didn't mean to . . ."

"You have *no* right to say anything." Catherine pointed a delicate finger back at Fred's face. "Just leave her alone." She lifted her chin and met his glare. "C'mon." She grabbed Poppy's arm, like a small child who needed help to cross the street. They walked quickly, but Poppy looked back. Fred, like a marble statue, stood in the same spot where they'd argued. His lips moved silently. It said more about him, his friendship with Geoff, and the estrangement than Poppy could bear.

"He's right," Poppy breathed, as she stumbled after her roommate. "I *am* cruel. I did a really bad thing. I told Meredith before the Candlelight that I really didn't want to do it. I said that everyone would think it was Geoff." She heaved a sob. "And they *did.*"

"I know, I know," Catherine soothed, and pulled her over to the empty bleachers across the street at Sandspur Field.

"The whole thing," she said. "Just horrible. I shouldn't have told Meredith about it at all. But being the good little *rule* follower I am, I obeyed chapter rules." Her high-pitched tone sing-songed. "I'm so mad at myself. I hate myself. Fred's right, I am mean." Poppy blubbered, and collapsed on the aluminum bleachers, and her wooden sandals made a *clonk* sound.

"Now wait a minute." Catherine stepped onto the riser beneath them and sat in the row in front of Poppy. "You are not," she said, as she looked up at Poppy. "You're one of the most thoughtful people I know." Catherine thrust out her hand like a stop sign. "And stop shaking your head no."

Poppy sniffled and exhaled several breaths to regain her voice. "I know it's sudden." Poppy's voice warbled in response to her roommate's unasked question—the question many probably had. "He just *asked* me. He and I haven't dated since high school," Poppy said, her words eking out. "I got a few letters from him. I even read them out loud to Geoff when we walked back from Beans and the mailroom." Poppy shook her head as if it didn't make a whole lot of sense to her, either. "It's been four years since I've even *seen* him." She looked at Catherine, whose periwinkle-blue eyes blinked.

Catherine grimaced and shook her head in an *oh my* kind of way. Her fingers twirled a bangle bracelet round and round her wrist, and the movement underscored the futility of trying to bring happiness to everyone involved. She stared at the grass, at a leftover red flag in the middle of the field from yesterday's flag football game. Catherine stared at Poppy. "So even though you just saw him a few weeks ago . . ." Catherine scooched forward, her bronzed knees up against the metal riser. "He asked you to marry him." Catherine's voice, gentle and inquisitive, sounded like that of a compassionate detective who was trying to gather information from a distraught and newly widowed woman.

Poppy nodded and hugged her knees. "It's hard to understand," she mumbled, as she stared at her shoe sliding back and forth against the grain of the ribbed aluminum.

Catherine wiggled her always-shoeless blackened toes on the risers. "Why didn't you tell me?"

"I don't know." Poppy shrugged. "I didn't tell anyone."

I'd finally updated Phillip, even though I knew he'd be disappointed with me. I noted what I thought had happened—that Poppy must have felt some uncertainty about her future and wanted to feel special, to have Geoff *show* her and *remind* her that she mattered—and would *continue* to matter. She'd looked to him for some sort of guarantee. She didn't want to be taken for granted.

*But she hadn't known how to ask in a clear way*, I thought, as I looked out the window of my haven onto Mills Lawn. Spring promised so much, but no answers for my couple.

In my scroll, I entered my reflections on what I thought had occurred. Poppy, who felt a great deal of insecurity about her romantic future with Geoff, the first man she ever trusted—loved—allowed her fear to overpower her ability to ask Geoff a direct question. *But to turn around and get engaged right away?*

Poppy found Rollins a magical paradise, a place where she'd explored the real essence of herself. Yet her parents and others reinforced the idea that college, especially Rollins, wasn't the *real world*. She didn't want to be *too* forward. Too overt.

I dumped my scroll on the sofa and took one last glance out the window, taking in nature's scenery of blossoms and birds. A sparrow hopped from branch to branch to stake out a habitat and provided a welcome distraction from putting things in an orderly, logical perspective.

In the sanctuary, I paced up and down the aisle, trying to sort the *unsortable.* Poppy had wondered what would become of them the next year. She expected Geoff—who had no idea that a problem existed—to subconsciously discern a problem. And to solve it. Make it better. Wasn't that what she always said? Geoff made things better? She needed Geoff to read her mind.

Yet, Geoff, like most twenty-one-year-old males, had the intuitive skills of a Guernsey cow. I frowned as I pressed my hands against the back of the pew. *Cow or no cow, I should've nudged Geoff to be aware of Poppy's feelings.*

*Wisdom is better than strength*, I thought, as I took in the beautiful chancel—the Rose Window's motto in the stained glass at the rear of the chapel. I admired it one last time. The Rose Window—the seven scholars—pillars of wisdom: Prudence, Knowledge, Fear of God, Counsel, Sound Wisdom, Understanding, Power.

I ran my palm along the solid pew in front of me. A gesture to the journey that I'd experienced at Rollins. As I stared at the circular Rose Window above the organ in the sanctuary, I thought I heard a pinging sound coming from my haven. I hurried through the nave and realized that my scroll, for the first time, had summoned me with a sound and a blinking notification.

Phillip's words crept across the screen:

> *Jesse, I understand your disillusionment at this time. I realize you believed Poppy and Geoff shared a deep connection as a couple. I, too, believed they shared that. Follow your good instincts—you were on the right path.*
>
> *Although it's not quite ready, I want to share the mysterious challenge I mentioned earlier, just with you for now. Not to inundate you with too much information, but I believe that you may be among the first to help us realize*

*the phenomenon of what I refer to as The Empathic Bridge. Our theory is that when two people reach a pinnacle of connection, and our relationship with that couple is equally as powerful, the Empathic Bridge will become a reality. We believe we will be able to hear their thoughts and feel their feelings.*

*More later. Just wanted to give you some hope.*

# CHAPTER 17

# Graduation

⁓

THE ROLLINS COLLEGE GRADUATION WEEKEND brought out a garden variety of emotions. Students, whose excitement burst out like bright tulips, compared to those who drooped, like soaked daffodils; those who didn't want to leave the sunny paradise. Although Poppy was venturing to a new life far away from campus, she appeared drenched by torrential rains of shame.

The week after the Candlelight, only one more entry appeared in Poppy's diary—undated—as if even the diary couldn't bear to properly document her thoughts: *It's painful to walk by the Phi Delt House. I can't wait to leave here. I don't even want to go to graduation.*

Poppy spent her remaining time at Rollins hidden in the art studio, exiled from others. She didn't eat at Beans with her friends. She avoided the common walkways where she might see Geoff. They had no overlap, no chance to discuss what'd happened. No chance to make things right.

Poppy wanted invisibility. Sequestered from her friends on campus, she wanted to remain as unseen as tan stucco on a campus dorm. While Poppy disappeared into the studio, Geoff found some comfort with his brothers, not his usual happy self. His dimple rarely made an appearance, and his moustache even drooped. Like a man blinded, like a tragic Shakespearean character, he went through the motions. *Social solitude.*

He, too, seemed ready for the school year to end.

For me, and for Poppy and Geoff, the last few weeks of the school year presented the kind of misery found in Dante's first circle of hell—the limbo in which good people with minor human infractions wait for liberation.

⁓

With several of his fraternity brothers set to graduate, Geoff remained at Rollins for Commencement. Fred's mother and father hosted a reception for parents of graduates at the Phi Delt House while their sons and daughters rehearsed for the ceremony.

Mayflower Hall changed from a Cheetos-infested swamp into a living room that passed inspection for moms and dads. Fred's mother brought a white linen tablecloth from home, an effort to bring a touch of civility to the frat house. For some reason, it made the building appear taller. More dignified.

The previous month, it had been a walled asylum for undomesticated college boys. This month, it was an almost elegant conservatory that appeared pleased to house gentlemen graduates of the Phi Delt House. The house had transformed from a lounge with a barefoot-cutting pop-top strewn floor into a ceremonial stage for parents who waited for Saturday's five o'clock rehearsal.

Gone were the crushed pretzels and potato chips from the floor, and the kegs from the alcove—including the keg that'd had a one-time appearance in the second-floor bathroom during a rush party. The bathroom keg was reserved for those who either chose not to or were wise enough not to drink the 180-proof grain alcohol and grape juice concoction known as Purple Jesus that sloshed in a Rubbermaid garbage can on the first floor.

A proper bar with large jugs of wine—Paul Masson and Gallo—along with vodka, gin, rum, and bourbon, and appropriate mixers of tonic, club soda, and ginger ale, replaced the typical fraternity fare. No Welch's grape juice or Kool-Aid as mixers. No grain alcohol or Mad Dog—MD 20/20.

The underclassmen in attendance mimicked the postures of their friends' parents. They dressed for the occasion in button-down shirts and khakis that'd spent the night pressed under mattresses. Each wrinkle of their clothing was a medallion of brotherhood activity to the Phi Delts. The boys' slacks—averse to the persistence of an iron—sprouted cuffs that looked like roof gutters. But they stood up straighter, their wet hair combed—some for the first time that day. They sipped their drinks as if they'd just taken an overnight course in chugging no more.

Geoff, in a pale-blue oxford and khakis, centered his moustache over the plastic cup and took a small sip of beer that he'd poured from a can of Schlitz. *The beer that made Milwaukee famous.* With his back to the kitchen, in the rear of the living room, Geoff took another sip, then abruptly winced and coughed when two smartly dressed adults walked in the front door. He recognized Poppy's parents.

"Oh shit," he said into his sudsy cup. His eyes darted left and right. No brother in sight to offer reprieve. He glanced at Valerie and George again, and his casual expression said, *I hope they haven't noticed me.*

Valerie's face brightened when she made eye contact with Geoff—an instinctive smile upon sighting a familiar face. Yet, her Chanel red lipstick faded into a polite expression. A dampened smile. Most likely the result of the realization that Geoff no longer played the part of *that kind* of familiar person in their daughter's life.

Geoff closed his eyes into his beer, as if to shut down the memories that were flooding back. He raised his head, fixed his lips into an *I can do this* smile, and walked to the center of the room.

"Hi Geoff," Valerie Terris greeted him graciously and extended her hand, a sign that a handshake would suffice.

"Hi, Mrs. Terris." Geoff shook her hand—the first-name basis jettisoned. "Hi, Mr. Terris."

George Terris greeted Geoff, and when he shook his hand, he demurred from his usual firm handshake—the *knock you off your feet* one. The heartfelt one he'd given Poppy's boyfriend in Wisconsin when Geoff had visited them just five short months ago. *A lifetime ago.*

"It's so nice of your friend to host this party for the parents," Valerie said, as her decorator's eyes took in the mantel. "This was the Pi Phi house when I attended Rollins."

"Yes, I remember. With Mr. Rogers." Geoff's pleasant smile spread—an attempt to muster a neighborly face.

"I'm sorry to see you again." Valerie smiled for a moment and looked down, as she fingered the napkin beneath her wine glass. "Under these circumstances," she said in a voice reserved for a widow at a funeral.

I watched Geoff as he spoke with Poppy's parents, his face pained. Like he, too, had attended the same funeral. It felt as though someone had died. Something *had* died.

*I'm supposed to be detached from the emotions of my couple.* But my entire philosophy about detachment rudely turned into Swiss cheese. Full of more holes than I could count. All my training, my planning, everything full of gaps. And yet, Phillip's words replayed in my mind, like minor chords in a tragic opera: *Hope in one scene; tragedy in the next.*

Although the blue sky and sunshine graced Mills Lawn for the graduation ceremony, it did little to chase the shadows present when I looked at Poppy *or* Geoff. No longer Poppy *and* Geoff.

The wooden folding chairs placed in neat rows contrasted with the lack of emotional order evident with Geoff.

In the queue to receive her diploma, Poppy's smile appeared rented, just as foreign to her as the starchy cap and gown.

In the back of the audience, toward the end of a row, Geoff sat next to Ernie. When the president shook the hand of the last student in the *S*'s and started the *T*'s, Geoff looked down and rolled up his program. When Poppy crossed the platform, he closed his eyes.

She walked off the stage and out of his life.

# PART II

# Last Love

# CHAPTER 18

# Clean Slate

~ ⌒

## 2010

ON WELL-TRAVELED HOLT AVENUE, TWO students walked past my window in Knowles Chapel at Rollins College, and the man's hand flopped lazily on the woman's shoulder as her arm and hand curled languidly around his waist. They stepped easily, as if the rosy-brick pavement were even. These past thirty-two years, that's the way Rollins life seemed for many students—easy and rosy. The paradise effect.

In more than three decades here at Rollins, I'd choreographed just under two hundred couples, just like the dreamy ones I was noticing outside of my room. Some of whom fit well together and later married, and a few others whom I'd nudged to go separate ways. All with Phillip's guidance.

After my first failure, with Poppy and Geoff in 1978, I quieted my own greed and ambitions and learned to focus on my couples. I honed my observation skills—listened humbly to Phillip's advice. Although I never really choreographed another couple so well-suited and as deeply in love as Poppy and Geoff had been. The ache of my failure in their relationship still haunts me.

I looked away from the strolling lovers and stared at my new device, the slate. Phillip had named his prototype after Idaho's Slate Mountain, near Mink Creek. The mechanism has taken him ten years to perfect.

While I didn't miss using the old scroll, or its sometimes unwieldy nature, I did miss its simplicity—like the typewriter that gave way to the computer. My sleek gray slate, enclosed in metamorphic rock, resembled a roofing tile. Its fine-grained composite structure was made mostly from quartz, hematite, and muscovite.

No more than half an inch thick, the slate resembled a child's Etch A Sketch toy without the knobs. Instead of the outer casing in red plastic, my slate consisted of foliated smooth rock with tapered edges, yet it was soft to the touch. Embedded in the front the 8x10 device, a 7x9 translucent screen presented Phillip's passionate work and more knowledge than I knew what to do with. The slate's capabilities included three-dimensional projections, holographic images, real-time information on individuals, but only those who were single and available. Couples still married or in a relationship did not pop up as potential candidates for relationships.

The device also incorporated microexpressions, voice inflections, and nuances. And of course, the slate held three decades' worth of data on the Empathic Bridge—the crowning jewel of Phillip's research and work.

Phillip had explained that when the ideal human connection is established, the Empathic Bridge could become a reality. We'd be able to hear people's thoughts, feel their feelings. Yet, after thirty years of waiting, and even though Phillip's positive messages pinged my slate on a daily basis, the Empathic Bridge remained elusive.

And as intrigued as I was with my slate, it did not give me information on past couples—those couples who'd been archived. Put to rest.

I sometimes still glanced at my old scroll, the burnished casing dented but still functional. And I knew the protocol on closed files: never interfere with married couples.

Along with the new device, Phillip had promoted me to master-level choreographer, which allowed me to work with adults as well as college students. I still preferred the college-aged couples, maybe because twinges of guilt from my failure with Poppy and Geoff continued to plague me.

My slate under my arm, the beloved scroll in my hand, I walked through the nave to the Knowles Chapel sanctuary. My eyes wandered to the chancel lectern where many students, including Poppy all those years ago, read scripture on Sunday mornings. *Poppy and Geoff,* I thought, just curious.

In the past—maybe once every two years—I'd glance at brief updates on Poppy and Geoff. Two years ago when I'd looked, I'd discovered that Poppy lived in Florida and had four children. The scroll noted that Geoff lived in North Carolina and had a son.

As I strolled outside to take in the rose garden, I had the thought that even though Poppy and Geoff were not together, I'd be lying if I said I didn't wish they were still together. That might relieve some of my guilt.

Much had changed in thirty years at Rollins College. Twenty-two names of the men who'd signed the Declaration of Independence still appeared on the stones of the Walk of Fame, and new names had been added. Mills Memorial Library had become a private meeting and event space. And even though the new Olin Library partially obscured my view of the gazebo and the water from where I stood on the walkway, my view of Lake Virginia still remained timeless.

The college's ski dock, although new and improved, appeared secured in the same place, just to the right of Alfond Pool. The original swimming pool now featured lounge chairs instead of cement bleachers that students in the seventies and eighties had enjoyed. To my left, I marveled at the great oaks that stood tall on Mills lawn and waved a hello with the Spanish moss that hung from their branches, like nighties drying on a clothesline.

Beneath my feet, I watched a spider make its way to the foot of an iron bench—an arachnid architect on a mission to create a webbed habitat. My slate emitted a vaporous pink cloud on the bench seat with dark-gray words that assembled in a weblike pattern. *Did you know that the spider connects the past to the future and creates possibilities?*

I smiled at my slate's observation as I made my way back into Knowles Chapel and into my haven where in my thirty-plus years I'd seen quite a few weddings. For a moment I closed my eyes and remembered a few of the brides, alumni I'd choreographed when they'd attended as students. My eyes took in the stone fireplace, inset on the wall to the right of the doorway. Next to the hearth, a blue wingback chair sat near the bronze andirons and showed minimal wear—Swiss dotting blended into the fabric like a Seurat painting and created a subtle and soft contrast.

The brides often sat on the edge of the settee in a dainty side-saddle pose and looked either at the oriental rug or at up at the portrait of Francis Bangs Knowles that hung above the fireplace. In 1931, Knowles had built the chapel that bore his name. I wondered if the giggles from the brides kept him young.

I pulled out my scroll and, at the same moment, my slate pinged. "A message from Phillip," I muttered.

*Jesse, I think it's time to retire the scroll. Your slate will provide what you need from here on.*

*What does Phillip mean? I won't be able to track Poppy and Geoff without the scroll,* I thought. My scroll, like a worn and tattered stuffed animal, brought me comfort. It kept me connected to Poppy and Geoff, who had shared a love like no other Rollins couple I'd ever choreographed. *I can't imagine not having my scroll.*

Phillip's words flitted quickly across the screen. *You're probably questioning my rationale. Please trust me, and I suggest you refer to the list of potential candidates for master-level choreography.*

"Is this something about the Empathic Bridge?" I mumbled, and stared up at the painting of Frances Knowles. *Like he has the answers,* I thought. I gave a cursory glance at the list of candidates on my slate. *I'm not sure what Phillip expects me to find.*

Phillip prompted me with another message: *Perhaps you ought to begin toward the bottom of the list.*

I sighed. "Roberts, Ryland, Samson," I muttered in a rote monotone.

*Skip to the T's, Jesse.* Phillip's words now rose in a lavender bubble above the slate.

I exhaled. "Taylor, Teague, Terris, Thompson." I walked around the floating list. I felt disbelief, as if I'd witnessed a magic trick. "Terris? That's *Poppy?*" I whispered. "It never occurred to me she'd be on *this* list—on our slates. I thought she was married," I said.

I stopped and stared at the suspended names. With the anticipation of greeting a loved one who has been away for years, my finger trembled as I traced the letters in the air. "Samson, Slade, Smithson, *Spencer.*"

I felt like I'd just received the *one* gift—the elusive, out-of-stock, no-longer-made thing that I'd always wanted. I took two fast breaths, and with my fingers, I pulled the two names from the list and drew a two-sided arrow between Terris and Spencer, their names now united in the air.

Another bubble of words appeared, encased this time in a honeyed gold color: *There's only one reason they're on the slate, Jesse. They're both unmarried and available.*

The slate began to pull up a plethora of information on Poppy. I read that she was divorced, and several of her friends had tried to set her up with available men.

The slate pumped out additional data. Very definite against dating, she'd told many of her friends—no interest. To everyone who asked, she'd said, "I'm focused on my children."

I sat in the wingchair and gazed at the portrait of Francis Knowles' wife, Hester Ann Knowles. The painting showed Mrs. Knowles with a bold expression—an open book on her lap, perhaps to reflect her eagerness to engage in an erudite discussion.

"But this isn't *any* man. This is *Geoff*—Poppy's first love," I said to the image of Hester Knowles.

I sat for several moments and reflected on how long it had been since the two of them walked hand in hand on this magical campus so many years ago. *It's been like thirty years.*

My slate dinged and jolted me from my reverie. *Thirty-two years, as a matter of fact. That's one billion seconds.*

CHAPTER 19

# The Bridge

~

I FOUND GEOFF.

In Davidson, North Carolina, he sat in a black leather office chair in front of a modular wooden desk, both found at Ikea. His home office looked out of a second-floor condominium bay window at Lake Davidson. Commuter cars lined a bridge, the north-south Charlotte Interstate 77 Causeway. Northbound brake lights flashed like blinking Christmas tree bulbs. A kayaker paddled below on chilly waters, as it passed the logjam of vehicles.

If I'd seen Geoff strolling for whatever reason on campus these past thirty years, I'd have recognized him immediately. His auburn hair, a little darker brown, was cut shorter than his college days, yet unlike many men in their fifties, he had a full head of healthy hair. His eyes, still the color of light caramel, focused on the monitor in front of him. His dimple still peeked out from beneath his signature facial feature—his mustache—that apparently had not left his face in more than thirty-two years.

I'd reviewed my slate's live updates and excitedly decided that I would nudge Geoff to reach out to Poppy.

Around four thirty this Monday afternoon, April 26, 2010, I watched Poppy on my slate. I'd discovered our slates—so versatile—allowed me to observe live action.

In a black skirt, a white-and-black polka-dot blouse, and black blazer, Poppy stood next to a man who I gathered was her father in an automobile showroom. She walked around a kiwi-green Lamborghini with sable leather interior. The sticker price was $483,000.

A sales manager approached, a blond woman with a professional, affable smile. "I'm so sorry. It'll take us another half hour or so to finish the paperwork." She adjusted her khaki suit, as if tugging at her suit could hasten the paperwork. "May I get you anything to drink while you wait?" she asked, as she fluffed her cowl-neck ivory blouse. She must have thought if she couldn't speed up the process, adjusting her attire would lessen her impatience.

"Nothing for me, thank you." Poppy smiled. "Dad?" She touched her father's arm, his navy-and-yellow long-sleeve polo shirt cuffs pulled to his wrist even though the outside temperature was in the mid-eighties. He looked frail. *Cancer,* I thought, and as I had the thought, my slate confirmed that George had leukemia. Cancer stole many things away from people. Including body warmth.

"No, thank you," George said. "I'll sit in there and watch TV." On his way into the sitting area, George eyed the flat-screen, where Wolf Blitzer talked excitedly above the CNN news banner. George tugged on his yellow trousers at the upper thigh as he sank into the oversized leather couch.

With maternal eyes, Poppy watched her dad settle into the lounge. Satisfied, she ambled aimlessly across the showroom floor, passing time as she glanced at a second vehicle, a snowy-white Lamborghini with a charcoal interior. "Jesus," she muttered and raised her eyebrows. "Who pays 500K for a car?"

In Geoff's home office, I decided, *Now is the time.* I looked up from my slate's live stream of Poppy. I watched Geoff close out his business on the Salesforce website. The computer clock read four forty-five.

As I concentrated on sending the right wavelengths at just the right speed, with the appropriate level of persuasion, I nudged Geoff to think of Poppy.

Geoff's facial muscles rid themselves of professional focus, and his expression loosened the way river log jams—when released—drive faithfully through a stream to a preordained destination. He squinted at the window that overlooked the lake and murmured, "Whatever happened to Poppy?" He swiveled in his chair, opened up a browser, and went to Google. He typed, *Poppy Terris.*

The entire first page of Google featured Poppy Terris on Facebook, on LinkedIn, as a Registered Art Therapist, as a professor. Geoff scrolled and leaned in close to his monitor. Facebook popped up first.

"Oh wow, Poppy Terris," he murmured. "That's easy." Below her photo, he pointed on the monitor. "Maiden name," he whispered. "It looks like she's divorced as well." His eyes scanned the screen. And as if she were there with him, he talked with her. "Oh, it looks like you've married and divorced twice. Like me."

"Hey, Coach Poppy, you have a website." He moved the cursor and leaned into the monitor. He squinted at the photo of Poppy's smile, and I wondered if he'd noticed a change. Diminished, with half the passion he might have remembered. The joy, part of her nature, replaced with a parental expression. But in her eyes was the same artistic nature he'd known. "There you are." He grinned with the recognition of a familiar face and time.

While he scanned, like a detective, the landing pages of the search results, he nodded slightly. "Here's your phone number," he mumbled.

With his eyes still on the screen, his hand groped for his Blackberry. He picked up the cell and smirked. "Oh what the hell, I'll give you a call."

As his eyes glanced back and forth between the number on the monitor and his phone, he paused before he'd finished entering the digits. "What will I say to you?" His gaze drifted from her photograph on the screen to look out the window for answers. For strategies to reignite if not the love of his life, then at the very least a friendship.

Answering himself, he mumbled, "What's the worst thing that'll happen? You'll get rid of me again? 'Nice chatting with you. Take care . . .' Oh, hell." He shook his head and grinned. "We can both laugh about being two-time divorcees." Geoff pressed the last cell phone key and put the phone to his right ear.

I heard the phone ring, and as I watched Geoff, his expression intrigued me. *Not anticipation,* I thought. *But rather an expression of memory, mingled with a wistfulness, a yearning.* A subtle thumping permeated the room. *A pulsation, a tempo of the heart?*

*Who do I know in North Carolina?* I heard Poppy's voice, but her lips hadn't moved. I jiggled my slate. *Maybe there's a glitch? Do I need to clean my slate?* Her cell phone caller ID read *North Carolina.*

But Poppy had *said* nothing, so how had I heard her voice say, "Who do I know in North Carolina?" I jiggled my slate again and checked the audio setting. I watched Poppy press the Talk button.

"Hi, this is Poppy." Her tone, friendly, noncommittal.

Geoff leaned back—rather, *lounged*—in his desk chair. His body language indicated he was settling in for a while. Behind his moustache, his dimple danced. "Is this Poppy Marie Terris?"

"Yes, who is this please?" She asked in a tone reserved for telemarketers.

"I'll give you a hint." Geoff curled the right corner of his moustache. "This is someone you knew from Rollins."

I looked back at the slate and saw Poppy pace the dealership floor, her eyes downcast. For a moment, she rested the cellphone on her shoulder and looked up to her right.

*Oh, the annual giving campaign. George and Molly need to be set up for college soon . . . not this year,* I heard Poppy say. Yet on my screen, I hadn't seen her say the words.

I looked at Geoff. He hadn't heard anything. He still curled his moustache, an amused final-round-of-Jeopardy grin on his face.

*Think! Who do you know from the Rollins annual campaign? I bet it's that one guy. Oh, shoot. What's his name?* She closed her eyes. *Andy, Andy! Andy Hoover, Andy Harmon, Andy Horvath. Hurry . . .* Poppy's words ran together.

*But she's not speaking. What's going on?* I wondered.

I stared at my slate and back at Geoff. *Why hasn't he heard what Poppy said? And why can't I see her lips move when she speaks?*

"Is this Andy?" Poppy said into the phone. I *heard* her ask the question, and on my slate, I *saw* her ask the question.

Geoff's chair rocked forward and he straightened. He hadn't heard her grasping for Andy's last name.

*Who the hell is Andy? Doesn't she recognize my voice?* I heard Geoff say as I looked right at him. Yet, just as with Poppy, his lips hadn't moved.

But I'd heard those two questions as clear as a sound check in a recording studio.

"No," Geoff said, with slight irritation. "I'll give you a much bigger hint. This is someone you dated extensively at Rollins." Geoff's head fell against the back of the chair, and his expression read, *C'mon, c'mon. Figure it out.* The chair squeaked as he reclined.

*Oh my God. Jeff or Geoff? One a horrible fit for me, the other—wonderful. One just a few dates, the other, my entire senior year of college. My first true love. Stop walking. I can't breathe.* Poppy exhaled and closed her eyes. *Breathe,* she thought. *My body feels like it's ringing. Please let it be the good Geoff. Please let it be the good Geoff.* Poppy squeezed her eyes shut and exhaled.

As I watched Poppy on the slate, I felt like I viewed someone who'd just stepped out of a board meeting to have a private conference with another person. Only Poppy hadn't talked with anyone else. Just with herself. *In her head.*

*I was still trying to process that I could hear her thoughts.*

I stared at Geoff. *She has to know who it is by now,* I heard him think. His lips curved into a smile.

*I hear both of their thoughts.*

From the slate, I saw Poppy place her mouth close to the speaker. "Yes, I know who this is." Poppy closed her eyes as if she'd readied herself to take a plunge from a dock into chilly Memorial Day Lake Michigan waters. "It's Geoff. This wonderful man who was so good to me."

Geoff took the phone away from his ear and stared at it as if he'd misdialed. *Wonderful man? Okay. Not what I expected.* Geoff's thought drifted through the room.

And I heard.

On my slate, I saw Poppy in the car dealership. I saw her talk—her voice clear on the slate when she'd spoken out loud to Geoff. I saw her eyes close when her thoughts wished it would be the good Geoff. But I heard her thoughts as if someone had pushed a mute button on and off. *Only we don't have mute buttons on our slates.*

*I can hear their thoughts.*

*How am I able to hear their thoughts?*

What had Phillip indicated about two people who are deeply connected? That with the bridge, we'd be able to hear their thoughts? Feel their feelings?

*Is this the Empathic Bridge?!*

My slate vibrated in my hand, and a veil of gold particles shot into the air and formed an arc. A shimmering bridge materialized, and vertical cables anchored themselves like dominos onto a platform. It flashed on and off like a Bellagio slot machine to the sound of applause and whistles.

At the same time, Poppy gushed and said what she most certainly had stored in her heart.

"Oh my God, Geoff! I've tried to find you. Three different times." As if she were in a race, she paced the showroom floor. "And, oh, Geoff . . ." Her voice faded along with her movement. She stared down at the tiles. "I'm so sorry." She closed her eyes and murmured. "I heard about your brother. I tried to find you. I didn't know where you were—where you lived."

"I'd wondered if you'd heard about Twig." Geoff rocked forward and grounded his feet on the floor. He rested his elbow on his knee. "I almost called you after it happened. I was in Milwaukee on business in 2002, a year after we lost him in the World Trade Center on 9/11."

"I'm so sorry, Geoff." Poppy held her elbow with her hand. "I heard about Twig when I took my daughter on a college trip eight years ago. At the orientation lunch, a nice lady told me. She knew Twig. I don't recall her name, but with 250 people in the room, I just *happened* to sit next to her. When she'd mentioned she lived in Cleveland, well, of course I thought of you. Told her we had been college sweethearts. That I knew your mom and dad and brother, and that's when her smile faded. She told me that her friend Twig had died in the World Trade Center." Poppy wrapped one arm around her stomach. "I was devastated. And sadly, she didn't know where you or your parents lived."

"Thank you, Poppy." Geoff looked out at the lake. "It was a difficult time."

"I can't even imagine." Poppy closed her eyes.

With one knee across his other thigh, Geoff said, "I'll send you an article written about me and my brother, and how I dealt with it."

"I didn't know anyone personally. Until you." Poppy paused, as if she weren't sure of the sensitivity level of the topic for Geoff. "I'd love to see it."

"Okay, I'll email it to you."

Poppy, still in place on the tile floor, shifted her weight from one foot to the other. "And how are your mom and dad? Jean and George? Are they still around?"

"Yes, sure." Geoff popped forward in his chair. "Mom and Dad are alive and well. They live in Florida—Mount Dora." Geoff added, "Near Orlando. Dad retired years ago. My mom couldn't wait to get out of Cleveland and the cold weather."

"Same," Poppy said, as she used to say in college. "My parents moved to Florida about twenty years ago. We live just a few blocks from each other." Poppy glanced in the lounge where her father leaned against the couch, one arm on top of his head—seemingly his comfort position. "Well, how are you? I can't believe you called me." Poppy began to walk on the tiles, taking baby steps. I bet you've called for the annual giving campaign for Rollins." Poppy ran her fingers on the sable leather seat back of the Lamborghini.

When I glanced closer at my screen to see Poppy, I suddenly felt a rush of energy emerging from the slate. A sensation completely foreign to me. I didn't understand it, as if my midsection were being squeezed by something.

*I can't believe this. I just tried to find him. When was it? After the Daniels' Christmas party. What if he's just calling for Rollins?* Poppy's thoughts came to me.

At the same time she had these thoughts, again, I felt a pinch in my gut

"No." Geoff shook his head as his jaw dropped, a hint of impatience. "I'm not *calling* for the annual giving campaign." He sighed. "I just thought, 'Whatever happened to Poppy?' and thought I'd give you a call," Geoff said, and his initial sense of being caught off guard quickly waned and hastened toward excitement.

*Oh my God. He's calling me. Just calling me. He's thinking about me.* I heard Poppy's thoughts and felt a ringing sensation—a slow crescendo of movement within my being.

"I mean, Geoff." Poppy looked out the showroom window. "I *just* tried to find you four months ago. In December. On Facebook." Poppy smiled, as her words cascaded out. "I found some guy who didn't look like you, or at least how I'd remembered you. I have no idea what you look like . . . but, you don't live in Australia, do you?"

"No!" Geoff said with a laugh. "I live in North Carolina."

"Well, there's a Geoff Spencer in Australia that looks like a hungover Santa." Poppy laughed.

I sensed lightness, a floating calm inside of me.

*Do I feel Poppy's feelings? Is this more of the Empathic Bridge connection?*

My slate jiggled, and above the gold bridge, words bobbed up and down. *Traits of the Empathic Bridge.* Like the Blue Angels flying over Lake Winnebago at the Oshkosh Air Show, bullet points from my slate swooped in, one word at a time. *You will feel the following sensations: Surprise, Excitement, Sadness, Anxiousness, Eagerness, Joy, Bliss.*

*Do I feel this way because Poppy feels these emotions?*

Gold stars circled the bullet points after my last thought.

"I just got on Facebook in January," Geoff said. He shook his head—still trying to process her comments.

His thoughts, now tangled with synapses in his brain, rushed around in tight circles. *She tried to find me? Reach me? Three times! I can't believe I'm talking to Poppy.* Geoff's thoughts collided and I heard them. From Geoff, I felt a thumping sensation in my chest.

"How'd you find me?" Poppy asked as she took small steps on the floor, as if the sales manager might've asked her to mark off and measure the square footage of twelve tiles. As if Poppy were using precise motions as a way to corral a multitude of emotions.

"I typed *Poppy Terris* into Google and saw you on Facebook. And the link to your website. Your phone number's right there." Geoff twirled his moustache. "So I called."

*After all this time I've wanted to find him, and he found me. So easily,* Poppy thought, and her lashes fluttered closed for a moment.

I felt a surge of emotion—a buzzing of positive energy. *Is it from Poppy? Or Geoff? Or both?*

"Geoff." Poppy stopped pacing. "I broke your heart, didn't I?"

Before he could answer, she added, "I never meant to hurt you. I'm so sorry."

I felt a grip of something. A tightness, with her last words. *A wave of sadness?*

Geoff's thoughts flooded my mind. *I can't believe I'm hearing this. How can this be?* He stood from his chair and pressed the cellphone closer to his eardrum. *All this time I thought something else. That she didn't really care. What had she said—"wonderful man?"* Geoff's thoughts raced.

"Yes. Yes, you did." Geoff's voice softened. A whisper.

And suddenly his thoughts stopped coming to me. Or maybe I couldn't hear them anymore. The Empathic Bridge and the list—still there—floated above the slate, and shined like the Golden Gate. I looked back at Poppy in the slate, where she stood on the tile. Anchored.

I still felt the ringing energy, a buzzing sensation from both of them.

"I'm sorry, Geoff. I was young. *We* were young. I tried to call you in 1990, after I divorced the first time. I called information in Orlando three different times and got three different operators." Poppy's words ran together. "But I couldn't find you." She blinked saltwater from her eyes.

"Nineteen ninety? I'd left Orlando way before then," Geoff said. He leaned forward and looked at a photo of Poppy at an event on his computer monitor. "I noticed you've married and divorced twice. Like me."

"Yes. I'm not proud of it." Poppy looked at her feet, her charcoal-gray leather sandals touching each other. "I know I look bad on paper. But I believe in marriage."

"I do, too." Geoff nodded into phone. "I feel the same way."

I sensed a heightened swell of emotion—still unable to distinguish if it came from Poppy or Geoff. I just felt it.

"Geoff, this is so unreal that I'm talking with you again. I want to keep talking, but I'm right in the middle of buying a car," Poppy said, her tone a wail when she said *car*. She looked toward the office at the sales manager, who'd stood up from her desk and stacked a small pile of paperwork. "May I call you back when I'm finished?"

"Sure. What are you buying?"

Poppy moved from where she'd stood frozen and began a leisurely stroll as she talked with Geoff. The conversation now seamlessly moved forward as old friends chatted, picking up where they'd left off.

"It's pre-owned. A BMW X3. I'm with my Dad." Poppy walked toward the waiting area to get a visual on her father. "Do you remember that both of our dads are named George?" Poppy grinned.

"Yes, I sure do." Geoff smiled as Poppy brought up the memory slideshow.

As I looked at my slate at Poppy, and back to Geoff, who grinned like he had when he'd first described Poppy at Rollins to his fraternity brothers, I felt a growing sensation—a collective ringing energy in my whole being.

Poppy nodded to her dad, who motioned her toward the sales office. "I hope to be done in twenty minutes, and I'll call you back on my way home. Would that be okay?"

"Yeah, that'd be fine." Geoff's cheek made a small pocket for his dimple.

"Thanks so much. I'm so excited to talk with you more." As if it were a Fabergé egg, Poppy held her cell phone with both hands.

"Me, too. I look forward to talking with you later." Geoff pressed the End button and fell back into his chair. "Holy shit," he whispered. "Poppy."

A sudden shift happened when the call ended. The same sensation humans have when a roller coaster ride comes to an end. A floating exhilaration, followed by a slow glide into the station—the aftereffects that still linger. *All of these sensations are new.*

The bridge that'd been projected above the slate sprinkled back into it, like fairy dust. I no longer heard Poppy or Geoff's thoughts, although I saw and heard Poppy on my slate. She walked with her father into the office at the dealership and sat opposite the desk.

"Dad!" Poppy said, wide-eyed. "Do you remember Geoff Spencer?"

George Terris reached his hand up to the side of his head and gently cupped the area where what appeared to be a tumor had begun to ravage his left ear. "Yes, honey."

I immediately witnessed an expansive paternal love for Poppy, but like a veteran businessman, he pointed to the blond, fresh-faced finance manager and said, "She's getting the title information right now." The woman straightened at her desk—every hair, like her organized financial documents, in place.

Poppy smiled and caressed her father's left arm. A smile that forgave his lack of hearing. "Thanks for doing this with me, Dad." She wiped tears from the corners of her eyes. Perhaps tears from a vast emotional terrain.

George Terris waved his right hand—an anything-for-you gesture.

When Geoff ended the call with Poppy, he sat in his chair and looked like the wind had been knocked out of him. His arms dangled over the sides of the chair, his head back; eyes staring at the ceiling.

He righted himself in the chair and leaned forward. He held his face with his hands. "Oh my God, I'm just blown away." He put his hands on his knees and looked at a wooden chair where an older-looking orange-and-white cat slept in the shape of a *U*. "Oh my God . . . I can't believe this," Geoff repeated. He staggered out of his office, as if the floor beneath him had turned into a college waterbed and he was floating on water.

In the living room, he paused next to a young man who was watching TV—lanky and form-fitted in a recliner, like Kokopelli, the magical fluted deity. "Jonathon. You'll never believe what just happened!" Geoff blurted out to the young man, who looked to be nineteen or twenty. *His son*, I thought.

Jonathon, on a blue pinpoint recliner and dressed in a faded Davidson Basketball T-shirt, reached down and pulled the wooden lever to lower the foot rest. "What?" His faced showed a son's yin-yang curiosity—his voice neutral, his eyelids raised.

"Ever remember me talking about my college girlfriend, Poppy?" Geoff said Poppy's name a little bit slower.

"Yeah, I guess so," the young man replied, and glanced back at the TV, as if trying to determine which might hold his interest more.

Unaware of his son's distraction, Geoff paced on the beige Berber carpeting. "I just had the most *unbelievable* conversation with her." He held his palms up like he was carrying something valuable that he should put down and didn't know where to put it. "I'm just blown away!" Geoff stopped in front of his son. "I can't believe this."

"What happened?" Jonathon looked at his father, one side of his mouth curled in a grin. The young man appeared to find his father's antics more intriguing than the TV.

"I just kind of thought about her and found her number on her website." Geoff paced again. "And I called her, and everything I'd thought about her for the past thirty years—well, apparently I had it all wrong." He fell into the chair next to Jonathon, the rocking stopped by his feet. "I can't believe it, Jonathon. She'd tried to find me." He shook his head, as if the reality of what he just experienced might've been a mistake.

Jonathon kicked the footrest back up and grinned at his father's confused state.

Geoff picked up Jonathon's lunch plate and took it into the kitchen. Over the running water in the stainless-steel sink, he spoke loudly. "She'd heard about Twig. Tried to call me then. And she tried to find me again a few months ago." He shook the water from the plate over the sink before placing it in the dishwasher.

Jonathon's eyes—the color of Tiger's-eyes stones—followed his father's movements around the room, the way dog owners are amused watching a new puppy.

He wiped his hands on the light-blue dishtowel as he stepped back into the living room. "I can't believe it."

"Yes, you've said that." Jonathon shook his head, his light walnut-colored hair bobbing in mirth.

"I was *crazy* about her." Geoff threw the dishtowel over his shoulder and headed back to the kitchen, as if only his feet controlled his mind and body. "This is unbelievable."

I understood the reeling sensation that the old lovers were experiencing, as I, too, began to process the realization of what had just occurred. Although thirty-some years had passed, I would've recognized Poppy: her soft waves of brown hair, shorter than she'd worn it in college, and a heart-shaped face with pink lipstick on her lips. But the distinctive sparkle in her chocolate-truffle-colored eyes transported me back in time.

My thoughts raced: *Poppy and Geoff, talking for the first time since that fateful night back at Rollins thirty-two years ago.*

# CHAPTER 20

# Cognitive Bypass

~⁓

GEOFF LEANED INTO HIS COMPUTER monitor and rapidly clicked on links to Poppy Terris' Google results, as if he had a limited time offer to recover a million dollars of lost assets.

He viewed her art therapy website, and I felt his joy. The site included photos of Poppy at a charity golf tournament and an assortment of photos of her speaking at conferences. With each page and each photo, his connection to her became visceral, and my intuition levels accelerated.

Armed with these new sensations, immeasurable hope filled me up, as if redemption for my past mistakes might be *possible*. I thought about it. *What are the possibilities with my Poppy and my Geoff?*

After fifteen minutes, he went back to her Coach Poppy website and clicked on her email address. In the subject area, Geoff typed the words "Catching up."

He moved the cursor to the body of the email and typed, *Holy Cow! Poppy Marie . . .*

~⁓

In my room in Knowles Chapel at Rollins, the Howard Miller chiming desk clock rested on the wooden table opposite the fireplace. The mahogany frame encased the Roman numerals, and the clock chimed six times. I looked out the window at a young dark-haired couple who held hands as they strolled on the Walk of Fame that circled Mills Lawn. Across from Gale Hall, where the X Club fraternity resided, the woman stopped and leaned her face up to the man. Their lips met in a familiar kiss. They could've been a couple from three decades ago—*my couple.*

I slid my finger through a sunlit ray of dust particles that streamed through the window. "The Empathic Bridge," I whispered. "It happened," I said to the portrait, ignoring Hester Knowles' inscrutable Renaissance-like gaze. *I heard their thoughts, felt something like intense joy.* My thoughts flooded out and tripped over one another like a five-year-old who tells a parent about what happened that day at the amusement park.

My slate in hand, I directed it to give me recent updates on the Empathic Bridge. The golden image appeared, this time without sounds and fanfare. *Amazing that I heard her thoughts even before she answered the phone.*

I stood and ran my finger over the top strands of the bridge. I peered under and around the holographic image like a construction supervisor at a final inspection. The bridge's golden stanchions held the cables like strong arms in a victory pose.

*What was that tingling sensation?* I wondered.

Just as I thought this, the slate re-projected the same list in the air: *Traits of the Empathic Bridge: Surprise, Excitement, Sadness, Anxiousness, Eagerness, Joy, Bliss. This list wouldn't have all of these emotions on it if not felt by both Poppy and Geoff.*

I used my hand to swipe and stow the image of the bridge and the list of traits back into my slate, and wondered about Poppy and Geoff's connection and how it had come and gone. *How had I lost connection to their thoughts, yet still felt the sensory energy from both of them?*

My slate immediately projected two green words: *Cognitive Bypass.*

"Cognitive Bypass?" I felt my brow cinch together. *I have no idea what my slate means.*

My slate displayed the words at eye level to me; black words on a white vaporous cloud: *Cognitive Bypass. Disconnect. Rare phenomenon. Thoughts are unfiltered. Pure delivery of message.*

My slate continued to further explain: *Cognitive Bypass is rare in relationships and involves thoughts, formerly filtered before spoken, which are suddenly pre-empted. A person's thoughts are not pre-selected. Instead, communication between the couple flows unfiltered—from one directly to the other without cognitive intervention.*

I blew air slowly from my cheeks. "The heart, not the head—more sensory communication than filtered conversation."

*The delivery of communicated ideas and feelings bypasses the fear center in the brain. Communication is pure and uncensored.* My slate's responses floated in even lines in the air.

I sat back in the chair and closed my eyes. I recalled that Poppy and Geoff hadn't been playing games—hadn't planned clever things to say. The Empathic Bridge was not broken. Poppy and Geoff had just stopped thinking ahead about what they might say. No pre-planning. Their words just *came out*—no sorting, and with no emotional armor for protection.

Across from me, my slate emitted more information. *Couples who have the courage to communicate, who are open and confident, and on the left side of the clock, can experience the phenomenon of Cognitive Bypass.*

"Those who speak to each other straight from the heart," I whispered.

A familiar ringing started to wash over me. *Poppy's calling Geoff. Her hands are shaking as she's punching his number on her cell phone from her new car.* I held my slate and saw her in a parking lot. *She hopes that he'll answer.*

Suddenly, a golden orb erupted from my slate and morphed into a pulsing, shiny hologram of a golden bridge, the color of a Tuscan sunset. "It's happening again," I said, and marveled at the projected image—admiring it, as if it were the Venus de Milo at the Louvre.

From my slate, I saw Geoff pick up his phone and smile. On the other half of the slate, in a split screen, Poppy, in her car, also smiled.

I felt a sensation in my midsection again—a tingling.

My slate displayed one word on the screen: *Butterflies.* More words and images of butterflies danced on the screen of my slate: *People get them all the time when they're excited and happy.*

# CHAPTER 21

# Time Warp

~

I watched Poppy's fingers tremble. She glanced at the Publix receipt on which she'd jotted Geoff's number, carefully written in case she'd deleted it on her cellphone by accident. *I can't believe he called me. I can't believe this is happening,* Poppy thought as she pressed the keys to dial Geoff's number.

As I felt her heart beat fast and sensed a buzzing—a ringing throughout my whole being, the illuminated bridge began to sparkle above my slate and shot little sprinkles of silvery-white dogwood petals—bracts—into the air.

*Physiological response. Heightened cellular activity.* The screen on my slate documented the sensations I was experiencing.

On my slate, I saw Geoff lean back in his desk chair—a quickened pulse.

"Hello, Poppy Marie!" Geoff's voice was a playful boom. "So, are you driving in your new car?"

"Yes, I love it." Poppy stopped at a red light and looked at her face in the rearview mirror. Her cheeks were flushed with excitement—an extension of her grin. "Tell me about you. I don't want to talk about my car."

Before Geoff could respond, Poppy added, "I can't believe you found me. I just looked for *you*. Do you still look the same? I bet you do!" Poppy's breathless sentences ran together, as if she might only have a few moments to talk with him. "Do you still have your moustache?"

"I do." Geoff twirled one corner of it. "I still have my moustache," he said, and his tone sounded relaxed; he was clearly savoring the moment.

"Oh my God! That great moustache. You *have* to send me a picture." Poppy took a breath. "Did I tell you that when I looked for you last month, the Aussie guy named Geoffrey Spencer didn't look anything like I'd imagined you looked?" Poppy's voice turned into a slight giggle.

"I'll send you some pictures later. I've already sent you an email," Geoff said.

"I haven't been home to check yet, but please do." Poppy's heart rate elevated. "So, do you have kids? And where do you live in North Carolina?"

Poppy drove 40 mph, just under the speed limit, as she headed north in the middle lane of Sarasota, Florida's Tamiami Trail.

"I have one son, Jonathon. He's twenty. He's a sophomore in college. And I live in Davidson—the Charlotte area—near Davidson College."

"Sure, Davidson," Poppy said, energized. "A family friend's daughter is there. Darling Annie Holcomb. Her parents, Stephanie and Ben, are the sweetest people on the planet. Stephanie is the kind of person who always remembers my birthday with a card."

I understood that they were still in Cognitive Bypass, and I also felt the butterflies—I think from Poppy.

"Do you still water-ski?" Poppy grinned. "I have great memories of you slaloming. And I recall when the boat crossed over the wakes, I had to hold my boobs from bouncing." Poppy chuckled.

Geoff laughed and threw his head back. "I skied until about a year ago. I live on a little lake. There's a slalom course I can see from my window as we speak." He cocked his head to the side as he gazed out the window.

"I remember my college boyfriend taught me how to water-ski." Poppy grinned.

"Yes, I did. I remember that, too," he said, his expression so pleased that his moustache tips tickled his cheeks.

The color of the bridge turned from a honeyed white-gold to a gilded persimmon.

I felt a warm sensation like when someone rolls up a window shade on a Vermont winter morning and they are awash in sunlight.

My slate dinged and alerted me to the reddish tones that were now spreading across the cables of the bridge. *The Empathic Bridge picks up emotional variances, represented by a change in color.*

On the slate, I saw and heard Poppy tell Geoff about her four children, their names and ages, her parents—her father's declining health. Geoff shared his work as a regional sales manager for a technology company in the higher education marketplace.

"Do you still sail?" Poppy's tone went up at the end, as if her voice were a limp spinnaker suddenly filled with a puff of air.

"I sure do," Geoff said. "Do you remember me talking about my family's Flying Scot sailboat?" He glanced to the right as he retrieved the memory. "I'll send you another item that will tell you the whole story—fill in what I did when I lost my brother."

"I'd like that," Poppy said. "Geoff, I remember you as a sailor and my grandfather calling you the 'sailor boy.'"

Poppy's thoughts emerged in a run-on of emotions. *Shoot, I'm almost here for this silly hair appointment. I don't want our call to end. Not after all this time. I can't believe I'm talking to Geoff,* she thought, and a little excited squeak that sounded like "eeh" burst from her closed lips.

"I look forward to reading your article." Poppy parked and shut off the engine. "Shoot, Geoff. I just arrived at my hair appointment. I don't want to end our call. Not after all this time," she said. Her voice suddenly tightened as emotion lodged in her throat.

And I felt it, too. I reached for my neck. My slate displayed an image of a neck with a bump in the center, a lump in her throat. *Verklempt.*

"What?" I felt the space between my eyes wrinkle. "Isn't that what people say after someone sneezes?"

The words bounced along the screen. *That's Gesundheit. Another German word. People feel verklempt when choked up with emotion. Overwhelmed by their feelings.*

"I'm sorry. May I call you back again?" Poppy asked. Her facial expression adjusted from joy to a barely hopeful wince.

"Sure." Geoff drew out the word. "It's been unbelievable to talk with you."

Both Poppy and Geoff, reluctant to sign off, paused to hear each other's silence. The gift of patience born from an enduring closeness few humans achieve.

I clearly heard Geoff's thoughts. *I can't believe I just talked with Poppy! This is so easy. I feel like I'm in some sort of time warp. It's Poppy. I'm talking with Poppy.* Geoff's thoughts toppled over one another like bowling pins in a strike.

*This is unbelievable. I feel like I've traveled back in time,* Poppy thought.

"Hi, guys," Poppy called when she'd opened the front door after a stop at her parents' home to tend to her father's ear. "Nickynoo. How's my girl?" Poppy scooped up a little dog, a Shih Tzu according to my slate, and walked back into her children's bedrooms. A young teenaged girl sat on her bed, a pile of papers and books covering the paisley bedspread. Poppy glanced at her the desk. "Hi, Molly! Did you empty your drawers and backpacks on your desk?"

"Very funny, Mom." Her daughter's long brown hair spilled over her notebook and brushed the pen with which she wrote. Her cocoa-colored eyes did not glance up from the spiral notebook on her knee. On her other knee, a laptop computer rested precariously. "How's Big George?"

Poppy dropped the little dog in the only open spot on the full-size bed. The dog circled. "He's good, I think. We did his ear. Big George and Val watched *Wheel* and *Jeopardy*. Same old," Poppy said in the abbreviated manner that most teenagers preferred.

Poppy stepped over Molly's swim bag and went a few feet into another doorway. "Hey, Georgie."

The teenager sat at his desk, strong fingers flying across the keyboard. A modular wall unit with drawers and shelves, designed for Spartan living, suited him. Minimalistic. Nothing on his desk except his computer and an upside-down paperback book. "Hey."

"What's my favorite seventeen-year-old working on?" Poppy sat behind him on the side of his twin bed.

"Stupid writing assignment." George's deep brown eyes were locked on the screen, his dark brown hair almost touching the monitor.

"Oh, c'mon. You're a fabulous writer."

"*If* I liked *Othello*. *Hamlet*'s okay. And *Macbeth*—but this is just drama bullshit."

"Oh, you mean Iago? And Desdemona?" Poppy stood and lifted the book on his desk. She flipped through the pages. "That's right, the whole handkerchief of death."

"C'mon, no real soldiers have women come along when they go off to battle." George stabbed at his keyboard. "Jesus."

Poppy rubbed his shoulder. "If you want to bounce any ideas off of me, let me know. I have to prep for one of my Ringling psych classes tomorrow morning."

At her desk, Poppy switched on her computer and the familiar *whirr* sounded. "Oh my God." Poppy clicked on the email message from Geoff. *"Holy Cow, Poppy Marie,"* she whispered out loud.

She reached in her purse and pulled out her cell phone. She tapped on the last entry and waited. Poppy walked around the four chairs at the dining room table and looked at the floor as she had in the car dealership. When Geoff's voicemail came on, she stopped.

"Hi Geoff, this is Poppy . . ." She smiled and closed her eyes—her radiant expression the same as someone who stands outside to embrace a long-awaited rain shower.

# CHAPTER 22

# Honch and Chief

~

I watched Poppy press the speed dial button on her cellphone.

"Hi, Kellbelle. I want to share something with you and Kimmy. Will you please do a conference call for the three of us?" Poppy poked at the jewelry on her dresser tray in her bedroom, the landline phone wedged between her shoulder and ear. She straightened the necklaces into neat ovals.

"Is everything okay, Mom?" Kelly sounded alarmed.

"Everything's great. I just want to tell you girls something." Poppy's voice rose into a giggle.

"Hold on. I'll get Kimmy on the line." Kelly's tone morphed into all business.

Poppy stood in the doorway of her room and slowly turned the handle on the door. She closed it silently.

"Mom?"

"Kimmy's on," Kelly said.

"Hi, girls." Poppy sat on the edge of her bed and quietly blew air from her lips.

"Is everything alright?" Kimmy asked, alarm in her voice. "Is Big George okay?"

"Yes, he's fine." Poppy's expression shifted from playful to solemn and back. "That's not why I'm calling."

"Okaaaay." Kimmy hung on the vowel.

"I feel like a teenager who just got asked to prom by her crush." Poppy laughed.

"What d'you mean?" Kimmy blurted out.

"What're you talking about?" Kelly asked at the same time.

"Do you two remember me talking about Geoff Spencer, my . . .," Poppy started.

"College sweetheart?" Kimmy filled in. "Yeah."

Poppy stood up, startled. "You do?"

"Mom, c'mon. You talked about him *all the time*," Kimmy said.

"All the time. She's right, Mom," Kelly added.

"I did not." Poppy paced in her room.

"Yes, you totally did, Mom," Kimmy defended.

"Totally," Kelly repeated.

"You said he was so nice, that you broke his heart . . .," Kimmy began.

"That he was so good to you—your first love. Yeah, you talked about him all the time," Kelly echoed.

"Really?" In the doorway to her bathroom, Poppy stared at her reflected image in the mirror. She massaged her cheeks where her smile extended. "Oh my God, K2, I can't stop smiling. My face hurts." She laughed. "He called me. Geoff *just* called me."

"Holy shit." Kimmy's expletive burst through the phone and echoed in the ears of her sister and mother. They both heard the sound of Kimmy's hand as it gently smacked her mouth in shock. Not only from her sudden swearwords but from the shock of her mother's news. *Their mother sounded, well, happy.*

"What? Oh my God, tell us." Kelly giggled. "What did he say?"

Poppy left the bathroom doorway and began to make small steps on her tiled floor. "I thought he was calling me about Rollins, to give money as an alum. But he said he'd just thought about me . . ." A remarkable energy, transmitted through the phone lines, electrified each of them.

At noon the following day, Poppy returned from Ringling College, where she taught a psychology course. She dumped her bag on the tile floor next to her antique painted desk and turned on her home computer. "C'mon, c'mon, email. Load," she muttered.

Earlier, when Geoff had sent Poppy the article, the Empathic Bridge had appeared with the same silvery-gold hue, but now its outline glowed amber red with a tinge of magenta, as Poppy opened Geoff's email and read the newspaper article about how he had rebuilt his family's sailboat, *Misty*, from a near scrap-pile mess to sail again. Geoff's brother had begun the process of restoring the sailboat, and 9/11 had stopped the process. Through a cathartic journey, Geoff finished what his brother had started.

"Oh my God," Poppy whispered, and dabbed the corners of her eyes. She scrolled back up on her computer monitor and looked again at the picture of Geoff on *Misty*. I watched as Poppy leaned closer to the screen, and her face embodied joyful recognition. "This is amazing. He looks the same. I would *totally* know it was him if I'd seen his picture somewhere. Same moustache—same warm brown eyes."

She sat back in her chair. *God, I can't even imagine.* She shook her head and closed her eyes. "What he must've gone through," she said. *He overcame his brother's death to honor him with personal courage.*

Poppy glanced at Nicky. *He's still the same wonderful guy,* Poppy thought. She clicked the Reply button on the email and began to type.

*What a touching story, Geoff! How wonderful that you not only rebuilt her—you carried the familial spirit with you, to finish line after finish line. Beautiful.*

She hit Send as the bridge glowed a soft pink.

~~~

Geoff closed the door to his bedroom. The latch made a quiet click. His gentle motion, a sharp contrast to his elevated heart rate, jumpstarted the beginning of a feeling within me, followed by the sensation of a cluster of butterflies. And as if following a stage lighting director's cue, the tint of the Empathic Bridge morphed into the color of ginger spice when Geoff picked up his cell phone.

"This doesn't seem real." Geoff pressed the Recent Calls button on his phone. "I'm calling Poppy Terris," he muttered.

I watched Poppy on my slate as she grabbed her cellphone off the counter. She shot a glance toward the hallway to George and Molly's rooms and tiptoed into her bedroom. Poppy closed her door with the same discreet motion as Geoff. "Is this my college boyfriend?" she asked on the third ring, her voice with a giggle embedded in it.

"It is." Geoff almost sang the two words in a baritone voice. He went to the chair—the ancestral rocker from the 1800s, and sat. The cherrywood in the Fairbanks rocker, despite the rich patina, creaked with age. "This a good time to talk?"

"It is." Poppy lowered her voice, mimicking Geoff.

With the two repeated words, the bridge glowed a flaxen red.

Poppy walked back and forth in her room, from the French patio doors to the closet, pacing the length of her bed and dresser. "I can't believe I'm talking with you."

"It's wild, isn't it?" Geoff rocked, smiling. "So what brought you to Sarasota?"

"The climate." Poppy laughed. "I think that was a part of it, but I wanted to be near my mom and dad." Poppy sat on the end of her bed and stared at the alabaster cross on her dresser top. "And my dad isn't well, so I'm glad I'm here."

"Oh, I'm sorry to hear that," Geoff said.

"He has leukemia. Ongoing treatments of chemo and radiation." Poppy stood. "Last summer the doctor wasn't sure Dad would still be here. He said that Dad just had a few more months. But I'm the ever-positive one with my parents and kids. And I pray a lot, too." She looked down at the floor and closed her eyes. Her signal of transition. "Tell me about you."

"Well, let's see . . ." Geoff twirled his moustache and began to summarize everything about his life, abruptly stopping to ask her more questions. They both continued to fill in thirty-two years of blanks. Seamless, flowing conversation that spanned two and a half hours. The bridge changed colors. When Poppy spoke of her father, the bridge turned a pale pink blush. When they laughed—which occurred frequently—the bridge became rubescent. When Geoff spoke of his brother or rebuilding *Misty*, the bridge had an aura of seafoam green around it.

Only once, when Molly came to Poppy's bedroom door and knocked, had Cognitive Bypass disappeared for a moment. "Excuse me for a minute," Poppy said, as she held the phone to her chest. "Yes, sweetie?" Poppy opened the door for her daughter.

"Sorry to bother you," Molly said, her five-foot-seven-inch frame leaned lightly on the door. "May I take the car and run to Walgreens? I want to get some stuff for my project that's due Thursday."

"Sure. Maybe George will go with you."

"No. Forget it. He'll insist on driving," Molly whispered.

"What?" Like sonar picking up the sound of a distant sub, George came around the corner from the kitchen and stood outside Poppy's door. "I'll go to Walgreens." George adeptly slipped his finger into the heel of his Sperrys. "Let's go, Molly."

"You can come, but I'm driving." Molly walked-ran to the front hall and snatched the keys from the ceramic dish on the front hall table.

"Fine. You can drive." He tsked as she slipped the keys into her pocket. "Jesus."

Poppy closed the door. "Sorry about that. Did you hear?"

"Yeah, some of it. Nothing surprising. Two teens arguing about the car." Geoff leaned forward to the side of his bed and stroked the cat's back. "I don't have sibling issues. Jonathon's an only child and has his own car."

"The car is *always* the point of debate around here." Poppy shook her head. "Oh shoot, Geoff. May I call you right back on my landline? My cellphone's about to die." Poppy hung up, went to her office, and plugged in her cell phone at her desk. She looked at herself in the mirror on the way back to her bedroom and smiled.

On the side of her bed, she petted Nicky's back. The dog swallowed a few times—a canine's response to a loving gesture. She punched in the number for Geoff's phone, which she'd written down on the receipt the day before.

"Hi there. And we're back," Geoff said in a radio host voice.

"Hi." Poppy laughed. "I still can't believe I didn't remember your voice yesterday." She looked at Nicky, who, on her back on the bed, encouraged Poppy with endearing eyes. Poppy grinned and stroked the dog's tummy. "Do you have any pets?"

"Sure do. Zippy's right here with me. My fat cat." He rubbed the top of Zippy's head. "How about you?"

"Yes, a Shih Tzu. Nicky. Saint Nick brought her in 2001." Poppy gasped. "Oh, the reason we got her was to bring some comfort to us all after 9/11."

"I understand that completely." Geoff leaned back in the rocker. "I've had Labs. In fact, Tucker, my yellow Lab, kept me company when I went to be with my parents two days after 9/11."

The bridge changed back to a softer hue, a coral pink. For twenty-five more minutes, both seemed to share an intuitive understanding of each other. Attentive and engaged, their voices ebbed and flowed with a natural ease.

"I suppose I should go before the kids return from Walgreens." Poppy grimaced.

"It's been so great to talk with you, Poppy." Geoff leaned forward, now on the edge of his bed.

"I know. I've so enjoyed this. I could talk to you for hours," Poppy said. "I don't want to hang up."

"We *have* talked for hours." Geoff grinned. "I don't want to hang up, either." Geoff nodded his head. "If it's okay, how about we talk again tomorrow night?"

"That'd be great." Poppy smiled. "Who's going to hang up first?" She giggled. "I feel like a seventh grader who doesn't want to end the call."

Geoff laughed.

Poppy's eyes filled. "Now see, if you'd laughed right away when you called me yesterday, I would've known *immediately* who it was. I've never forgotten that laugh. *Your* laugh."

❀

Twenty hours later, I watched Geoff's movements on the slate, and as his call to Poppy connected, the bridge presented itself once again—a golden-amber hologram. With Poppy at her home, I watched her as she sat on one of two wrought-iron chairs on her front porch—her legs crossed. The sound of cicadas buzzed from the treeline at the property's edge, their recent arrival singing praises to the humid southwest Florida evening. She swept away stray hairs from her forehead. "It's so good to hear your voice again. I've taken you outside tonight."

"That sounds nice. Where are we?" Geoff lay sideways on his bed, his elbow propping up his head.

"Not very exciting. Just my front porch." Poppy eyes rested on the stone angel statue.

"I glanced at our old Tomokans." Geoff smiled as he looked at the pile of three Rollins yearbooks on the corner of his desk. "Do you keep in touch with any Thetas?"

"Yes. I saw Maggie last November when I sold my original-design art therapy kits at a conference in Dallas. And I talk with my shoeless, braless roomie, Catherine, and a couple of others." Poppy stood from the cushionless chair and arched her back. "And a few on Facebook. You?"

"I talk a little bit with Fred." Geoff anchored the pillow at his lower back and settled in. "And Ernie, of course."

"Ernie!" Poppy shouted. "He was so cute. Our roommate, right?" Poppy's cheeks flushed—the words out of her mouth before she'd had a chance to censor them.

Geoff laughed. "Yes, he was. Do you remember Fred was my roommate the year before?"

"Oh God. Fred. I'll never forgive him for tricking me with those magic brownies." Poppy groaned. "Besides, he hated me, anyway." Poppy used her sandal to clear dirt from the grout on the porch. "Because of our breakup," she murmured.

"He doesn't hate you." Geoff's voice lingered on the last word.

"He yelled at me. Called me cruel for hurting you." Poppy's voice, tinged with remembered guilt, softened. She straightened her posture on the hard surface of the chair. "I can't blame him. He was being your friend. Loyal."

Geoff leaned forward from the pillow. "I'm sure if I can get over it, he can."

Poppy didn't speak right away. She wiped her eyes with the back of her hand.

"Are you there?" Geoff got off the bed.

"Yes, I'm here." Poppy also stood. "It's still upsetting to me, that's all. Our breakup." Her mouth trembled. "I remember calling my dearest friend, Cecelia, in Milwaukee, whom you met at my home in Wisconsin on New Year's Day thirty-two years ago. I told her of our split. Even *she* was really upset for us. She knew of the guys I'd dated in high school and college. She knew we were different. 'Special' is what she'd said of us." Poppy's voice quivered.

"Wow. I never knew . . ." Geoff exhaled. "From everything that we've just learned about each other, you have nothing to worry about. No need to be upset anymore."

Poppy nodded. "I know, I know," she said and swallowed, although her facial expression hadn't yet caught up to her statement.

"Poppy," Geoff began, his voice gentle. "Your words two days ago when we first connected completely changed how I look at all of this. It's okay." Geoff's tone sounded like a caress.

She walked to the majestic palm in the corner of the porch. Poppy tugged at a dead leaf and shook it from the tree, along with her sad feelings. She inhaled. "Thank you for saying that, Geoff." Poppy looked toward the treeline, the sound of the cicadas a welcome distraction to thwart unwanted emotion.

Her unsettled memories caused the Emotional Clock to fall back to Four O'clock—Shame and Guilt.

Geoff, as if he had a front-row seat to our bridge, intuitively turned to face the now-darkened Lake Davidson. Like a balladeer with an upbeat key change, Geoff asked, a smile in his voice, "Do you remember where we first met?"

"Of course," Poppy said and turned back to face her house. "The Pub." Poppy began to pace on the porch, and her momentum returned along with her cheerful intonation. "And you were wearing a rugby shirt. Green and navy stripes. White collar."

The hands on the clock swung quickly to Eight O'clock, Forgiveness, and the bridge sparkled with a full 3-D radiance as if it were a visual recording that'd been rewound.

"God, how do you remember what I wore?" Geoff lowered into the family rocker. "I remember telling you about getting electrocuted—and dying. I made you cry."

"What?" Poppy stood still. "I remember you were electrocuted, with the sailboat. That was awful. But I *cried?*" Poppy's eyes widened.

"You did." Geoff laughed. "I kept telling you I was fine."

"So silly of me." She shook her head. "Well, I cry all the time. Big sap."

Geoff ran his finger on the grooved arm of the chair. "I gave a speech on that in Doc's class. Remember Doc Rivers?"

"Of course I do. I gave *my* demonstration speech on how to jitterbug, and I had my college sweetheart dance with me." Poppy giggled.

Geoff spoke in a low, booming voice. "That's right. I did." With a deep bass resonance, Geoff imitated their communication professor's voice. "'You're great dancers. No one's ever danced in my class before.'"

Poppy laughed and wiped the corners of her eyes, shame tears and happy tears now gone. "You sound just like him. That's great." Her laugh trailed off. "And you taught me how to water-ski."

"I did, didn't I?" Geoff looked up at his ceiling.

"I remember when you came to Milwaukee for New Year's. And my Poppy Bowl party on January first." Poppy walked back and forth on her porch.

"Yeah, I froze my ass off in your stone guesthouse."

"I'm so sorry we froze you. I feel terrible." Poppy winced.

"I snowmobiled for the first time with you," Geoff said.

Poppy returned to the house. "That was fun." She sunk back against the arm of the living room sofa. "I remember our nicknames, Geoffrey. You were Chief . . ." Poppy closed her eyes as she brought her knees to her chest.

Geoff got up from his chair and lay on his bed, his elbow behind his head. "And you were Honch."

"That . . . I've *never forgotten*." Poppy sat up straight and picked up a feather that protruded from the cushion on the sofa. "So, what other memories do you have of us at Rollins?" Poppy sat back against the pillow and curled a lock of hair with her finger.

"Well . . .," he started, then stopped abruptly for a fond memory and added, "Some of the memories are fun!" Geoff smiled. "I remember some *very* clearly."

"Like what?" Poppy fluffed the throw pillow in the center of the couch.

"I remember that we were in my room one time, and you put on my ski gloves."

"Awww," Poppy uttered as if window-shopping for a new puppy.

After a moment of silence, Geoff added, "And that's *all* you wore."

Poppy leapt up as her hand flew to her mouth. "Oh my God! Oh my God." She strode into her bedroom and shut the door. "I hadn't remembered that until right now," she whispered. "What else do you remember?" Poppy chewed her lower lip.

With a grin on his face, Geoff leaned back on his bed. "I remember we celebrated my twenty-first birthday at the Park Plaza." He held both hands behind his head as the phone rested on his shoulder.

"Oh, yeah." Poppy squinted. A foggy memory. "We had dinner, right?"

"Yeah." He waited. "Don't you remember we *stayed* there, too? I don't remember much about dinner, but I remember being in the room. The only thing you wore until the next morning was a smile." Geoff's mouth curved up into his cheeks.

"OH MY GOD!" Poppy said, as she paced in her bedroom. She opened her bedroom door a crack, covered the mouthpiece, and peered into the family room. She tiptoed back inside and silently closed the door. "I can't believe this," she whispered. "I was a good girl. You corrupted me, Geoffrey Spencer."

Geoff laughed for several seconds. "And I remember that we went to our family condo at Cocoa Beach. Remember the teakettle?" Geoff closed his eyes and shook his grinning face side to side.

"The teakettle?" Poppy's eyebrows inched together in confusion.

"Yeah, the teakettle. When we got up the next morning, you went to make some tea. You came back to bed, where we got distracted, and . . ."

Poppy gasped. "I burned the teakettle." Poppy exhaled into Lamaze transitional breathing. "I can't believe it, Geoff. I was a slut!" She raced into her bathroom and closed the door. She stared at herself in the mirror—half-smiling, half in shock. "I'm horrified!" She sat on the cover of the toilet seat, and with her head in her hand, she nodded. "Okay, so I was a slut. Okay. A slut."

Geoff sat up straight. "You were *nothing* of the kind." His laugh popped out of his mouth like a runaway balloon. "Come on, Poppy," Geoff said, laughing. Don't you remember any of this? I mean, you were *there*." He chuckled.

"Stop laughing!" She blurted out. "This is terrible."

"I'm sorry. I can't help it." He giggled. "Why are you getting so upset about this?"

"Because I hadn't remembered any of it until right this moment. After our rough breakup, I think I blocked everything. Even this." Poppy got up and walked back into her bedroom. "So, what you're saying is, all you remember about me is me being naked? Do you have *any* memories of me with my clothes on?" she shout-whispered.

Geoff was silent. The bridge radiated a crimson-red glow from the gold center. *God this is so funny,* Geoff thought, and leaned back. He closed his eyes, and his dimple made a parenthesis on his right cheek.

"Seriously, Geoff? You have to rack your brain to come up with a memory of me clothed?!" Poppy's mouth fell open.

She put her hand on her forehead. *Holy shit,* she thought. *He can't remember anything except fooling around. What about holding hands and walking to Beans? Dancing and laughing hysterically at the Pub?* She wondered to herself.

"Hold on. Hmm . . . I think I have one . . .," Geoff began, still laughing.

"Stop it! I can't believe you have to work this hard to come up with a socially appropriate memory!" Poppy smiled in mock irritation. "What about Beans? And dancing? The Pub?"

"Of course I remember all of that. I'm just having fun with you." He sat up in bed. "I remember very clearly you had a cropped navy-striped velour pullover that you looked so cozy in. Oh c'mon, you were adorable. I was crazy about you."

Poppy exhaled like she'd just taken a drag on a cigarette. "I remember we were M&M's, and you were such a good sport."

"Yep. I remember." He grinned. "I was the one with the nuts."

Poppy smiled and stood. "You know, it's really funny." Her accordion closet door squeaked as she slid it open. "Hold on a sec. I'm taking you into the closet with me."

"The closet? Aren't you already out of the closet?"

"Haha. I just remembered this past summer, I was looking at old photos with Molly, and I found our M&M picture, and the one with you at the farm with my cat. You looked so cute." Poppy reached for the plastic baggie of photos from the third shelf.

Geoff looked up to his left. "Those silly cardboard things I had to wear. Taking shit from my fraternity brothers for wearing tights," he mumbled.

"Here it is. I found it." Poppy sat on the bed and cradled the phone on her shoulder. "I can't believe I'd placed these pictures of you in a different place than the rest of my photos that I keep in the garage. I hadn't considered why I'd done that. Weird, right?" She held up the M&M photo and stared at it.

Just then, the bridge changed from bright red to a softer russet red, and Poppy's eyes watered. I felt the tug of her emotions.

"This is so unreal, Geoff, because I haven't seen these pictures in more than fifteen years. I just *happened* to come across them. Just *happened* to put them in a safe place." Poppy's jaw fell open, and her expression expanded from casual enjoyment to frozen wonderment. "And then you call me." Poppy jumped up, opened her top dresser drawer, and removed a hand-painted box—marine blue with pink-and-white flowers. She gasped as she lifted the lid. "Geoff," she breathed as she grasped an opaque white shell. "I have a white shell—a baby's ear. It's the one we found on Cocoa Beach," she said, and cradled it in her palm as she'd done more than thirty years ago.

"The same shell?" He whispered.

"It is. This is amazing. I hadn't remembered where I'd gotten it until tonight. Until we connected," she murmured, and tucked the shell in the silk lining of the box.

"See? A memory where you had clothes on, Honch." He laughed. "And you kept it." He mused.

Molly came to Poppy's door and knocked softly. "Mom? You still on the phone?" The teen asked, her tone laced with parental disapproval.

Poppy put the phone facedown on the bed. "Yes, Moll. I'll be right there. Mary's in Seattle, three hours behind us."

Molly walked back through the kitchen toward her room. "Sorry, Geoff. I pretended with Molly that you're my good friend, Mary, who lives in Seattle. Molly knows that Mary and I talk for hours. I don't want her to be suspicious. Even though I'm divorced, I'm not ready to tell the kids that you and I are talking."

"I understand. You don't have to explain any further."

"I better go—talk with the kids again before they go to bed. And I have another psych class first thing tomorrow." Poppy hugged her stomach. "I can't wait to talk with you, tomorrow, Geoff. Chief."

"Me, too, Honch." Geoff twirled one corner of his moustache. He pressed the End button and dropped the phone on the bed. He shook his head with a slight movement of disbelief. "No wonder I fell in love with this girl thirty-two years ago. She's perfect for me."

# CHAPTER 23

# Healing a Wound

~~

"YOU KNOW YOU DON'T HAVE to sit here with me." George Terris glanced away from the CNBC stock ticker on the flat-screen. "I'm fine, honey," he said, his hazel eyes watery with emotion.

He sat in an ivory leather chair with a matching ottoman. In pale-yellow slacks with a long-sleeved white cotton knit polo—the sleeves covering his wrists in spite of the warm setting of the thermostat—George kept his right hand on the back of his head. On my slate, I noted this gesture as one that soothed, offset, and balanced the discomfort from the tumor—the wound—that'd begun to take over his left ear.

"I know, Dad. I want to be here. This is the only time I get to be with *just you.*" Poppy sat a foot away at a small round table covered by a French silk tablecloth. She stroked her father's left wrist and rose to clear the wrappings and dressings from the wound on his ear.

The two of them, along with Nicky—who happily perched on the edge of George's ottoman—spoke of world news and local news, as they did each Tuesday and Thursday afternoon when Poppy's mother, Valerie, played bridge.

When Valerie returned home, I watched the three of them—a relay race of passing the baton of levity and good cheer. Of optimism and hope. Of love. George deflected his own pain to revel in his wife's joy of a victorious day at the bridge table and express pride to his daughter. Valerie had left the world of play she enjoyed for a few hours each week to face her worst fear every time she looked at her husband—and a wound that couldn't be healed. And Poppy tried to be the anchor leg of the race, to muster enough positivity and daily encouragement to keep the family in good stride. Where normalcy became a quest. A luxury.

~~

At five thirty that day, now with Geoff in North Carolina, a flaxen-colored bridge emerged from my slate, even before he'd called Poppy.

*I think I'll call her now—choir practice in about an hour,* Geoff thought.

On my slate, I saw Poppy sprinkle oregano on six chicken breasts in a Pyrex baking dish. She opened the oven door and slid in the pan.

"Hi, Chief!" Poppy answered the phone in her kitchen. "Just finished preparing dinner and waiting for the kids to get home. How are you?"

"I'm good. I thought I'd call before my choir practice at seven." Geoff sat on the sofa in his living room and elevated his feet on the Scandinavian wood coffee table.

"Wow. I didn't know you sang in a choir." Poppy set the timer on the oven. "What kind of church?"

"Methodist." He sipped his Propel. "Davidson United Methodist Church."

"Oh my gosh. Same," Poppy exclaimed like a middle-schooler. "I go to the Methodist church here." Poppy walked into her living room and sat on the green sofa, next to Nicky.

"I'm also the choir chaplain," Geoff said. "I say a prayer after rehearsal."

"The chaplain? So you're like a sous minister? A sous chef?" Poppy laughed.

"Sort of." Geoff chuckled. "I just get called upon for our group prayer. People share their concerns. And I just say whatever's in my heart at the time."

"That's beautiful." Poppy closed her eyes. "I imagine you're wonderful at it."

"I'm comfortable doing it on the spot, and it feels good to be able to share thoughts that bring comfort." Geoff picked up an errant kernel of popcorn from under the table and walked into the kitchen. "So how was your day?"

"Well, I had my last psychology of social interaction class. I gave a final exam. Students had to give a presentation and write a paper." She sighed. "These kids are so talented." Poppy straightened the candle in the holder on the coffee table. "I usually feel a letdown when the semester ends, but talking with you has taken that away," she said, her tone both solemn and sensual.

"Well, glad I could help." Geoff matched her seriousness and added a playful redirect. "I couldn't wait to call you."

Poppy's face flushed. "After my client session, I went to my mom and dad's house." She caressed Nicky's head. "My mom is a few hundred points away from becoming a Silver Life Master player. She competes every Tuesday and Thursday afternoon. I like to hang out with my dad while she's gone."

"Life Master Bridge player. Sounds pretty serious."

"She's really good. And it gives me time to spend with my dad. I don't spend much time with *just* him. Only when, as a kid, I went to Packer games with him. My mom always worried that it was too cold, and even though I totally froze—like 35-below wind chills—I'd say I was just fine." Poppy got up and walked around the living room. She took a kitchen towel and dusted the tables in the formal room. "It's because of the connection with my dad, who's a huge football fan, that I'm a Green Bay fan for life." She flipped the towel over to dust the antique wooden Bombay chest.

"So how is your dad?" Geoff set the utensils on the round dining room table.

Poppy laid the rag on the table and sat down next to Nicky. "Um, he's okay." Poppy took the pillow out from behind her and inched back against the sofa. "He's so proud—never complains about the pain I know he feels." Poppy's eyes teared. "He's always taken care of all of us. On our three trips to France, we never spent one franc of our own money."

Geoff started for the kitchen and paused. "Three trips to France? Wow, he *has* taken great care of you." Geoff pulled out a dining room chair and sat.

Poppy closed her eyes. "My dad's the ultimate protector. He rarely asks for anything. And his mind is so sharp. Sometimes we still play golf together when the chemo treatments don't affect him too badly. It's hard to explain it, yet my dad and I seem to have a really good unspoken sense of each other. We get each other very well."

"At one of my mom and dad's parties in the early nineties, I showed up without the guy I'd been seeing for a few weeks, post-divorce. I'd just broken off with him—a trust thing for me. My dad saw in my eyes that I was un-settled." Poppy stroked the fringe on the throw pillows. "My mom didn't see it—kept asking where he was, why he hadn't come with me, would he come later." Poppy sighed. "With one look, my dad captured the entire picture and in his very stern voice said, 'Valerie, he's not here.' Which meant 'drop it.'"

Poppy set the pillow aside and stood. "It was very telling for me. My dad understood the whole of the situation in one glance and communicated to my mother in four words and in a way that she'd understand: Our daugh-ter's upset. Back off." Poppy ran her finger on the beveled edges of the base of the lamp. She wiped the dusty residue on the bottom of her skirt. "My mom doesn't like changes in plans," she murmured. "My dad could've cared less that the guy wasn't there. He only cared that *I* was okay."

"I'm sure he loves having you there, Poppy—and certainly it's a relief to your mom to have you nearby." Geoff uncurled the edge of a woven place-mat on the table in front of him. "May I call you back after choir? I need to get a quick bite before I leave."

Poppy stood up and smoothed her skirt. "Of course. I didn't mean to keep you."

"I'll be back around quarter to nine or so."

Poppy looked out her bay window at the angel statue in the front yard. "I look forward to hearing your prayer."

~~

A dozen men ranging in age from their forties through their late seven-ties gathered in the choir room for the men's sectional rehearsal. From his cubby, Geoff pulled out his music folder and two loose pieces of music.

Geoff sat in the middle of the first row of chairs. An older gentleman, already seated next to him, glanced at Geoff and did a double take. "You seem in especially good spirits." The slim man grinned, as the fluorescent lighting reflected off his white hair.

"Larry, I'm in phenomenal spirits. I've had the most incredible thing happen." Geoff steadied his hands on the music sheets in his lap. "I haven't told anybody," Geoff said, his voice an animated whisper. "I've talked to my old college sweetheart, whom I haven't spoken to in thirty-two years."

Larry, with twinkling green eyes, turned in the padded folding chair to face Geoff. "I don't think I've ever seen you like this. This excited." He studied Geoff's expression, the moustache that curled into his dimple.

"Larry, I can't even begin to explain this." Geoff stared up at the acoustical tiled ceiling as though Michelangelo might still be up there painting it. "We've only been talking for three days. It's like we've never been apart."

~~

Two hours later, Poppy turned on the lamp in her bedroom and smoothed the comforter on her bed. "What did the choir chaplain offer as a prayer tonight?" She answered the phone without saying hello, as if she couldn't waste any more time or years with formalities.

"I talked about surprises." Geoff lay on his bed and stroked Zippy's back. "And thanked God for the surprises that come our way in life. Surprises we don't expect that are wonderful." Geoff paused. "And I asked that He please continue to keep our hearts and minds open to new possibilities."

Poppy's fingertip wiped a tear from the corner of her eye. "That's beautiful."

I felt an inner calm, similar to what people describe when they first sip chamomile tea and warmth flushes over them—a peacefulness that spreads throughout the being.

"I'm comfortable with taking my emotions and putting them into words I hope will resonate with others," Geoff said.

"You sound like a minister," Poppy said, as she played with the gold cross necklace she'd worn every day since high school.

"I've been told many times that I should've been a minister. But I'm *way* too fallen for that." Geoff tsked.

"I can attest to that. The fallen part," Poppy scoffed. "You made me fall for you."

"Haha!" Geoff laughed. "Yes, I guess I did. I fell for you, too, you know."

Poppy straightened a pad of paper on her nightstand. "I wanted to talk about something if you don't mind. I know I touched on it when you first called the other night. Gosh, doesn't that seem like years ago? Like we've talked now for weeks and weeks?" Poppy stood and walked to her jewelry chest. She opened the third drawer and began to pair the earrings that'd been randomly scattered.

"It *does* seem like we've talked for ages," Geoff murmured.

"I wanted your thoughts about what happened. During our breakup. It was *so* sudden. I really never knew how you felt." Poppy sat on her bed.

"I never understood any bit of it—why we broke up." Geoff stared at his reflection in the dresser mirror. "I thought you just didn't want to be with me anymore. You broke up with me and got engaged right away." Geoff's words came out fast.

Poppy nodded, her arm tight across her stomach. "I know, I know." She closed her eyes. "I just didn't know any better. Right before we broke up, I'd asked you one night, 'What do you think will happen next year?' You said you'd be captain of the water-ski team." Poppy slid off her sandals and put her feet up on the bed. She hugged her knees to her chest. "I already had a job lined up in Milwaukee. I meant to say, 'What will happen with *us*?'" Poppy blinked. Her crow's feet now served as corridors for her tears.

"Yeah, I'm sure I hadn't thought ahead." Geoff shook his head. "Not back then."

"Of course. But here's what I thought. I couldn't stop thinking about the future—going home, being far away from you. I wondered if we'd maintain our relationship. Write letters once a week to each other. Call on Sundays. See each other like we had that Christmas." Poppy traced the quilted thread-ing around the comforter. "I'd had all of these uncertainties and wanted *some* reassurance from you, but I didn't want to come right out and *say any-thing* because I feared that would have been be *too forward*. Not proper."

Geoff put his fingers on his forehead, his jaw open. "Okay . . ."

Poppy spoke quickly. "And I wanted to hear that you, too, had thought of the next year. Because in my twenty-one-year-old brain, that would've confirmed that I was special. That you really loved me. That I was some-thing more than just a filler for the year."

"You definitely weren't a filler," Geoff scoffed.

Poppy's voice quivered. "When I didn't hear the words I'd hoped for." She paused and closed her eyes as if confessing her greatest sin. "I assumed that I wasn't *that great*. That I wasn't important to you after all." Her eyes brimmed with fresh tears.

"You had to know that wasn't the case. I was crazy about you, Poppy." Geoff stood up, his free hand on the dresser.

"Geoff, it wasn't until I began to break us up that I realized that," she said, her tone distraught and remorseful. "I realized too late that you cared because you got so upset. Before that, I hadn't known."

Poppy rose and walked the length of her bed and dresser. "I know I sobbed and could hardly breathe. And then you cried and I was surprised, and thought, *Why is he crying? Why is he so upset?* And I could hardly speak, and I wanted to take it all back and say, 'Stop! Let's talk.'"

Poppy sank on the bed as if she'd fallen into a dense jungle of emo-tional vines.

As Poppy railed through her confessional, I felt my insides being thrashed—a forestry excavator as it cut through the thicket.

"But you were up and leaving. You didn't want to hear any more." Poppy shivered and stood. Now in the bathroom doorway, she stared at her damp-ened cheeks. "I was in shock. Speechless. Because I hadn't expected you to care if we were together or not. No words had formed in my head.

"You shook off my hand," she whimpered. "I pleaded, 'Don't go. Wait!' But it was too late. You were out the door." Poppy breathed air from her pursed lips—a steadying of her emotional breath. She walked back to her bed and sat. With closed eyes, she finished. "It was one of the most traumatic events in my life, Geoff." Poppy pushed herself upright.

"I know. It was awful," he muttered, his tone that of a bystander at the scene of a bad wreck. "I couldn't understand any of it. I kept asking you, 'Why are you doing this? Don't you still love me?' And you kept saying you didn't know why, but yes, you still loved me." Geoff lowered onto the bed and closed his eyes. "And then that frigging Candlelight . . ." His voice melted into disdain.

Poppy stopped pacing. "I didn't want to do the Candlelight," Poppy whispered. "I came back to school after Mother's Day—engaged." Poppy stared at the tile on the bedroom floor. "I was such a good little rule follower, so I told Meredith, our Theta president, that I'd gotten engaged. I begged her not to hold the ceremony. And I told her I wasn't engaged to *you*." Poppy closed her eyes again. "I told her that all the sisters would assume it was you. No one really knew we'd broken up."

"Yeah, neither of us said a word about it to our friends. I know I was in a fog," Geoff murmured.

Poppy leaned on her dresser, one arm holding her stomach. "Meredith insisted and said it would be fine. And of course it wasn't. It was a nightmare. And the worst *did* happen. Everyone *did* think it was you." Poppy's voice broke. "I'm so sorry, Geoff. I've felt guilty all these years. It's still upsetting. Just thinking about it. That I would hurt this wonderful man who'd been so good to me." Her voice splintered.

"Poppy, ahh." His voice, a whisper. "I had no idea."

"I see that now." She nodded, and tears fell on her blouse.

"I was sure you wanted nothing to do with me. That you just cast me aside without any further thought," Geoff scoffed. "That damn Candlelight was the final blow."

"I didn't know what to do. How to be assertive. How to share my fears with you and possibly burden you. After that Sunday night, I didn't think I had the right to talk with you again. I didn't deserve you." Poppy's mouth contorted as she continued to sew emotional stitches. "And the day after the Candlelight, that's when Fred approached me as C-Bell and I walked to class. He blasted me—told me I was terrible. That I was cruel to hurt you. And I just stood there and nodded, completely agreeing with him. He was right. I was an awful person," Poppy said, crying again.

"I never knew *any* of this, Poppy." Geoff rested his head against his fingers.

"D'you know, I don't even *remember* my graduation. Not where we held it. Not if my parents came. *Nothing.* I've repressed it. That's how traumatic our breakup was."

Poppy went into her bathroom, removed the designer cover from the tissue box, and took the cardboard container back to the bed. "I became a hermit. Hid out in the art studio for the last few weeks of school." She sniffled. "Took circuitous routes to make sure I wouldn't cross paths with you."

"I remember your graduation," Geoff said, as scorn seeped into his tone. "And I remember seeing your parents," he tsked. "It sucked."

"Really? You do?" Poppy bolted up from the bed, the tissue wadded in her hand.

"I remember you walking across the stage, and out of my life," he said, the defeat of that memory dredged up in his voice.

"I can't believe I don't remember *my own* graduation." Poppy blew air from grimaced lips. "Geoff, I teach this stuff. All about defense mechanisms and Freud. How we repress memories that are too painful. Clearly, I'd suppressed all the memories of me with my clothes off, from what we shared last night. And I think I have a pretty good memory." Poppy's laugh came at the end of her crying, like a gulp with hiccups.

Poppy dabbed the tissue to her nose. "I remember our breakup. You sat with your right leg and foot on the floor, and your left ankle tucked under the back of your knee."

Geoff's lips parted in disbelief. "You remember how I *sat* on your bed, but you don't remember graduation?"

"Well, up to the point of the breakup, I thought I had a clear perception of being dispensable. I hadn't expected you to be upset with the breakup." She shivered. "Geoff, the trauma was *so intense* that after that night in my room, I blocked a lot out." She exhaled again. "And all that was left was me believing that I was . . ." Poppy's voice faltered, and she softly added, "Unworthy of such a good person."

"Wow, Poppy. I know it's hard to resurrect this again. To relive all this pain." Geoff's arm lay across his chest—his hand over his heart. "I never really understood what'd happened until right now."

Poppy held the Kleenex box in her lap. "I've felt ashamed. Guilty, all these years."

~⌣

"So, that's what really happened," Geoff mumbled to himself. "I've been wrong about it all along." With deliberate steps, he trudged to his desk. "I never knew."

He clicked his mouse and refreshed the screen on his computer. He typed an email to Poppy.

*I want to thank you for the wonderful conversation we shared earlier. I especially want to thank you for healing a wound that I have had in my heart for thirty-two years.*

CHAPTER 24

# In a Dream

~⁀

I SAT IN THE ORGAN loft's first pew of the Knowles Chapel at Rollins and gazed at the magnificent stained-glass window, a circle with vivid cobalt-blue sections. The famous pipe organ—custom built against the choir loft's wall—surrounded the panorama of glass. Golden wings, these stair-step and evenly spaced cylinders of the instrument, stretched toward heaven. I imagined the music, the choir, and the hymns. And a memory from decades ago.

My slate on my lap, I glanced to the altar, covered with day-old flowers. From this viewpoint, I had a quiet view of the sanctuary below—the altar the focal point for many poignant events at Rollins College.

The screen of my slate suddenly projected an image of a thirty-year-old Poppy, sitting cross-legged in three-inch-tall rye grass. Dressed in khaki shorts and a turquoise short-sleeved blouse, she leaned back, her arms propping her upright.

The screen image—mercurial—floated from my slate. "A dream," I whispered. "Poppy is dreaming."

Barefoot, Poppy wiggled her toes—manicured with a pale-pink polish. As she moved, the polish shimmered and created mystical shapes of roses, and the fragrance, roses in full bloom, filled the air above the slate. Next to her, Geoff—also in his thirties in a navy-blue polo shirt tucked into khaki shorts, plucked an iridescent blade of grass between his two thumbs and readied his cheeks to blow.

A purple spotted swallowtail butterfly landed on Poppy's sandal.

Poppy extended her bronzed legs in front of her and crossed her ankles. As Geoff began to blow through the blade of grass, he stopped and looked at Poppy. His dark caramel eyes shone from the sunlight, and his dimple became a continuation of his smile. Poppy smiled back at him and said, "I love you, Geoffrey."

The dream image evaporated, and I now stared at Poppy on my slate. Her eyes blinked open, her head on her pillow. "I love him." Tears dribbled from the corners of her eyes onto her cheeks and the pillowcase.

She looked at the digital clock—4:31. "That was so real," she breathed. She collapsed against the pillow and closed her eyes. "I told Geoff I love him."

~

A few hours later, I studied Geoff in his office chair, as he sipped his cappuccino. He held his china mug with two hands as he looked out the window, the sun rising over Lake Davidson. The sun sparkled through the trees each time the breeze moved the leaves, and it appeared as though fireflies were dancing in the poplars. Latte foam rested on one corner of his moustache like of seafoam on a beach.

Geoff's curious expression—a half smile from one side of his mouth and one eyebrow raised higher than the other—looked as though his face was juggling many thoughts and emotions at once. He punched in a number on his desktop phone.

"Hey, Geoff. What's up?" a woman's husky voice asked.

"Lucy, how's my favorite Stephen minister?" he asked, and rushed into his next sentence. "I couldn't think of anyone else who knows me as well as you do to share this."

Before the woman could respond, my slate—unsolicited—shot up the words: *Stephen Minister: a Christian layperson who offers one-on-one confidential counseling and care to someone in need or in transition.*

"Share what?" Lucy prompted, her voice casual. Conditioned to be calm.

Geoff blurted out, "Lucy, I think I've lost my mind." He crossed his ankle over his knee and twirled his moustache, his contemplative self-soothing habit.

Lucy chuckled. "I'm sure you haven't lost your mind, Geoff. What's going on?"

"Four days ago, I just happened to have a thought about my old college sweetheart, Poppy. I was madly in love with her." Geoff glanced out his window and watched a slow-moving fishing boat in the distance. "She just popped in my head. I looked her up, called her, spoke to her." He shook his head. "And it's been the most unbelievable thing. We talk each night. For hours, Lucy. We're having the time of our lives reconnecting." Rocking forward, he put his foot back on the ground. "It's like we've never been apart."

Geoff stared at a faraway fisherman as if he'd held the answers. "Lucy, this just doesn't make *any sense.*"

For a few seconds, Lucy said nothing. Her deep voice came through the speaker. "Let me ask you two questions, Geoff." She paused—her tone—a lawyer during a cross-examination in a court session. "First, why did you call her?"

"Becauuuusse." Geoff's eyes darted around the ceiling. "I feel unfulfilled in my life?" Geoff's voice lifted into a question.

"Um-hmm. Okay. Second question." Lucy hesitated. "Are you still in love with Poppy?" Lucy asked, her voice now softer.

Geoff's head fell back on the chair's padded headrest, his mouth slack. The side of his face toppled into his open palm. "Yes," Geoff said, his eyes glazed with new awareness. "Yes, Lucy, I *am* still in love with her."

"Well," Lucy began with a lilt in her voice.

Geoff stood up, and sent his chair sliding backward. "Oh my God, Lucy. I'm stunned." He walked to the window and raised the accordion blind. "I just realized that all this time, I've never fallen *out of love* with her." He leaned on the windowsill. "She was a few months older, and we only got split up because she graduated the year before me. There was never anything *wrong*. Never a fight. We were together my entire junior year." He talked into the windowpane. "Oh my God, I feel like I'm walking around in a dream."

"Well, Geoff. Sounds like you've answered your own question," Lucy murmured.

He stared at the phone as if she were right there. "Lucy, thank you."

With his head down, he put his hands flat on the dresser and leaned into it, not so much for support, but rather to steady his newly discovered realization. "I've been in love with Poppy this whole time," he murmured. "This explains so much." He whispered, "We never fell *out of* love."

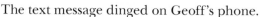

The text message dinged on Geoff's phone.
*You free?*
*Yes!* Geoff punched in the letters on his Blackberry.
"Hi!" In her kitchen, Poppy filled her water glass.

"Good morning. How are you?" Geoff cleared his throat.

"Good. I've been awake since four thirty. I'll tell you why later. I've been to spin class and back. I resisted the temptation to call you right when I woke up." Poppy laughed.

"Good!" Geoff bellowed. "Four thirty? What in God's name were you doing awake then? And at spin class? I'd be unconscious. And I *was*."

"Well, I had a dream that woke me up. You were there." Poppy grinned.

"I was? What was I doing in your dream?" Geoff asked, his tone, playful.

"It woke me up. I had tears soaking my face. I even tried to go back *into* the dream. I wasn't sad or anything." Poppy walked slowly around her dining room table.

"Crying?" Geoff sat up, and dropped his foot on the floor. "What happened?"

"I woke myself up with my own talking." Poppy sat at the breakfast bar.

"So what did you say?" Geoff asked—his tone both curious and bouncy.

"Well, you and I sat in a green field. You tried to make a horn sound with a blade of grass. And I smiled at you. You had your great dimple on." Poppy chuckled. "And . . . I," Poppy closed her eyes. "I said, 'I love you, Geoffrey.'"

The bridge glowed a bright blue-green, the colors of an expression of love. I felt a thumping in my core as if someone had pounded on a locked door that never should've been locked.

In slow motion, Geoff walked to the living room. He slid the throw pillow over and lowered himself to the couch. *God, I can't believe I'm hearing this,* he thought.

*This feels a little bit scary to say this, but I do love him,* Poppy thought.

"I love you, Geoffrey." Poppy's eyes filled with fresh tears and her heart pounded with truth.

"I love you, too, Poppy," Geoff said. His voice, soft and filled with memories, transmitted a tenderness he had forgotten he had.

"I didn't say that, Geoff, to fish for a response. I said it because it's in my heart. And when we broke up at Rollins, I was in my head. Now, I'm expressing what I feel." She paused. "From my heart."

"I hadn't just said it, either, Poppy. I was just on the phone a few minutes ago talking with Lucy, from church—the person I mentioned to you yesterday." Geoff stood up and walked toward the kitchen. "She asked me two questions," Geoff said, his deep voice confident. "Why had I called you and was I still in love with you?"

"Seriously? That's so wild." Poppy hopped off the barstool.

"I felt unsure about the first question, but I know I wasn't fulfilled. I shocked myself with the answer to the second question. Yes, Poppy, I *am* still in love with you."

Poppy didn't speak right away and swallowed to contain her emotion. She wiped her cheeks. "Geoff, I just can't believe I could feel this way . . . so quickly. I mean, the joy and love I feel for you—*for us*—is so easy. So complete." She pushed back hair from her forehead. "It just doesn't make rational sense."

Geoff smiled. "You know what my opening words were to Lucy? 'I think I've lost my mind.'" He walked to the window in the living room and stared at the bridge that separated Lake Davidson and Lake Norman—the fishing boat now hidden behind the island bend. "So, yes, I understand that it doesn't make rational sense."

The Empathic Bridge radiated a vivid shamrock-green prismatic crystals shimmering around its edges. And in mere minutes from daybreak, on a glorious morning, the hearts of two people reached across hundreds of miles and retrieved what'd been lost. After three decades apart, four days of phone reconnection, and sight unseen, Poppy and Geoff anchored their love—rekindled and reawakened—to twelve on the Emotional Clock.

"I mean, who falls in love in four days?" Poppy's laugh caught in her throat.

"We didn't fall in love in four days, Poppy." Geoff smiled. "We fell in love thirty-two years ago." His thumb wiped his wet eyes. "We never fell out of love."

# CHAPTER 25

# Spiritual Dimension

⁓

THE TWO OF THEM HADN'T spoken since Friday afternoon because Geoff had been competing with the reborn *Misty* in Lake Norman's Great 48 Regatta. Geoff had received two texts from Poppy wishing him success on Saturday and sent a one-word response of *Thanks!*

Sunday morning, I sat with Poppy in a rear pew at the Church of the Redeemer, the Episcopal church she often visited. Her thoughts of Geoff—very intense—caused her to visibly tremble. At the beginning of the church service, the bridge had appeared above my slate and glowed violet—a fitting hue for the sacred setting.

On my slate, I watched Geoff and his crewmember, Dan, on Lake Norman. With tight maneuvers, they tacked *Misty* and jockeyed for position at the starting line. Just as the committee boat sounded the race-warning gun, Poppy slipped her hand in her purse, pulled out her phone, and—though many might wag their finger—sent off a silent text to Geoff.

*I hope you have nice weather today and know that I'm with you in spirit. I know you'll be stellar.*

The bridge brought her thoughts to me, like a prayer. *Geoffrey, I want you to feel my thoughts and desire for you to feel great today.* She sniffled. *Dear Lord, please let Geoff feel the love in my heart that I'm sending across the miles. Please let him feel my love to inspire him in all ways.*

Two teardrops fell onto her bulletin. "Amen," she whispered.

*Why am I crying? Why am I so emotional?* she thought, and slid her fingertip along the lower edges of her eyes, her finger a squeegee on her lids. *I haven't talked to him since Friday. I wish I could connect with him, share these powerful feelings I have.* Poppy's eyes pooled and she opened them wider, forbidding tears to fall again. *I'm happy beyond belief, and still, this yearning ache, like my insides are pinched.* She blew air out in a measured release.

The bridge changed quickly, the violet turning to a bright—almost blinding—white. And I felt Poppy's gripping inside of me, the bittersweet, the yin and yang of contrasting emotions. The hurts-so-good syndrome. I watched her brush back her hair—a brunette wave that had shielded her eyes. A strand of hair tangled in her dark, almost black eyelashes, and she carefully used her fingers to pull it out. She breathed in a deep breath and wiggled back into the hard wooden pew. She closed her eyes. Her cheeks were pink—a softer shade from her magenta lipstick. She ran her tongue on her upper lip and exhaled. *C'mon, Poppy. Steady,* she thought.

*Nice steady breeze. Misty feels good. I feel ready,* Geoff's thoughts broke through—clear as if he were here, sitting in the pew. *Left side of the course looks a little bit fresher. Get a good rhythm with the waves. Don't over steer it.* Geoff's thoughts came in a calm flow.

Poppy's palms lay flat on the pew, her body immobile and her eyes still closed. *Just use your guided imagery. Geoff steers his boat on smooth waters, and he'll know exactly what to do,* Poppy thought with a slight nod of her head.

*Keep good speed as we round the weather mark,* Geoff thought. *You know what to do—nice, smooth rounding.* Geoff gently turned the tiller as they rounded the first mark of the course.

The bridge, still illuminated a translucent white, shimmered like a large diamond. Poppy's focus shifted from conflicted thoughts to one constant stream of positive support for Geoff. And I felt the shift as well—a swell of momentum and excitement.

*I know my crew, Dan, will get the spinnaker up quickly,* Geoff thought. *Trim the boat for downwind speed. Stay in clear air. Don't get covered.* Geoff's thoughts rolled out in a steady stream of consciousness. *Look for the puffs, sail to the puffs, up in the lulls, down in the puffs. Thank you, Dad, for teaching me that.* He looked up at the chute, its blue stripe standing out against the billowed white background. *Keep an eye on the rest of fleet. Cover the closest boat. You know how to do this.*

Geoff looked up to the top of the mast and thought, *Keep masthead fly pointed to clear air. Maximize speed.* Geoff took his eyes off the spinnaker and looked over his shoulder at the competition. *You're okay.*

As *Misty* rounded the mark, Geoff pulled in the mainsheet. *Nice, smooth, wide rounding,* he thought. *Trim for upwind.* He glanced again over his shoulder. *Okay, breathe. Relax. Position us to cover other boats upwind. Stay calm. Keep the boat going. Maximize speed.* Geoff's head moved around the sails as his eyes made a visible checklist. *Keep going. Keep covering. Keep her driving. Just relax. Keep her going. Feel the boat* . . . Geoff's thoughts cycled—a meditation. A mantra.

In the pew, Poppy sat, smiling, and the bridge still glistened. I'd picked up both Geoff's heightened energy and Poppy's calmness.

Geoff repeated his chain of thoughts two more times around the race course. When they rounded the final upwind leg to the finish, Geoff's thoughts burst. *Just bring it home, Geoffrey. Relax. Keep it going.* One of his hands on the tiller, the other on the mainsheet, his head and torso moved rhythmically with the waves, the same way a jockey does when in sync with his horse.

Geoff pounded his palm on the deck. "C'mon, *Misty*, keep it going, old girl!"

Geoff and Dan crossed the finish line first—their gloved hands raised in victory.

At the exact moment, Poppy shook hands with the priest as she left the church.

She paused on the sidewalk that faced the marina and stared at a sailboat as it headed out on Sarasota Bay. The sun's reflection on the mast, like nature's Morse code, blinked silvery dashes across the water. Poppy raised her hand over her eyes and squinted. "Thank you, Lord. I know he did well," she whispered.

When the regatta ended, Geoff left *Misty* at the dock and headed to his car. Before he started the car, he picked up his cell phone. He clicked on a text message Poppy had sent earlier that morning.

"Oh my God," he murmured and stared out the car window, as though he needed a witness. "She was with me the whole time," he whispered. "And stellar?" He smiled as he tapped his response. *I was!*

On my slate, I watched the azure waters of Sarasota Bay nudge anchored sailboats like a mother cat grooms her kittens. The Empathic Bridge had just begun to fade and was no longer brilliant white but an aqua blue. Cerulean. As Poppy drove off from Sunday services, I stood across from the marina and wondered what I'd just experienced with her and Geoff.

The link between them—unmistakable. The energy. The symmetry. I felt a new spiritual dimension to their rediscovered relationship. The luminosity of the bridge, the intensity, a testament to that.

With more than five hundred miles separating Poppy and Geoff—who remained unseen to one another for thirty-two years—how had they been able to share such a powerful sensory connection?

# CHAPTER 26

# Wildest Dreams

~∿

IN THE CAR, POPPY TURNED on the ignition and peeled open an envelope she'd received from Geoff. Inside was a crystal CD jewel case with a Post-it note on top. Scrawled on the shiny disc in black Sharpie: *From Chief to Honch.*

*Thought you might enjoy hearing this,* Geoff's handwritten note read.

She inserted the CD, and a baritone voice filled the car with the song "Unforgettable," a Nat King Cole rendition.

"Wow...," she said. "This is a pretty song." For several blocks, she smiled and listened. *I wonder why he sent this song to me,* she thought.

When the male voice crooned, "How the thought of you does things to me," Poppy gasped and blurted, "Oh!" Poppy signaled to turn into a parking lot. "It's *Geoff.*"

I felt the familiar drumming inside—when people first experience something new and exciting. She put the car in park, listened to the rest of the song, and looked around the parking lot as if to wonder if anyone was witnessing her wonderment.

She exhaled when the song finished and squeezed her fingers on the steering wheel at ten and two. The next song began— "Mona Lisa." She closed her eyes.

When the third song played, Poppy leaned in close to the speaker, as if being closer would help her to better hear the lyrics.

"But when I meet the right one, I know that I'll be true . . . my first love will be my laaaahhhhst . . . When I fall in love . . ."

"Oh. My. God." Her hands fell from the steering wheel. "Did he just sing *my first love will be my last?*" Her mouth dropped open again and her thoughts staggered out. *I'm, like, in a dream here.*

Tears formed, readying themselves to tumble onto her print blouse. Her fingers trembled as she pressed a speed dial button on her cell. *Please answer,* she prayed.

"Hi there!" Geoff's voice could've been Nat King Cole's.

"Oh my God, Chief! You're unbelievable." Poppy's voice quivered. "And I'm crying again." The tears dripped on her cheeks before she could catch them. "The CD is so beautiful. I can't believe your voice." She took a breath. "And oh, the *words*."

"I thought you might like my surprise." Geoff crossed his leg over his knee and grinned. "I recorded that song ten years ago. There's a little story behind this. I recorded it for my mom as a gift because she's a big Nat King Cole fan."

"It's amazing—you're amazing," Poppy whispered.

"The funny thing is, I'd sung 'When I Fall in Love' for a couple of friends' weddings. But it wasn't their first wedding, so I'd changed the words." Geoff chuckled. "I had to sing, '*This* love will be my last.' And when I pulled the recording out on Friday to send it to you, I listened to it and said the same thing you just said: 'Oh my God.' I'd forgotten those were the opening words to 'When I Fall in Love.'" Geoff grinned, adding, "So you like it?"

"Like it? Are you crazy? I love it!" Poppy's eyes filled with new tears. "It's the most wonderful gift I've ever received."

I'd watched Poppy and Geoff for several days—sometimes with Poppy when she'd spoken with Geoff on the phone, other times with Geoff in his condo. And twice in my old haven at Knowles Chapel. But no matter where I'd stood, the Empathic Bridge, independent of location, projected clues to my couple and their emotional state—as if in stand-by mode. It'd appeared first in a silvery gilt—vermeil. And the hue altered, depending on the context of their thoughts and conversations.

When they'd shared joyous dialogue, the bridge had shone vibrant—vermillion red and orange. When they'd discussed challenges, the bridge turned cerulean blue, reflecting openness and candor, and forest green when they'd touched on emotions from the right side of the clock—Anxiety, Anger, Shame and Guilt.

On Wednesday evening, Poppy and Geoff had talked for an hour.

I watched Poppy walk back and forth in her bedroom, and she paused once to use her hip to close a dresser drawer.

Geoff lay on his bed, one hand behind his head, ankles crossed. "What do you think happened with your marriages?"

Poppy sat on the end of her bed and slid a cluster of rolled athletic socks to the center of the spread. "I've thought about what'd happened, hindsight being 20/20." She sighed. "I realized I just didn't like myself—as a mom. As a wife. Or even as a person." Poppy looked at her bare feet. "I wanted my children to have healthy role-modeling."

"I agree with you." Geoff rolled over onto his elbow. "I never wanted Jonathon to experience negative behavior. I tried to spare him from that."

"Totally. You know, Geoffrey, in the past, I think I unconsciously allowed and enabled disrespect. And it occurred to me—what am I teaching my kids?" Poppy stood and, at the window, twisted the rod to close the vertical blinds. She laughed a self-deprecating chortle. "Besides, I'm the mama grizzly bear when it comes to my children. Don't mess with them." Poppy's voice rose in a pretend threat.

"I see you that way." On my slate, Geoff nodded with a knowing smile.

"When I divorced, a couple of my friends said, 'Well, what about the kids?' And I'd told them, it's *because* of my children. For my children," Poppy said. "And I look at my parents and wonder why I haven't had what they have."

"Mm-hmm." Geoff stood and wandered into the living room. "My parents have been married sixty-five years. I've also said, 'I'm not one to condone divorce, yet I believe it fitting to expose children to something more wholesome and healthy.'" Geoff straightened the paper napkins in a sailboat-shaped marine-blue kiln-fired napkin holder.

At her dresser, Poppy placed two picture frames of her four children at right angles to each other. "I believe in marriage. My parents also have a loving and respectful marriage, 'respect' being the operative word."

"Mine, too. I don't think they've ever disagreed on anything. Never a harsh word between them." Geoff looked at his parents' framed portrait on the fireplace mantle. "They're wonderful partners."

Poppy picked up a pink quartz heart from her dresser tray. "I'm not one to cast stones or blame. I wasn't able to cultivate a home with the respect I knew possible. I learned from my parents what a respectful dynamic looks like." Poppy rubbed the heart stone on her knit skirt, making it shinier.

"I learned the same lesson from my parents," Geoff said, his chin and lips wrinkled in reflection.

"And I don't bad-mouth an ex—I don't believe it's right." Poppy tsked. "My friends, Mary and Cecelia, both told me I got an *A* in divorce. I mean, why would I want to say anything bad about the father of my children? That would be a terrible message to give my kids."

"I'm sure you got an *A*. And yeah, I'm not one to dwell on mistakes I've made. I try to understand and learn from them. Figure out *why* I did certain things." Geoff stood at his living room window and watched the car taillights on the I-77 causeway. "And I try to look at the things within my control and address them right away."

"So important." Poppy nodded. "To talk through concerns as soon as possible." Poppy put the heart back on the dresser tray. "For me, the respect factor is really big—the foundation of a healthy family. Without it, the well-being of the family crumbles."

Poppy looked at her reflection in the bathroom mirror and touched the corners of her wide smile, as if newly surprised that joy had found its way so easily to her face. She rested her palm on her cheek, as the emotions beneath revealed the familiar safeness they'd shared at Rollins. "Besides, if I'd chosen to be stuck blaming others, I wouldn't be able to . . ."

"Move forward?" Geoff nodded.

"Exactly." Poppy exhaled. "And I never dated or saw anyone when I was in the divorce process. I made sure that both of my divorces were finalized. I focused on my kids. I knew I had to take time for some introspection so I'd be in a good place for my children."

"I've seen so many friends who can't get beyond their anger." Geoff shook his head and picked up a cushiony ball—a cat toy—from the living room carpet. He lobbed Zippy's favorite soccer toy in his hand and caught it again in a one-handed juggle.

"I know. It's bad. Everyone suffers. The person—the kids. And many people start a new relationship right away without learning from the last one."

"Right." Geoff sat in the recliner. "They have to take a self-inventory."

With a sock ball suspended in the air, Poppy said, "It's so easy to talk with you, Geoff. I feel like I'm able to share parts of me I've tucked away. Little slices of myself that've been dormant for thirty years."

"I experience the same thing." Geoff gently rocked in the recliner. "A rediscovery of who we are and who we *were*."

"I think I got away from myself." Poppy squeezed the sock ball. "Who I was *with you*." She closed her eyes for a moment. "Who I was with you," she murmured, the revelation just beginning to sink in.

On Thursday evening, I followed Geoff up the stairs to his condo after his choir practice. He grinned at his phone, which still illuminated Poppy's text: *Look what found its way from my stomach into the grocery store!* She'd sent a photo of a cellophane package—a giant crafted decorative butterfly with lavender gossamer wings.

"She's so funny." He shook his head. Without stopping, he dropped his keys in the pewter dish and strode into the bedroom. Like Poppy, he dispensed with hello and started to speak, as if their conversation from before choir continued seamlessly.

"Do you know the hymn 'How Great Thou Art'?" He paused, adding, "I'm doing a solo at the end of the month."

"Oh Lord, my God, when I in awesome wonder," Poppy sang softly. "I like that one," she said and crossed her legs on the bench in her bedroom. "That song is in the movie *Prancer*. A Christmas movie with Sam Elliott. I bawl my eyes out every December." With her finger, she dusted the frame of the antique French poster.

"I don't think I've seen that one," Geoff murmured.

"What's your favorite Christmas carol?" Poppy said and animatedly gestured as if she were holding a caroler's lantern. "Wait. Hold on. Let me tell you mine first— 'O Holy Night.'" Poppy stood, and her bare toes traced the tile edges on the floor in her room.

"That's the one." Geoff took off his topsiders and lay back on the bed.

"What d'we have for her, Bob? A new car!" Poppy dramatized in a low voice.

Geoff laughed. "Have I told you that the past couple of Christmases, I've performed 'O Holy Night' a cappella—live. You know, no accompaniment."

"That's so neat." Poppy closed her eyes. "Um, okay, favorite Christmas movie?"

"Easy. *White Christmas*." He cleared his throat.

"I remember getting excited for Christmas as I watched the Macy's Thanksgiving Day parade on TV. I wore those feetsy pajamas, also my Christmassy and Saturday morning cartoon-watching uniform." Poppy chuckled.

"TV, a bowl of cereal, and PJs." Geoff grinned. "I had a similar dress code."

Poppy fluffed the throw pillow under her neck. "I watched TV with my brother, on the rare occasions he treated me nicely." Poppy scoffed. "Okay, favorite cartoon?"

"There's no way you could have the same one. If you guess this, I'll marry you on the spot." Geoff sat up and grinned.

"Favorite cartoon. This is easy! *Jonny Quest*," Poppy said.

"No way!" Geoff shouted and bounced up from the bed. "You've got to be kidding me. There's *no way* you like *Jonny Quest!*" Geoff paced, barefoot in his room.

"Sure there is. Hadji. Bandit, Race Bannon. And the pterodactyls. Arhhhghh, arhhhghh, arhhhghh," Poppy crowed, as she imitated the cartoon's flying dinosaurs.

"Seriously?" Geoff stopped in the middle of his room, his hand on top of his head. "How can you have watched that?" His mouth gaped open. "Girls didn't watch that shit."

Poppy giggled. "If Stacy watched it, I watched it."

"I was sure you would have said something like *Scooby-Doo* or *Tom and Jerry*." On the edge of his bed, Geoff smoothed the royal-blue duvet cover.

"Well, I never got to choose what was on TV. And my brother was so mean," Poppy said in an elementary school voice.

"Oh I know, my brother, too. It wasn't until we were young adults—me in my late twenties and Twig in his early thirties—that we became good friends."

They hung up the phone after eleven o'clock, as they'd done each night that week.

*I think I just told her I'd marry her,* Geoff thought, as he brushed his teeth. He shook his head, and rinsed the brush. "*Jonny Quest*. Unbelievable," he mumbled.

Geoff sat at his desk, one hand on a mug handle, one on the computer mouse. He looked out the window at the grayscape—a cinereous veil in front of him. Friday morning fog concealed the causeway bridge and hung like an opaque shower curtain over Lake Davidson. He leaned back and sighed, his released breath the sound of bittersweet memories. His thoughts came, and the Empathic Bridge, now bronzed, shined above my slate. *There was a song we always used to listen to. What was that Moody Blues song that Fred and I played?*

Geoff slid the coffee mug forward and straightened in his chair. He clicked on Google and typed in "Moody Blues." His eyes scanned the list of songs. "That's it," he murmured. He sat up and inhaled, filling himself with air. "Oh, I dreamed last night I was hearing, hearing your voice," Geoff sang and rocked forward in the chair. He quickly moved the cursor over the red triangular Play arrow. From the speakers, the voice of Justin Hayward filled the room. "If there's a time and place to begin love, it must be now."

I felt a swelling within me. Much more powerful than the butterflies I'd first experienced. A flooding of warmth. I looked at Geoff—his mouth open—tears collecting on his moustache.

*Oh my God. This is it. Like a musical blessing. I had the opportunity before and let it slip away. Now this is it. I've been given an incredible chance all over again.* Geoff's thoughts flowed. *I can't wait to tell Poppy.*

He reached for his cell phone, and at the exact same moment, the phone chirped with a text message notification. *Good morning, Chief. How is the MIL?*

Geoff pressed the Talk key, and before Poppy spoke, he said, "The man you love is..." He swallowed.

"Geoffrey? You okay?" Poppy stood, and her eyebrows met in concern.

"Yes . . . I'm very okay." He wiped his eyes. "Just a little emotional." He rocked his chair back. "Do you remember the Moody Blues song 'I Dreamed Last Night'?"

"Yes, I do. It's pretty." In slow motion, Poppy lowered herself onto her desk chair, as if intuitively aware that something meaningful would follow.

"I just downloaded it. I'll send it to you." He opened up a new email and attached the music. "When I heard this song again after so many years—not really paying attention to it—I felt like I opened up an idle quadrant of my heart. Like *Misty* on the water, I feel like my luffing sail caught a god-send of a breeze."

Geoff looked up at the ceiling. "And here's this piece of me that I'd tucked away. I have it again, and I don't want to lose it." His voice was a whispered plea.

The bridge glowed a bright green, and I felt a waterfall cascading within me.

Geoff closed his eyes. "Remember back in college how much these songs *meant* to us? And we were passionate about each and every lyric?"

"You're so right." Poppy breathed. "Powerful heartstring-tugging songs. Like Barry Manilow's 'Even Now.' I start to cry on the first chord."

"How'd we get away from that? Become so dulled as adults?" Geoff murmured.

Poppy steadied her breath.

"Poppy? Are you there?" Geoff asked, his voice like a soft knock on a summertime screen door.

"Yes, I'm here." She wiped a tear from her cheek. "Sorry. These connections." Poppy's lips turned to a smile and buckled, the force of her deep emotions tugging against the corners of her mouth, the contrast of joy and resurfaced pain expressed on the human face. "Every time I feel this incredible happiness . . ." She crossed her arm over her stomach. "I re-feel the trauma of our breakup."

"I know," Geoff whispered. "And I've pushed that aside. It doesn't matter anymore. I'm right here, Honch."

Poppy tried to smile. "I know," she sniffled. "It's just a lot of colliding emotions."

Geoff paused, his thoughts like a tow rope to pull her forward to this moment. *Tell her about the other songs,* he thought. "Do you remember 'Wildest Dreams'? And a song—appropriate for *you*— 'I Know You're Out There Somewhere.'"

"Yes, of course. My brother had all of the Moody Blues albums. We listened to them nonstop in the taproom at the farm."

Poppy opened his emails and began to read the lyrics. "Geoffrey!" Poppy's lower lip trembled in a free fall. "You'll make me cry all over again."

"I thought you might like these." Geoff gestured to his screen. "Like they're written for us." He pointed to a line on the monitor. "In my wildest dreams," he read.

"They're amazing," Poppy breathed. "I feel like we're living in a dream."

"If someone had said to me, 'Geoff, Poppy Terris has been looking for you. In fact, she's tried to find you *three times*—as recently as this past December. And she never meant to hurt you. She'd be *thrilled* to hear from you. All you have to do is pick up the phone. You'll be back together again. And it'll be *even better* than when you were twenty-one.'" Geoff snickered. "I would have said, 'Yeah, right. Like that would ever happen in my *wildest dreams.'*"

CHAPTER 27

# To Have and to Hold

~⌐

WITH A SOFT GOLD-ILLUMINATED BRIDGE still glowing above my slate, I smiled at an email from Geoff on the screen. *Will you be in the greater Sarasota area Monday through Wednesday, May 17–19?*

They had yet to see each other. And of course, they'd each received cautions and warnings in the past two weeks: *Be careful. You might get burned. Don't rush into things. Do you really know him/her? What about your children?* But the well-meaning people hadn't seen what I'd seen.

~⌐

On the phone the night before Geoff left his parents' home in Mount Dora, Florida, he tried to cajole Poppy into meeting him at Rollins the following morning.

"It's only a couple of hours for you. C'mon, Honch. Zip over here. I'll meet you at Beans," Geoff said, a Huck Finn coax in his voice. "I had the vision today when I drove down here. Us meeting there when I call on the Rollins IT Department."

At her dining room table, Poppy let the ribbon fall from her hands. "That's so tempting." She pushed back her chair and stood at her dining room doors. "I have to be on an eight thirty plane on Thursday morning to attend our family reunion in Milwaukee." She looked back at the round glass table and eyed the groupings of miniature silver picture frames, sealed packets of chocolates from Burke Candy, and two dozen tiny pink quartz hearts. "I wish I could, Geoffrey." She looked out the doors. Her eyes followed a blue jay that flitted from tree to tree, as if on an invisible pogo stick.

"Just sneak over, like you used to do from the Theta House," Geoff teased.

"Agh. I have back-to-back clients scheduled on Wednesday. I'll be away from Thursday to Sunday." She bent to pick up errant pieces of kibble from the side of Nicky's dish. "You know I'd love to see you at Jolly Rolly Colly." She dropped the uneaten dry dog food into the wastebasket.

"I know. I just thought I'd throw it out there," he said. "We'll have many other opportunities." Geoff glanced toward his parents and son. "Jonathon's excited to have my dad's Honda Civic. My dad is not driving anymore. Thursday, we're off to Universal for some quality father-son time. We'll both head back on Saturday. He'll follow me."

"And we'll see each other on Monday. The day after I return." Poppy put her elbows on the table, her fists nestled in her cheeks. "Do you know how excited I am?"

"I sure do," he said and nodded. The fantasy was coming to life.

Poppy walked to her desk. "While I don't have a voice as wonderful as yours, nor will it bring tears to your eyes as your CD brought tears to mine, I'll send you heartfelt messages for your car ride home."

They finished their phone call, and on the slate, I saw Geoff walk through the living room and into the dining room to join his family. Poppy half-sang, half-hummed as she packaged her gift bags. "I know you're out there somewhere, somewhere . . ."

On Saturday, as Poppy attended her family gathering, I accompanied Geoff on his drive home to North Carolina. After Geoff stopped for lunch, his eyes fell on the package of CD's he'd placed on the passenger seat from Poppy. He pulled out the case and shook the bubble package upside down. He unzipped the case and noticed a folded piece of paper on top of the plastic-sleeved CD holders. He unfolded it and stared at the personalized stationery.

*Poppy* was printed in red on the bottom of the fine paper.

"Wow, *Poppy*," Geoff murmured. His eyes followed each word. When he finished reading, he held the note out in front of him. "Her name. *Poppy*," he whispered. "With hearts. And she wrote, *All my love, Poppy*."

He ran his finger along the bottom of the page. The paper, parchment, with a beveled edge—elegant and thin with a barely perceptible flower watermark. His thumb rested on the lower right corner where a pink lipstick kiss, the color of Bougainvillea, caused him pause. "Her lips touched this. She handwrote this." He breathed. The note trembled in his fingers as he looked up, unaware of the children in the play area and their watchful parents. *This is real. I'm not imagining this. Never in my wildest dreams . . .* Geoff's stream of consciousness trailed off.

The note was yet another proof of Poppy's re-emergence into his life. It was the time taken to create, address, stamp, mail, and wait for the response—the cause and effect of giving and receiving. Of acceptance and recognition. The waiting—the anticipation—generated excitement and the basis for deeper sensory connection. *A gift to one's emotions.*

Poppy had touched the paper. Written on it. Drawn hearts on it. Folded it. Tucked it into a case. She'd sealed it. Mailed it. Geoff—the next person to touch the contents.

I followed Geoff's eyes as they drifted back to Poppy's note. I wondered if a letter, a CD—talismans of any sort—were all pieces of artwork? When Poppy had received the CD of Geoff's songs, tears had formed in her eyes. The personalized stationery and written love sentiment had evoked a similar response in Geoff.

Poppy's letter, now a tangible object, to have and to hold from this day forward.

Geoff read the personalized note one more time.

> *Dearest Geoffrey! These CDs are by no means the incredible breadth of talent that you demonstrated on your CD, yet the "positive feeling" reminders (not that we need any!) have a good premise.* ☺
> *All my love, X ♡ O, Poppy.*
> *P.S. Have a safe trip ♡!*

"I can't believe I'll touch her in two days," Geoff whispered to the piece of stationery.

# CHAPTER 28

# His Walk

~⁓

"CAN YOU BELIEVE YOU'LL SEE Poppy today?" Geoff said into his bathroom mirror. He stretched his chin out as the razor glided underneath.

The bridge, the same bright green as the inside of kiwi fruit, radiated above me.

Geoff's feelings immediately transmitted to me, and I recognized the sensory excitement of a field of fluttering wings within me. It felt like a sudden immersion into the Smithsonian Butterfly Pavilion. I felt lightheaded—giddy.

*I get to kiss her again,* he thought, as he ran his finger along his jaw. *In four hours.* He rinsed the razor under the running water and tapped it once on the sink. He leaned closer to the mirror and used both hands to curl the corners of his moustache.

"It's unbelievable." He stood up straight and smiled. "I'm going to see Poppy."

~⁓

*Oh my God. I'm smiling like crazy, I can't even put on my lipstick.* Poppy's thoughts tumbled out. *I'll wear the black cotton top and gray silk skirt. Earrings . . .* Poppy set down the MAC tube of lipstick and went to her jewelry chest.

"Here, the turquoise ones from the kids," she muttered as she lifted them from the velvety drawer. She placed them on her dresser. "And this ring, from Mom." She held up a turquoise-and-gold ring and laid it next to the earrings.

Her thoughts came out in a meandering stream. *What did he say when I told him that I don't look anything like he remembers me? Was he okay with that? I mean, I sent him the pictures from the reunion last week. And at Ringling's graduation with other faculty. I wore a black tent for God's sake. So, he wouldn't be on the plane if he didn't like the way I look, right?* Poppy picked up one turquoise earring and a silver-and-black teardrop earring already on the dresser, and held one up to each ear. She tilted her head side to side in the mirror and dropped the black-and-silver one back onto the dresser tray. "Just stick with the turquoise. Stay with the first one you picked," she murmured.

~~~

"Okay, when we go out, I'll need dress shoes, socks, belt." Geoff tucked a dark-brown leather belt inside the compartment of his carry-on. In his open suitcase, he laid three dress shirts and a navy blazer, all in plastic dry-cleaning bags. He folded the arms in. "I've got Dopp kit, pair of shorts, polo shirts." Geoff stuffed the edges of the bag in as he pulled the zipper around. He turned around, glanced at the dresser, and said to Zippy, "Okay, got it all."

~~~

"I can hardly breathe." She exhaled on the last word. "Nickynoo, Geoffrey's coming!" She raised the pitch of her voice. Nicky's head cocked to one side. "He's coming, girl." Poppy cupped the Shih Tzu's face in her hands, and the dog's furry jowls squished together. "He's on his way to me!"

~~~

"The very thought of you, and I forget to do the little ordinary things that everyone ought to do," Geoff sang as he turned on his blinker and merged into the right lane to the entrance to the Charlotte Douglas Airport. "I'm living in a kind of daydream. I'm happy as a king . . ."

~~~

Poppy stuffed the king pillow inside the sham and sang along to the Moody Blues CD that played from the portable player on the bedroom bench. "Once beneath the stars," Poppy sang, as she fluffed the throw pillows on the bed. "The universe was ours . . .," Poppy crooned along with Justin Hayward.

"I wonder if you think about it. Once upon a time in your wildest dreams," she sang as she dusted the nightstands and dresser, her hand in a widowed athletic sock.

She turned up the volume and left the room. At her desk in the living room, she peeled off the sock and stowed binder clips and pens in the drawer. Her hands, as though she were playing a shell game, moved papers and folders into stacks until two large piles remained on a shelf next to her desk. She smiled at her dog, now on the green couch. The dog lifted her head—alert. "That's good enough, right, Nickynoo?"

~♪

As I watched both Poppy and Geoff on my slate, I wondered if they felt each other's excitement. That rich anticipation I felt—and *still feel*—from them. Their parallel actions, each of them singing as they prepared to meet, now made the bridge glow a velvety indigo. *I wonder what will happen to the bridge when they actually see each other,* I thought.

Like Poppy, who'd stood in the mirror second-guessing herself, I, too, questioned my expectations. *What if they don't feel the same vibrant energy when they come face to face?*

~♪

The hostess at the US Airways Club greeted Geoff. "Hello, Mr. Spencer. How are you this morning?" The Southern-accented woman returned Geoff's membership card to him. Her wide smile—straight white teeth against her dark skin—automatically made everyone smile in return.

"Hi, Darnelle. I'm fine, thank you. In fact, I'm *fantastic*." Geoff smiled.

"Well, gooood," she drawled, her blue-tinted eyelashes blinking in expectation. "Goin' somewhere special?"

"I am." Geoff leaned into the counter and raised his eyebrows. "I'm off to see my college sweetheart, whom I haven't seen in thirty-two years."

"*Go awn!*" Darnelle put her hand to her chest. "You've been in contact though?"

"Nope. I just found her three weeks ago today." Geoff grinned. "It's like we've never been apart."

Darnelle waved to the man behind Geoff. "I'll be right with you, Mr. Hansen." Darnelle stood and pressed her American flag manicured finger on the counter. "Now, you need to tell me *awwl* about it when you get back, okay? That's something real special." She rubbed her arm. "I got shivers."

~♪

"It's today, Mary!" Poppy leaned over to polish the glass table in the family room, the Windex in her left hand, a rag in her right. "He's at the airport now."

"Oh, Pop." Mary's throaty voice came over the speaker phone. "You sound great. I'm so happy for you. Awww." Mary said "awww" like a woman at a baby shower watching an expectant mother open a gift. "I can hear it in your voice."

Poppy eyed the reflection on the table. "Mary, I'm so excited right now. God, remember when we were Brownie leaders and I couldn't figure out what friggin' color of paint to buy?"

"Oh Pop, a real low point for you," Mary tsked. "You were a mess."

"This is the exact *opposite* of that. I'm floating." Poppy giggled. "I'm cleaning to quell the energy. I haven't scoured my house this fast in I don't know how long."

"God love you." Mary laughed, her raspy outburst, hearty—like award-winning chili. "Call me as soon as you can. Like right after you guys *do it.*"

"Stop it!" Poppy's face reddened. "I'm not going to sleep with him," Poppy said, her tone like a defensive teenager.

"Oh yeah." Her laugh exploded. "*That* was convincing."

Geoff slid his roller bag and backpack in the overhead bin above seat 1A. He sat down in the window seat, alone in his row. He placed a paperback book in the mesh pocket of the bulkhead and smiled as he accepted a cup of orange juice from the flight attendant.

A woman with saggy eyelids and creased flesh near her temples, like brown file folders of skin, stopped and sighed in the aisle next to Geoff. A young man in his twenties stood in the aisle and groped in his opened suitcase in the storage compartment of row 3. The boarding line in the Jetway—thirty people deep—caused the petite flight attendant in the galley to peer around the cluster of motionless bodies like a bird in a cuckoo clock. Geoff looked out the window and smiled. He watched the busy ground crew on the tarmac below and knew they were unaware of the exuberant passenger in the first row of the plane.

*I'm on my way to see Poppy.* Geoff's thoughts—only of Poppy—not in the least bit distracted by the aggravations of travelers jockeying for storage and seats.

*I'll let her know I'm on my way. What should my text say? I know . . .* Geoff thought, tapping on his Blackberry, his dimple peeking out from beneath his moustache.

*On my way home to you, Honch.*

At the marina, Poppy smiled as she and Nicky walked past the slips of boats. When they came to a banyan tree that bordered a cut-through across the park, she let the Shih Tzu off leash. "Ready girl . . . run!"

Nicky ran, and her paws moved so quickly, they became a blur of beige. Poppy picked up her pace and smiled at others she passed. *Can anyone here tell how excited I am?* Her inner monologue sped up with her feet. *Geoff's probably on the plane, ready to take off. To come here. I feel like my whole body is ringing.*

Nicky sniffed the same area of grass over and over, as if she were saying, *I know it's here somewhere.*

Poppy's cellphone dinged.

"Hawh." Poppy gasped, taking a sharp breath of gulf beach air. "He thinks of me as home." She looked up from Geoff's text message, and her eyes scanned the park to see if anyone had heard her outburst. Her mouth quivered.

*I wish there were someone here I could share this with.* Poppy's thoughts traveled toward Nicky, who fixated on a root of the banyan tree. *You know what I feel, right girl?*

The dog lifted her head and right paw, waiting for a noteworthy command.

Poppy pressed the keys on her phone and texted in the message thread under Geoff's words. *I'm waiting for you with an open heart.*

Geoff lifted the window shade to the top. The bright sun reflected light in the shape of a trapezoid on the royal-blue carpeted wall. He reached in the seat-back pocket for his book, David Baldacci's *The Camel Club*. He opened to page 97 where an old boarding pass stub had held his place. He filed the stub toward the back of the book and began to read. Moments later, he laid the book facedown on his lap, its binding making a steeple.

He looked out the window and his thoughts filled his head. *I can't wait to see her. To touch her.*

⌒୨

Poppy stepped from the fifth window at Johnny's carwash to the sixth. *Hurry, please,* she thought and stared at her white BMW as it chugged along the rollers. *C'mon, c'mon. What if his plane is early?* she thought, and didn't consider that her desire alone would not speed up the machine.

After she'd paid at the counter, she stared at the pegboards on the wall that featured a variety of air fresheners. *Oh, I've got to stop my heart from racing.*

The cashier, a fresh-faced brunette with large eyes like large malted milk balls, followed Poppy's happy gaze. "Would you like an air freshener?" she asked, as her hand, like Vanna White's, swept the air toward the wall where little packets of every scent imaginable hung.

*Sick,* Poppy thought, as she touched the piña colada cardboard. "No, thank you," she giggled. *I'm losing it here. Why the hell am I even looking at this stuff? Air fresheners are gross. And I'm smiling like I've just won the lottery. Well, actually . . .* Poppy laughed, entertaining herself.

⌒୨

The flight attendant walked through the cabin with a white plastic bag in her hand. A voice came over the loud speaker. "Please make sure your tray tables and seat backs are in the upright and locked position, and your seat belts securely fastened."

Geoff leaned forward, and his eyes took in the azure waters of Sarasota Bay. *This is happening. I'll be on the ground in a few minutes.* He picked up his book from the seat next to him and noticed the stub still marked page 97.

⌒୨

*Thank goodness—I'm breezing right through these lights,* Poppy thought, as she drove north on Highway 41, Tamiami Trail. She passed Ringling College and stayed in the right lane, then turned right onto University Parkway, a block away from the airport entrance. *Oh . . . breathe.* She let out air from her cheeks.

⌒୨

*I'm here,* Geoff thought, as he saw the airport building. *She's right there. I'm going to see Poppy in just a few minutes.*

⁓

Poppy pushed the red button for a ticket at short-term parking. "I'm still shaking. Breathe," she said, and blew air out. "Phew, it's not crowded here." She swung her car into the eighth spot from the baggage claim. She parked, grabbed the two cold waters from the passenger seat, and dropped them into her purse. "Keys, water. Oh! My sign in the back seat." She opened the back door where an 11x17 piece of paper lay on the seat. "Oh my God, I'm going to see Geoff," she said, and clicked the lock on her key fob.

⁓

The plane taxied to Gate B3 and stopped. The interior lights came on, and a two-bell signal chimed. "Here we go," Geoff whispered, and stooped to clear the overhead compartment. *Nice; I'm the first one off.*

⁓

Poppy walked up the stairs, and her kitten-heeled sandals slid on the edge of each step. *We'll ride that—together,* she thought as she looked at a couple descending the escalator next to the stairs. When she reached the top, she glanced at the empty massage chairs to her right. To her left was the giant fish tank—the hub of the terminal. Above the fish tank, the arrival and departure monitors blinked. Poppy made a vertical and horizontal tracing with her finger. "At gate," she whispered. "He's here!"

Four rows of chairs faced the gate area and the security checkpoint queue. Fewer than a dozen people sat in the chairs, many of them elderly. Like theatergoers, they looked as though they were waiting for a movie to begin.

Poppy walked to the first row of chairs and sat. She craned her neck around the airport displays and security signage. "Hmm," she muttered, and moved two seats to her right. "Better," she said softly, and dropped her purse into the empty seat next to her. She held the paper sign she'd brought from the car, the ends touching—the center not creased, just bowed. Inside the loose paper, a single word, *Soulmate*, was written in pretty script. "Just a few more minutes," Poppy breathed.

As passengers began to stream out from the arrival gate, Poppy lowered her head and looked beneath the overhead signs that blocked her view. She only saw people from the waist down, their upper bodies obstructed.

*I forgot to ask him what color pants he'd be wearing,* Poppy thought. She opened the 11x17 paper she held in her hand and smoothed it on her lap facedown.

~⁊

Geoff looked in the bathroom mirror, right to left. *Should I brush my hair?* he thought. *It's fine.* He reached into an outside pocket of his backpack and got a wintergreen Lifesaver. *Time to see Poppy.*

~⁊

Poppy licked her lips and inched forward on her chair in front of the security railing. Some passengers with expressionless faces had already exited. People came out in clumps, making gaps between the exiting passengers. Poppy smiled as a little boy ran to a white-haired woman and shouted, "Grandma!" He got sucked into her bosom.

Poppy looked back to the gate concourse. "Oh my God," she whispered. She got up from the chair in slow motion, her head still, her eyes fixed on the approaching lower torso of a man in beige pants.

She put her hand to her mouth. *I remember. Walking together on campus. To the Pub! Geoff walking up the hill from the ski dock, walking over from the Phi Delt House under the breezeway, to meet me at the Theta House. Seeing him walk away as he went up the steps to Orlando Hall. I remember.*

"Oh my God," she murmured, as she stared at the khaki pants coming her way. "I remember his walk." Air escaped from her open mouth. "I know *his walk.*"

CHAPTER 29

# At First Sight

~

I stood near the security line at Sarasota's airport and watched as their two bodies closed the few yards of remaining distance between them. My inner core rang, the pounding so intense it seemed to drown out the roar of jet engines on the tarmac. My slate vibrated in my hand, and with it, the sound of a drum roll that built in intensity. The Empathic Bridge now pulsed with their rhythms and transformed from indigo to fuchsia. The vivid pink edges of the bridge, outlined with blinding-white crystals, glittered and floated.

A three-yard section of the walkway allowed passengers a brief glimpse before they'd disappeared behind a freestanding screened wall. Like a curtain pulled back and quickly shut, the opening revealed Geoff for a flash of four seconds. His pink polo shirt highlighted the color of his flushed cheeks.

Poppy walked sideways, as her hands displayed the sign. "He's here." Her voice quivered. *My Geoff. He's here*, she thought and jumped up and down. A cheerleader at the moment the team wins in overtime, she waved her handmade sign so enthusiastically it created a tropical breeze for bystanders.

*That's my Poppy!* Geoff smiled as he walked behind the screen.

Like a barely contained fan at a championship football game, Poppy stood inches from the *Do Not Enter* sign. Her eyes locked on his face—the face that three decades hadn't changed. "He's the same." Poppy breathed, and her eyelids collapsed ever so slightly to capture the moment forever, the emotional realization that *Geoff's really here.*

On the floor next to the PGA Tour Shop, Poppy dropped her purse. Breathless, with her mouth forming a quaking smile, she held up her sign.

"Ha! It says, *Soulmate*." Geoff beamed, his moustache almost reaching his ears.

Poppy bounced on the balls of her feet and wiggled her sign. "Oh, Geoffrey!"

Geoff slid his arms around Poppy's waist and pulled her close. She draped her arms on top of his shoulders, as her sign swung down his back. "You're here." She inhaled against his chest and squeezed her eyes closed.

He wiggled off his backpack and leaned it against the wall—his eyes unwilling to move away from her face. Like a high-speed download, they scanned each other's faces—as their liquid-brown eyes tried to fill in the thirty-two-year gap.

The pulsing from the bridge illuminated a shimmering white glow, and the slate's drum roll culminated in a crescendo, like cymbals clanging together.

"There you are, Honch," Geoff whispered, and gazed into Poppy's pooling sable-brown eyes.

"You're here," Poppy breathed again. "Nothing's changed. You're the same." Drops of emotion spilled from her eyes onto her cheeks. She reached her finger to Geoff's face and stroked his dimple. "I've never forgotten this." Her mouth quivered, no longer able to maintain just a smile. "Nor your beautiful soft-brown eyes."

Geoff smiled. "There's that same beautiful smile." He leaned in. "There's my Honch." He pulled Poppy closer and lowered his lips to hers.

Her eyelashes fluttered. *Oh . . . his kiss. This ringing in my body. His moustache, feathery on my mouth. A sensual tingling.* Poppy's thoughts floated through the in-between space of a misplaced memory and a dreamy reality.

*I can't take her in, drink her in fast enough. Her lips are just as luscious as I remembered.* Geoff's thoughts drifted out. He held Poppy's chin, as his eyes circled her face. He lifted her chin and brought her mouth to his.

Poppy's fingers trembled as they touched the familiar muscles in his arms—an amnesiac who relearns how her lover's skin feels. *I can't even think straight. Or speak. So many feelings. Sensory overflow.* She stared at her hand as it stroked his wrist, as if it, too, needed further evidence of his physicality.

Geoff's eyes followed Poppy's sweeping hand. He circled her hand and wrapped his fingers around hers. He raised it to his lips. Teary, he held her hand and nodded.

For a few moments, they stared at each other. Poppy wiped her unremittingly moist eyes. "I can't believe this is finally happening."

"I know." Geoff's finger dabbed at the corner of Poppy's eye and gently absorbed her emotion with his touch. "I couldn't get off the plane fast enough."

"I can't stop looking at you." Poppy's whisper escaped from her smile.

Geoff looked over his shoulders. "Um, Honch? Everyone's gone."

She put her hand to her mouth and giggled. "I haven't paid attention." Poppy picked up her purse, her sign secured between two fingers. "I'm busy with my soulmate."

Geoff put his backpack over both shoulders and gave it a small jerk to center it. His luggage in his left hand, he said, "I'm consumed with you, too." He took Poppy's hand in his and smiled at her as they approached the escalator.

Poppy turned around on the escalator to face Geoff. "This doesn't seem real. I know I keep saying that, but I can't find the words," she said, as her thoughts attempted to keep pace with her heart.

"It is, Honch. I'm *really* here." He tilted his head. "I can't stop smiling, either."

They walked hand in hand to the parking lot, oblivious to the eighty-three-degree sunny day. Oblivious to the TSA agent who whistled at an idling car. Geoff lifted his bag into the back deck of the BMW. Poppy stood next to him and gaped—her expression similar to someone who'd just found a photo album of treasured family memories hidden in an old attic.

Geoff looked over at Poppy. "What?"

"I just . . .," she began, and shook her head. "It's incredible . . ." She took a step closer to Geoff. "It seems so normal. Like I've picked you up at the airport for years."

Geoff stroked her arm. "It does seem so comfortable."

"I have a surprise for you," Poppy said, and slid into the driver's seat. She started the car and handed Geoff the cold water from her purse.

"Thanks." Geoff unscrewed the top and took a drink.

"Not that." Poppy giggled and pressed the Power button on the car radio. "Did you know I only listen to tracks ten and eleven?"

The psychedelic introduction of the Moody Blues' "Wildest Dreams" began to play.

"Ha! That's great. Perfect, Poppy." Geoff grabbed her hand and pulled her closer. They both leaned in, their lips meeting—lingering.

When their lips parted, Poppy's head fell against the headrest. "How d'you expect me to drive after that?" She panted.

"Do you need me to drive?" Geoff grinned.

Poppy laughed—a tinkling escape of breath. "Nothing's changed." Poppy exhaled, her contentment spilling into the car. "You still give me butterflies thirty-two years later."

"I'm glad that I still can." He caressed her arm and nestled his hand on top of her shoulder, his desire to maintain their connection of energy strong.

At a stoplight just outside the airport exit, Poppy pointed. "That's the Ringling Museum straight ahead. You know, for once I'm glad that our traffic lights are three minutes long." Poppy stretched across the center console. An apparition of a kiss and a familiar ritual ignited the air between them.

They both laughed. "Where are we headed?" Geoff murmured.

"To one of the best beaches in America. The *world*, really." Poppy turned left onto Tamiami Trail. "We're creating our own new memories."

Poppy and Geoff traveled over the arched walkway to the Gulf of Mexico. The crystalline sand was so soft I mistook it for enriched flour. The pedestrian bridge from the parking lot to Siesta Key Beach resembled Monet's often-painted bridge at the French artist's home in Giverny.

They held hands as they crossed over. I'd finally witnessed this moment when, against all odds, *here they were*, crossing over a bridge to one of the most renowned beaches in the world. *In love. Again.*

The Empathic Bridge, still a crystalline white, glistened like a star sapphire. I didn't know if my slate was toying with me or if my eyes deceived me, but the bridge appeared as a mirror image of the walkway they'd just crossed—the oyster-gray cedar slats on the gulf bridge now pale-lavender planks on the Empathic Bridge.

When they stepped off the cedar platform, Geoff removed his socks and shoes and rolled up his khakis. Poppy slipped out of her sandals and rested her hand on Geoff's arm for balance. She gazed up at him. "Here we are at a beach again, Geoffrey."

"This is beautiful. Brings up some wonderful memories with you—*of you*—at Cocoa Beach." Geoff bent down, and his lips brushed hers. He raised his hand to his forehead and shielded the midday sun. His eyes surveyed the vast beach. "Wow, from here to the water is as long as a football field." Without looking, his right hand found Poppy's left, and they sunk into the sand as if they were walking on rows and rows of pillows.

When they reached the water's edge, Poppy squinted up at Geoff. "I feel giddy. Almost as though I shouldn't be here." Poppy looked down at their linked hands. "Like we've just snuck out of school. A couple of truant teenagers."

"It does feel like we're getting away with something, doesn't it?" Geoff bounced his eyebrows up and down.

She giggled. "Everything with you feels"—she looked up at him— "so right. So familiar." She squeezed her right hand on his arm. "Just like it did thirty-two years ago. How can that be?"

They faced the gulf, the horizon a cobalt border with infinite possibilities.

My slate shuddered in my hand as the bridge once again transformed, deepening to a pink sapphire. The bridge's rosy stanchions and cables spanned over the gulf to an ethereal vanishing point.

"You know, Honch, it *does* feel as though we've been together the whole time." Geoff turned, and gazed at her. "Like we've existed in some sort of parallel universe."

# CHAPTER 30

# Something Good

~⁓

STILL HAND IN HAND, POPPY and Geoff stepped on the wet sand, ignoring the Gulf of Mexico surf that'd washed around their feet. The distinct impressions of their feet quickly morphed into organic shapes that resembled opals.

"I've often thought about what happened between us." Poppy squinted up at Geoff. "I don't remember a whole lot. Only that I felt I didn't matter to you."

"And I wondered why you abruptly cut us off." Geoff gazed out. A half mile away, a motorboat bumped along the waves. "I didn't think you cared for me, either." He nodded. "In fact I felt certain of that for thirty-two years."

Poppy paused, the water pooling around her feet. "I know we've discussed this on the phone," Poppy said as she looked out on the water. "I wanted reassurance from you, in your words and actions, that I was special. She looked down at the rushing water. "I made an assumption, and said in my head, 'He doesn't care.' I'd already made up my mind before I broke us up. I didn't have the wisdom to give you a chance to chime in," she said, her last two words swallowed by a soft, rolling wave.

"And I didn't have the maturity to question it, even after you asked me to stay. I just went away. Hurt." Geoff pulled them out of the reservoir of saltwater at their feet.

"It's funny how we can remember our physical actions. I tried to reach out to you—grab your arm." Poppy reenacted her plea. "To stay. In that sliver of a moment, I realized I'd made a mistake, but you pulled away," she said, as her arm fell limp.

"Well, I'm here now." Geoff hooked his elbow under hers. "You know, Honch," he glanced down the empty stretch of beach, "I think what happened to you and me was what happened to couples during the war."

"How do you mean?" Poppy tipped her head.

"Imagine in World War II, a young man from let's say Iowa leaves the love of his life and goes off to war. He might have been injured. Imprisoned. MIA. Letters stop coming. She moves on. Nothing wrong between them."

"Often promises were made. Commitments for the future," Poppy whispered.

"And I'm sorry I wasn't smart enough to do that. Didn't *know* to do that."

Poppy laced her fingers in his. "Neither of us did. *We* didn't know to do that."

~~~~~~~~

Geoff slid the striped keycard into the door lock. A green dot flashed. "After you." Geoff held the door for Poppy.

The mirrored sliding closet made up a short hallway to a sitting area of the ground-floor room. Opposite the couch, Geoff dropped his rental car keys, room keycard, and wallet on the desk. A familiar ritual. He rolled his bag over to the stainless-steel luggage rack and lifted his suitcase onto the black straps.

In the center of the room, Geoff cupped Poppy's elbows and drew her in. He stared at her face. He smiled and lowered his parted lips onto hers.

Her bottom lip trembled and her breath softly escaped.

As he pulled back from their kiss, Geoff's smile faded. "What's wrong, Honch?"

The corners of her mouth sloped down, and her eyelashes, wet from emotion, fluttered open. "Nothing." She shook her head and whispered, "Nothing at all. "I'm just . . . overwhelmed. I haven't felt this way in . . ." Poppy fanned her face with her hand.

"In thirty-two years?" Geoff smiled and pulled her close. He leaned his head back and widened his eyes. "Your face looks like you're upset—a pained expression."

"I don't mean to," Poppy began. "It's just that the feelings I have." She swallowed. "These feelings I have coursing through me are so powerful. So real. I'm having trouble taking all of this in. You. *Us*," Poppy whispered. "I'm so happy." Her eyelashes released her tears, and they spilled onto her cheeks.

"I feel like Maria in *The Sound of Music*. Where she and the Captain are in the garden gazebo, and she says, 'Can this be happening to me?'" She imitated Julie Andrews' accent.

"Yes." Geoff smiled. "She was awestruck. That's *just* what you looked like." He grinned, relieved to discover Poppy's emotions revolved around joy and rediscovery, rather than any disconcerting thoughts she had about their current connections.

"Somewhere in my youth or childhooood. *Or college*," he sang. "I must have done something gooood."

"Of course you did something good." She reached up and smoothed the lower part of his moustache with her finger.

"Honch, *we* did something good." Geoff brushed her wet cheek with the back of his hand. "We fell in love. And we're still there."

Geoff walked over to the bed and patted it.

For twenty minutes, they sat on the king bed. Poppy rested her legs on top of Geoff's khaki pants. They shared an intimate pose, face to face, where their eyes continued to relearn everything about each other. With fingers interlocked, as if they were on a playground rocking horse, their position, almost meditative, resembled a yoga pose. A visual and tactile opportunity to soak in, absorb, and savor.

"I wonder how many hours we spent doing this in college?"

"Dozens, I'm sure," Poppy chuckled. "Yeah, pretending to study."

"I remember we sat in your room in the Theta House. Cross-legged on the bed, just like now." Geoff smiled.

"And at the Phi Delt House. Studying. Ha." Poppy leaned in and kissed Geoff on his dimple. "We have muscle memory, you know. Like right now, all my cells are saying, 'Whoa. I remember him.'"

"My cells are saying the same thing, Honch." Geoff grinned. "Why don't I have my cells call your cells to set up a meeting?" He raised his eyebrows.

Poppy inched closer, their fingers still interwoven. "I would love to have you come with me to see my mom and dad. I check in on them every day."

"Sure, I'd love to see them again." Geoff smiled. "What is it?" he asked, his smile fading. "You have that face again."

Poppy hesitated. "I didn't expect you to be so easy about everything."

"If you think I'm as easy as I used to be, you're right." Geoff grinned.

Poppy's eyes sparkled with fresh tears. "You're wonderful."

After a brief reintroduction to Poppy's parents, where Valerie's eyes had glistened with something good for the first time in months, Poppy and Geoff walked hand in hand through the Ritz lobby, their shoes echoing on the inlaid marble floor. Above, the crystal chandeliers bounced light off the gilt chairs, upholstered in Italian silks of aqua, coral, and lavender.

The veranda of the Ritz-Carlton, with its Tuscan influences, overlooked Sarasota Bay. Just inside the rear patio doors of the nine-year-old hotel, the Ca d'Zan lounge displayed a hickory-paneled bar, designed to resemble John Ringling's library, and it maintained the circus king's preference for Florentine style.

For more than an hour, Poppy and Geoff parted hands only to nibble on the Margherita pizza they shared. Like radar, their adoring eyes swept each other's faces, just as they had the night they'd met at the Rollins Pub all those years ago.

"The view here is beautiful," Geoff said, and wrapped his hands around Poppy's.

"It is gorgeous." Poppy looked over her shoulder, the cement balustrade framing the sunset over Sarasota Bay. The palm tree fronds floated in the balmy evening air.

"Oh, that." Geoff peered over the ledge. "I meant you, Honch."

Poppy looked down and folded her napkin. Her head rose to reveal tears.

For a moment, it seemed as though Poppy was vacillating on the right side of the clock: Four O'clock, Shame and Guilt. She had an expression I'd seen before on her and others—an unworthiness that'd sometimes crept into a human psyche.

"You've got that expression on your face again. Maria's 'Something Good' look." Geoff reached over to Poppy's face and dabbed at the corner of her eye.

"I'm not used to hearing that." Her voice quivered.

"Well, it's true." Geoff grinned. "You'll have to get comfortable with it."

"You're the only man, besides my dad and granddaddy, who's told me that."

"They are wise men." Geoff smiled.

A little after ten they arrived at Geoff's hotel and parked near the rear entrance closest to Geoff's room. The floodlight near the door illuminated the parking lot and cast a bluish-white light onto their faces and inside the car.

"I wish we didn't have to say goodnight." Poppy turned in the driver's seat as the car idled. "My kids think I'm with a coaching client." Poppy gave a half smile. "I haven't told them about us. They're alone. And even though they're old enough . . ." she paused.

"I understand, Honch. We'll have plenty of time." He reached into his pocket. "Here's an extra key card for the room. Just in case." Geoff tucked it in her hand. He turned in the passenger seat, and with two fingers, he lifted her chin and tilted his head to bring his lips to hers. He drew away slowly. "I'll see you tomorrow."

"Thank you," she whispered. "For making this day so wonderful. Even more wonderful than I'd imagined. I've loved every second with you. *My Geoff.*"

A piece of white paper rested on top of the granite counter.

The paper lifted up when the air conditioner recycled from the vent above the kitchen countertop. In Poppy's familiar handwriting, the word "Mom" was written above the letterhead. She'd scratched out the more formal *Poppy* on the note she'd left for George and Molly.

*Hi, guys. Like I mentioned last night, I'll go to spin. If I'm not back before you leave, there's fresh berries and oatmeal ready for hot water on the breakfast counter. Nickynoo's been out. Drive safely and HAGD. Text me later. I love you. Mom*

Poppy turned off the car in the rear lot of Geoff's hotel at 5:57 a.m. She'd made the seven-minute drive in silence. The Empathic Bridge, visible all the time, and now bright red, flushed with Poppy's excitement and love.

I felt her heart quicken as she quietly slid the keycard in the rear entrance to the building. When she reached Geoff's room, Poppy swiped the card one more time to his door, making a soft click. After she stepped into the room, she eased the door closed with another small click.

She blinked a few times as she stood in the center of the room. The drapery— not closed all the way—exposed a sliver of light from the window. Poppy's heart rate beat four times as fast as the rhythm of Geoff's even breathing. She stepped out of her sandals and shed her black Lulu lemon pants, black shirt, and sports bra in the darkness of the room, and noise-lessly placed her clothing on the desk chair.

Barefoot, she padded over to the bed, drew back the covers halfway, and lowered herself into bed.

"Mmm, you're here," Geoff whispered.

"Yes, and I brought butterflies with me."

Raisin Bran, Special K, and Frosted Flakes, upright in their stainless racks at the breakfast bar, faced the entryway to the modest dining area at the Hampton Inn. A man in a suit with no tie sat near the window, his still-sleepy eyes grazing a *USA Today* newspaper. He folded the business section inside out while he blindly reached for his coffee cup. His fingers groped air until he peered down to make contact with the handle.

In a booth in the lounge, Geoff looked euphoric.

Poppy walked toward the booth. Her sandals, barely visible beneath her workout pants, flapped on the tile floor. She set two extra creamers in front of Geoff, who stirred a spoon in his steaming oatmeal. Poppy sat and put both hands under her chin. She openly stared at Geoff. The expression on her face, more peaceful than a glissando on a harp, gave her the angelic features Geoff remembered from their college days.

Geoff hesitated before he emptied the creamers, the plastic cup sus-pended in mid-pour. "I can't believe how comfortable all this feels. Sharing the shower like we did at Cocoa Beach."

"And at the Park Plaza." Poppy grinned.

"And at the Theta House." Geoff smiled, and stirred the creamer he'd just poured. "It feels so"—he looked up—"so normal." Geoff set down his spoon and took hold of Poppy's hands.

"I know." Poppy nodded, as fresh tears formed. "When I crawled into bed and touched you for the first time . . ." She stroked his arm. "It felt like a time warp. When we made love this morning, everything came back in a rush. Even in the dark, it's like we said yesterday, our bodies have muscle memory. And every muscle in my body remembers you, Chief," Poppy whispered.

"It is just so *easy* with you." Geoff's eyes widened as he shook his head. "It's . . ."

"Are you calling me easy?" Poppy feigned insult and giggled. "I know what you mean."

I felt another familiar sensation as I watched them. Just like college. They didn't need any nudges. I didn't think they needed choreography at Rollins. But they did. My wise supervisor, Phillip, had known it. Known they'd needed subtle guidance with their communication. Phillip would've noticed from my reports what *wasn't* being said. *What if I'd paid more attention back in college? Maybe they would've been together this whole time. Maybe they were always in that pathway—a parallel universe.*

It doesn't matter. *They're together now.*

At the Island Park Bayfront Marina, Poppy and Geoff walked hand in hand like seasoned dance partners. On the sidewalk, a couple walked a Yorkie; the little dog's feet flitted back and forth across the walkway as if on a slalom course. A hundred yards out, moored sailboats bobbed in the aqua water—an inexpensive parking lot for them—and dinghies lay lopsided on the ribbon of sand and shells at the water's edge.

Geoff raised her right hand to his mouth and brushed it with his lips. "I love you, Poppy." His eyes watered. "It still surprises me to hear myself say your name."

Poppy's head burrowed into his chest. "My Geoff."

Geoff's gaze paused on the rock wall where two seagulls searched the crevices for Sarasota's best waterfront fare. He kissed Poppy's temple. "I feel badly we have to have an early dinner and cut it short. I'm meeting my business associate at eight."

"Me, too," Poppy murmured. "But I need to check my dad's ear, and I can't be gone again tonight when the kids are home. I need to be there." She swung their hands. "I thought we'd go to Sarasota's oldest restaurant, a Mediterranean place—Columbia—on St. Armand's Circle. Another place where we can create new memories."

The next day, Geoff's morning business appointment left them only forty-five minutes for lunch at Michael's on East—located just off Tamiami Trail on East Avenue in Sarasota. Michael's was the only four-diamond restaurant in Sarasota. The intimate décor offered the luxury of a Silversea's cruise liner without the obsequious waitstaff.

Poppy reached across the white cloth and pushed the sugar container aside. She caressed Geoff's hand. "Our lunch was so rushed," she said to their hands.

Geoff glanced at his watch. "I'm okay. I won't check bags, and I already have my boarding pass." He took Poppy's hand in between both of his.

"You made a hand sandwich." Poppy's half grin evolved into a downcast glance, and she seemed to memorize their lovingly packed palms, fingers, and wrists.

"Don't be sad." Geoff met her eyes with genuine tenderness. "I'll be back soon."

"When?" Poppy whispered, and her lips worked against gravity—a smile that wanted to be there but drifted into a submissive frown.

"How about in less than two weeks for Memorial Day weekend?" Geoff caressed her shoulder.

"Really?" Poppy's expression brightened. "Maybe Thursday night?" Her voice raised an octave. "Maybe we can go to our other favorite restaurant—the Bijou Café."

"Sure. What date is that?" Geoff asked.

"May 27, a week from tomorrow." Poppy inched closer.

"Okay, we'll do it." Geoff signed the credit card slip, his signature like a doctor's.

"It's just that I want something to look forward to." Poppy leaned back against the chair and exhaled. "I can handle eight days."

"For once I wish we were delayed by the departure queue, so we could have more time together in the car," Poppy said, outside the US Airways terminal.

Geoff opened the cargo hold and yanked out his luggage. "It's only eight days, okay?" He, too, tried to smile, but it turned into a grimace. On the curb, he stroked her upper back. "Ain't got nothing but love, babe, eight days a weeeeeek…," Geoff sang. "There, Honch. I'm a walking jukebox."

Poppy's tears fell on his right shoulder in another embrace. "I love you, Geoffrey," she said into his blue oxford dress shirt.

"I love you, too, Poppy. I'll miss you like crazy." Geoff, to lift her spirits, continued to hum "Eight Days a Week."

As Geoff pulled up the handle on his carry-on and walked toward the terminal, the Empathic Bridge that had fluctuated between red and indigo for most of their visit now suddenly changed into a spring green. The color of love. A soulful, aching love.

Poppy sat in her car and, through watery prism-like eyes, watched Geoff's familiar gait disappear into the departure doors. *After all this time. These precious moments together, and he has to leave right away.* Poppy's thoughts cascaded out in unison with her gulped breaths. *You can do this.* She lowered the visor and flipped open the illuminated mirror. She slid a finger along her puffy lower lids. *He'll be back in a week,* she thought, and realized her French manicure had lasted throughout his visit. Something unexpected. Something good.

I felt the heaviness in both of their hearts.

*I can't stand to leave. This sucks,* Geoff thought, as he stepped onto the escalator to the gate. *I'll come right back. Be back in no time.* He held the escalator rail and looked up. The empty corridor in Sarasota's lightly used airport mirrored his aching void.

The unimaginable joy they'd just experienced crashed against the hollowness of leaving, like a Flying Scot sailor who suddenly catches a great puff and planes the soft chine of the hull down a wave, only to feel the boat bogged down in the trough between the waves. That sailor had to wait patiently for the next puff. For something good in the wind.

# CHAPTER 31

# Cool in the Pool

~⁓

"As soon as homework is done, everybody in the pool." Poppy walked down the hallway to her children's rooms.

"Yay." Molly looked up from her laptop. "I have one more paragraph to type."

"I'm done." George rolled his desk chair back on the tile floor, and the leather back bumped against his bed. "I call the raft."

Molly dumped her computer on the bed. "No, George. I get it first this time."

"Okay, guys. No need to get excited here." Poppy picked up a ponytail holder from the entrance to Molly's room. "Come out when you guys are ready."

"I'm in." George opened his Henredon dresser and pulled out a wad of surf trunks. He dropped all but one back into the drawer and shoved the drawer closed with his thigh, two suits still protruding. He went into the bathroom and shut the door.

Poppy stepped into her son's room, opened the drawer, and patted down the obstructing clothing. "See you out there, Moll."

In the pool, a red-white-blue-and-yellow Air Force SportsStuff raft floated lazily along, bumping the sides of the pool. The raft was big enough to hold two, with a circumference the size of a baby's wading pool. George came out the dining room doors, took two long strides, and shouted something that sounded like "Hioh," before he cannonballed into the pool and sent the raft further into the corner of the deep end.

"Nothing subtle about your entrance, Georgie." Poppy tried to block the tsunami of water he'd displaced. "I can forget about keeping my hair dry." She grinned.

George hoisted himself onto the raft and lay like da Vinci's Renaissance-era Vitruvian Man, his arms and legs like compass points. "Ahh," he sighed on his back.

From the corner of the back yard, Molly tiptoed across the grass and held her index finger to her mouth—the "shh" sign. From the pool step where she sat, Poppy smiled and looked at George, who'd closed his eyes on the float.

Stealthily, like a stalking lion, Molly slipped through the row of red Jatropha shrubs and jumped in, inches from the inflatable. She tipped George over in her attack.

Molly smiled as she wriggled onto the raft. "So how are you, Mom?"

"You're so dead, Molly." George came up spewing like a whale. He tugged at the corners of the float in his effort to tip her, but she held onto the side of the pool.

Nicky, under cover in the shade, ran to the edge of the pool and barked.

"Come out of that water at once," Poppy spoke in an Austrian accent. "Nicky thinks she's Captain von Trapp. She doesn't like you two horsing around." Poppy swam over to the side of the raft. "C'mon, guys. Don't fool around near the edge of the pool."

"Mom, help me tip her," George whispered beneath the inflatable.

Poppy shook her head and swam back to the stairs in the shallow end.

George dragged the raft to the center of the pool and flipped Molly, who relinquished the raft and swam to join her mother.

"So George and Moll." Poppy squeezed out water from the ends of her hair. "I have a couple of things I want to talk with you about."

"Shit." George's head popped up. "Molly, what d'you tell her?"

"Tell me what?" Poppy looked at both her children.

Molly went underwater and came out with her hair sleek from the water, showing her delicate oval features. "Hmm?" She tipped her head to help water drain from her ear.

"Alright." Poppy looked back and forth between them. "You better tell me. Who broke something? Who got an F? Who got a ticket?"

"Nothing happened," they said at the same time.

"You're not going to give us the sex talk again, are you?" Molly groaned.

"Oh, Jesus." George paddled to the far corner of the deep end.

"Well, I don't know. Do we *need* to have the sex talk?" Poppy waded back toward the three steps.

"Nooooo." Molly rolled her eyes.

"As long as you brought it up," Poppy began.

"Good job, Molly." George scoffed.

Poppy plucked four leaves from the pool and laid them on the cement deck. "I hope you'll remember what we've discussed. Use safe practices when you choose to be sexually active."

George slid off the raft and flopped his arms on the deck. "So you want to buy me a bunch of condoms?" George grinned.

Molly went under, did a handstand, and her legs flopped backward.

"If I need to, I will." Poppy lowered herself onto the second step. "I'm just saying, please be careful. Don't just *do it* with anyone, either." She turned and cupped water and drizzled it on the cement. Steam rose. "I was twenty-one, in college, when I made love for the first time. And it wasn't with just *anyone*. It was with a man I completely trusted. I was in love with him." Poppy faced her children.

"Jesus. I can't believe I'm having this conversation with my mother. *Again*." George dove under and came up on the opposite wall in the shallow end.

"Yes, we know. And you broke his heart and yours, too. 'It was awful,'" Molly raised her voice. She pushed the water back and forth, making figure eights.

Poppy turned to look at her daughter. "Really? You remember me telling you about my college sweetheart?" Poppy stood on the third step.

"Yesss, Momm. Like twelve times I've heard the story." The sixteen-year-old girl groaned and splashed water on the deck.

"Geoff was so wonderful. So good to me." Poppy smoothed the top of the water with her hands. "I'd dated other guys—a huge contrast to him."

George coughed and muttered "assholes" at the same time she said "guys." It was an intentional obfuscation that everyone in the pool heard but didn't object to, because the goal with all teens is for the ambiguous to be unambiguous.

Poppy shook her head. "That's why when I met him, the time was so obviously right to be intimate with him."

"That's cool. I respect that. Good for you for holding out for the right guy." George dragged his arm across the water as he made swells and waves.

"I have to tell you something," Poppy murmured.

"What?" they both said in unison, stopping their movements.

"No, it's good." Poppy looked from one to the other. "I've been talking with Geoff."

"I knew it!" Molly smacked the water. "I told you, George. You owe me five bucks. I *knew* you weren't talking with Mary or Jennifer or any of your friends at night like you'd said." Molly flicked a few drops of water in her mother's direction.

"Well, I didn't really *lie*." Poppy raised her eyebrows above her aviator glasses. "I also talk with Mary and Jennifer at night."

"So where is he? In Florida?" Molly bobbed on the second step next to Poppy.

"No, he lives in North Carolina."

"Shit, that sucks." George leaned back against the deck.

"When was the last time you saw him?" Molly scrunched her nose.

"It *had* been thirty-two years." Poppy hesitated. "Until five days ago."

"I so called that," Molly blurted out, smiling. "'I have a client meeting on Monday night,'" she mimicked her mother with a squeaky voice.

"I sort of did!" Poppy protested. "He might be a coaching prospect."

"Oh right, Mom." Molly laughed, and splashed a handful of water at her mother.

"Jesus," George said. "So when do we get to meet this guy?"

"Next weekend." Poppy smiled.

"This coming weekend? Memorial Day?" Molly stood on the step.

"And you need to be nice!" Poppy pointed at her seventeen-year-old son.

"Why are you pointing at me? Molly's making funny looks." George shoved a large wave of water at his sister.

"Yes, this weekend. And you know what, guys? He's *still* wonderful." Poppy dipped her fingers underneath her sunglasses and wiped her eyes. "I'm so happy."

"Yeah, you've been too happy and agreeable lately," Molly chirped.

"Oh, so I'm mean as a snake normally?" Poppy teased.

Both teens smirked and nodded.

"No." George raised his chin—a mature adult. "I'm glad you're happy, Mom."

Geoff gazed out the window. He held his coffee mug and watched the seven a.m. rush hour traffic along the I-77 causeway. Last night, they'd spoken for two and half hours and had switched between cell phones and landlines when batteries had expired.

I nudged Geoff and watched as his Dell PC made a warming-up sound, halfway between a meow and a groan. He typed an email to Poppy. *You need to get on Skype so we can see each other. It's free and easy, just like me!*

*I'm surprised they haven't thought of it sooner,* I thought. But then again, I wondered, if they both had decided to meet on Skype during their recent conversations, before their first airport greeting—well, it wouldn't have had the same sensory impact. Might have lessened the significance of their first encounter and their first face-to-face contact in thirty-two years. Electronic devices seemed to diminish the impact of human contact. And then there was the glory of anticipation. No amount of pixels could compare to the real thing.

*I use Skype! Let's go.* Poppy responded in an email message six minutes later.

Poppy sat upright at the edge of her chair at her desk. Skype made the noise of a French police siren as it opened. With her mouse, she clicked on the tab that said, Answer with Video and leaned forward. "Oh, hi, man I love." She smiled.

"Good morning, beautiful lady." Geoff smiled back at her.

"I can't believe we didn't think of this sooner." Poppy straightened, no doubt an unconscious comportment message from her middle-school years in poise class.

"I think we were so caught up with finding each other that we didn't think about it." Geoff adjusted the angle of the detachable camera on top of his computer.

"Transported back in time." Poppy's eyes glistened. "Remembering and savoring all the good memories."

"Right. *Our* form of communication from long ago." Geoff smiled.

"We just gravitated to the familiar, you know?"

"I do know, Honch. I like to see that gorgeous face. Your beautiful smile."

"I feel like Maria in the gazebo again. You say such wonderful things to me."

"Just speaking from my heart." Geoff patted the left side of his chest.

Three days later, Poppy stood in the upstairs terminal at the Sarasota airport, the loosely folded *Soulmate* sign in her right hand. As Geoff approached the entrance, Poppy opened the sign and waved it back and forth like a temp assigned to pace a sidewalk holding a sign that said, *We buy gold here.*

Poppy wrapped her arms around Geoff's waist. "You're here, you're here," her muffled voice said into Geoff's blue-and-white-striped oxford.

"I am here, Honch." He lowered his lips to hers and hugged her again.

"As I said over Skype yesterday, we'll first go to my parents'; you can leave your stuff at their house." Poppy grimaced. "I still can't believe my mom. 'It wouldn't be proper for Geoff to stay with you, with the kids there.'" Poppy mimicked her mother and rolled her eyes. "I'm sorry, Geoffrey. Thanks for being a good sport."

"C'mon, Honch. It's not a big deal." Geoff lifted his suitcase into the rear deck of the BMW. "Besides," he added. "I get to be with you for four days."

"And you'll meet the kids, after we get you settled at Chez Terris," Poppy said with a protective flash, and with thoughts about unfamiliar territory in her single mother's eyes. "Molly's at swimming now, and George is at crew practice."

Geoff fastened his seat belt and turned to face Poppy. "They *have* to be great kids." Geoff kissed the side of her face. "They have a wonderful mother."

"Hi, guys," Poppy winked at Geoff. "We're in here," she shouted from the sofa in the family room.

George shook his head at Molly and rolled his eyes. "Jesus," he mouthed.

In the front hall, Molly put Nicky down and swiped at his arm. "Be nice." She mimed, indicating a smile on her cheeks with two fingers.

"Nickynoo, bring those two kids in here," Poppy called out.

As George and Molly came around the corner into the family room, they smiled—both nervous and happy. Geoff rose from the couch and extended his hand.

"I'm guessing you're George." Geoff shook George's hand.

"Hi, Geoff. Nice to meet you." George looked him in the eye, a bit longer than social graces allowed and less than polite.

"Hi, Molly." Geoff shook her hand. "It looks like you just got out of the pool."

"Hi, Geoff." Molly grinned. "Yes, I did." She held up a chlorinated clump of wet hair as evidence—a strand of chocolate taffy.

"It's good to meet you both." Geoff smiled. "I've heard all about you."

"Uh-oh." George looked at his sister, and his mother. "What did you say?"

"I told him the truth. That my children are perfect. Have impeccable manners. They never fight. They are A-plus students." Poppy rocked her head like a bobblehead.

"Well, one of us is." Molly grinned and sat cross-legged on the floor.

"Oh, you B . . ." George's face reddened. With a few fingers, he pulled up a chair from the wall next to the TV.

"Ahem," Poppy interrupted. "As I've told Geoff." She smiled. "Perfect."

"I'd expect nothing less." Geoff caressed Poppy's forearm.

Molly and George exchanged looks when Geoff touched their mother. Poppy observed their interchange and gave them *the look*—that universal mom look that all children know.

"You're on the crew team? I have a colleague who's a master rower," Geoff said.

"That's cool." George nodded.

"I heard you're a state champ." Geoff said with a nod.

"Yeah." George's tone said, *I'm chill with all this.* "Our team won eleven trophies at States."

"Wow, that's great!" Geoff leaned forward, elbows on his knees. "And you're in the two-man?"

"Yes, the pair." George fidgeted with the cording on his Sperry topsiders.

"It was so awesome, Geoff. When the team held their trophies in the photo, it looked like they had robbed a trophy store." Poppy looked at Geoff and grinned.

Molly looked at George before her eyes locked on the rug. George reached into the pocket of his shorts and pulled out his cell phone.

Neither Poppy nor Geoff had noticed George's expression when he looked at his sister.

Under her towel, Molly pulled out her cell phone partway and texted her brother, while her eyes remained on her mother. *Is that a moustache, or did Nickynoo's squirrel go missing?*

George also texted without looking. *LOL. Since when is Mom into wildlife?*

Geoff, oblivious to the texting banter, raised an impressed eyebrow to Poppy's youngest. "Molly, I hear you're quite the breaststroker."

*LOL. Look at the googly eyes they give each other.* Molly jerked her head up.

"Well, I don't know about that," she said, self-effacing. "But I like the breaststroke."

"She's great, Geoff. I know I'm biased," Poppy admitted. "She has a beautiful stroke."

*Before this gets serious, Mom has to watch the movie* The Stepfather. Molly sent the text and suppressed a smile. She looked up and pretended to straighten the towel as if some mysterious force had tangled it up.

George sneered. *That would be hilarious. If he even tries something like that, I'd totally take him.*

"I swam competitively in high school as well. As a sprinter. Freestyle. Fifty-free. Anchored the relays." Geoff sat back on the sofa and draped his arm around Poppy.

"Oh, that's cool." Molly nodded the teen-to-adult nod. That formal gesture that says, *I'm being polite and not sure what else to say.*

"I used to swim a half mile almost every day at Rollins, although there was no swim team then," Poppy said, lovingly staring at their joined hands on the sofa. "And my college boyfriend was on the water-ski team."

*JK. He seems nice. And Mom is so giddy,* Molly texted. With a side glance, she monitored her mother, who hadn't stopped smiling at Geoff.

*I know. Jesus.* George fired off a quick text.

"So we both did water sports like you two." Poppy grinned. "We went to school in paradise." She rubbed Geoff's arm. "The Thetas were right next door to the Phi Delts."

*A frat guy. Oh no,* George texted.

Molly smiled, halfheartedly. "Yes, I've heard this. *Several* times." She raised her eyebrows at her mother. "I've seen the picture of the M&M's." Molly tucked her phone away and laughed.

"That was ridiculous wasn't it? Your mother made me do it." Geoff tsked. "Had to wear tights."

George set his phone down—he'd found common ground with Geoff over his mother's ridiculousness. "Oh, Geoff. Sorry man. She makes us do shit like that all the time, too."

"You both probably have some homework, right?" Poppy looked at George.

His ears flushed a rosy color. "Why are you looking at me?" He stood up and avoided answering his mother's question.

As the teens retrieved their backpacks and passed through the family room to their respective rooms, Geoff leaned forward and said, "It's good to meet you both."

"You, too," George mumbled, as the shadow of prospective homework crossed his face.

As if an English teacher had asked them to provide a more formal response to Geoff's comment, Molly smiled. "It's good to meet you, too, Geoff."

Poppy grinned. "They were up to something. Texting some secretive messages to each other. Probably making fun of us for holding hands. That'd creep them out."

"I expect them to make fun of us. My moustache is easy fodder for jokes." Geoff leaned back, his arm around Poppy.

"With teenagers, it's a crapshoot. I think being real—knowing that they'll make fun of us, it'll give them what time they need to process. Being open in our communication is the best we can do." Poppy sighed. "Kids have laser-sharp detection abilities. They know when parents aren't being up-front with them."

Geoff kissed her hair. "I'm an open book, Pops. What you see is what you get."

~~~

I knew one thing. As a mother, Poppy had an intuition about how her children felt about Geoff. Her maternal radar searched 360-degrees of their emotional state. If they didn't care for him, or if they rejected him emotionally, intellectually, or irrationally—*heaven forbid*—she'd already decided Geoff wouldn't be a part of their lives. *Of her life.*

*Research.* I would plan for days of research on available resources on blended families. Divorce. New relationships. Coping mechanisms of adolescent and young adults. *Poppy and Geoff's reunion is much more than either of them imagined. Yet, if their offspring refuse their renewed relationship and the idea of it, as well as the reality of it, research may all be for naught.*

On the wrought-iron chair next to me on Poppy's front porch, a question popped out of my slate popped: *Research? I can help.*

I smiled at my slate's readiness. "Please provide research and stats on blended families. Children of divorce. Behavior of adolescents and young adults in transition," I said.

A light melon-colored bubble floated up. *Is this what you're looking for?*

The slate's screen displayed twelve pages of information on blended families, adolescent stages of identity, divorce statistics. Parenting. Coping mechanisms. Group dynamics. Families in transition. Timing and trust.

"Excellent. Let's start with divorce statistics and remarriage with blended families," I requested.

My slate made sounds like Chicago winds whistling down the corridors of Michigan Avenue at Huron Street. Data appeared on the screen.

*Divorce and Remarriage Statistics:*
*As of 2006, the divorce rate for remarried and stepfamily couples var-*
*ies, but it is at least 60 percent. Second marriages, with or without children,*
*have a 67 percent rate of divorce. Seventy-three percent of third marriages*
*end in divorce. Almost 65 percent of all remarriages end in divorce. – US*
*Census Bureau and the National Center for Health Statistics*

"Seventy-three percent?" I held my slate closer as if I hadn't read correctly. "Those are daunting numbers," I murmured. "I wonder why they're so
high."

New information appeared on the screen.

*There are several reasons why remarriage in a blended family ends in*
*divorce. These are the most common: disputes over parenting, money, pri-*
*vacy, responsibilities, boundaries, traditions, and holidays. Feelings of being*
*unappreciated. Disrespect. Children acting out. Parenting differences over*
*values. Loyalty conflicts to biological parent. Couples feeling overwhelmed*
*or discouraged about a stepfamily. Step-sibling relationship challenges.*

I stared at the list displayed on the screen and felt anxiety wash over me.
"These are serious issues." I grunted.

I stared at the stone angel statue. My thoughts went to Poppy, who'd
struggled with her son's acting out. His disrespectful behavior to his mother and sister. *George thinks of himself as the man of the house. And Poppy's worked*
*for eight months to change his perception and reclaim respect in the home.*

Although Geoff had just experienced a good first meeting with George
and Molly—and even though first impressions are important—this was not
a real-world situation. Not a day-to-day interaction with the adolescents.
And Jonathon. No one had met Geoff's son yet. Nor Kimmy and Kelly. *How*
*long might it take for all parties to feel comfortable with one another? If ever?*

*I should stop right now. Not make them endure anymore. It would cause too*
*many changes in the children's lives. They may never have a positive group dynamic.*
I gripped the top of the black iron chair and exhaled.

At the treeline in Poppy's front yard, dozens of red asterisks floated like
fireflies—beamed from my slate—to get my attention.

"You have something to add?" I mumbled, and looked at the steady
stream of red stars. "I'm afraid these are irrefutable statistics, and besides,
I'm way ahead of myself. No one's talking marriage."

*A recent study claims that lost loves who marry one another have a less than 2 percent divorce rate.*

My slate projected a yellow smiley face after the word "rate."

"Really?" I asked. "I'm sorry I overreacted."

Under the golden Empathic Bridge, still illuminated, a river of royal-blue water flowed in a steady stream. The screen on my slate brightened with the words "Water under the bridge."

My slate's happy words marched out.

*The reason there is a 98 percent success rate in this particular kind of remarriage is documented below:*

*Dr. Nancy Kalish, who has researched rekindled love, says that, "Couples [who] shared friends and values, whether they were from the same hometown or met in college, spent formative years together and became each other's standard for all romances since."*

"Each other's *standard for romance?*" I stared at the findings, my mouth open.

Poppy had said as much when she'd spoken to her daughters before they went to college. I felt hopeful. I remembered that Poppy had told her girls that Geoff was the "template" for men. That he was "wonderful."

From my slate, a vapor of silver mist with cobalt-blue writing splashed out onto the tiled front porch: *Geoff was—is—the standard.*

CHAPTER 32

# Family Matters

~

"Wow, IT LOOKS LIKE THE Knights of the Round Table gather here," Geoff joked as he pulled out the dining chair in Valerie and George Terris' dining room. "How many does this table seat?"

"Ten. Eleven is tight," Valerie said, and placed her napkin on her lap. "Our table on the east side of Milwaukee sat twenty-six."

"Holy cow." Geoff laid the napkin across his khakis. "That's a big crowd."

"Mom and Dad fit twenty in here." Poppy pointed to two identical bistro tables that each sat four comfortably, five snugly.

George Terris lifted his water glass to Geoff. "Good job on the steaks, Geoff. They're cooked perfectly." He smiled at the grill master.

"Yeah, really good," George said, and the teen plopped a large piece in his mouth.

"Very good," Molly said, at the same time.

The teens' rote responses—automatic, as politeness had been taught in the crib—provided a barely mannerly reply, just enough to allude to their innate graciousness. Yet, within Poppy's family, they were transparently superficial. An indication that the jury was still out on Geoff.

Valerie smiled. "So what time do you two travel to Mount Dora tomorrow?"

"We'll head out in the afternoon." Geoff squeezed Poppy's hand under the table.

Molly saw their arms move, looked at her brother, and rolled her eyes.

Big George cleared his throat. "Poppy tells me your sister-in-law has never remarried. How is she doing?"

"No, not remarried." Geoff set down his fork. "She's doing okay. She gives most of her attention to her kids and grandson in Utah. Her mother lives in Bonita Springs, and she spends quite a bit of time there."

Poppy's children, who had kicked each other under the table right after Geoff had taken Poppy's hand, stopped and instantly gave their attention to Geoff.

A learned response.

I noted that Poppy's family had an intuitive understanding, a core understanding, that compassion for the human condition is ageless. Within certain families, compassion is a natural trait, while in many other families, external examples—from church, community, a school environment—supply models and paradigms for behavior.

"I'm sorry, Geoff. Mom told us about your brother," George murmured respectfully.

"That must've been awful for you," Molly said, after her brother.

"Thanks. It was hard." Geoff paused, collecting his thoughts and restraining buried emotions that emerged at unexpected times. "I felt very lucky that we had a great friendship and shared some wonderful sailing adventures before we lost him."

Poppy's parents, eyes tearing, stared at Geoff, their expressions appearing to say: *No parent should ever lose a child.*

Poppy's father pushed his plate toward the center of the pine table. "I read the article about you rebuilding the boat. Terrific what you did." He turned his good ear toward Geoff and looked at him intently. The expression on the eighty-eight-year-old man's face was solemn and reverent, as if they'd both been soldiers together who'd faced adversity and overcome it.

"Thank you, George. It was a cathartic exercise for me. It let me move on. Not let tragedy be the end of my brother's story."

Poppy's son slid his plate to the side at an empty place setting. "How long did it take you?" He folded his arms on the table and leaned toward Geoff.

"About six months, George." Geoff sat, levelheaded and composed, but memories of Twig piled up on the empty plate in front of him. A sip of water prevented any emotional spills.

"Did you have help?" Molly said, her heightened female intuition fully powered.

"I'd received a lot of help from people at the factory who told me how to do it. Friends and neighbors had shown up at the right time with tools and support. But ninety-five percent of the actual effort was mine." He looked past the two adolescents to the patio doors. "The boat was a wreck—I wasn't sure if I should've taken it to the dump, or rebuilt it."

"Do you sail it now?" Poppy's son asked.

"Sure do. In fact, as your mom is well aware"—he looked at Poppy—"I just won a race at a major regatta at our club. I beat the boat builder, who sailed a brand-new boat."

"Oh, wow. Congratulations." Molly smiled. The energy around the Terris round table rebounded from a heartbreaking memory to making and sharing new memories. *A testament to the strength of family. Poppy's family.*

After the two teens cleaned up and Valerie oozed her appreciation to them, the kids left to attend to their Friday night plans. George Terris rose from his chair to signal his goodnight. He put two fingers on his mouth and blew a kiss to Poppy. On his way out, he hand-delivered the kiss to Valerie's cheek.

Valerie stared after her husband as he walked past her and rose. She said her goodnights to Poppy and Geoff.

"Well, I thought that tonight was gre—" Geoff looked at Poppy's face. "What's the matter, Honch?"

Poppy wiped her eyelids, where tears had formed. "I just can't get over how comfortable." She hesitated. "How *right* it is with you here." Her voice low, she touched his cheek, lingering on his dimple. "Like you've been here for years."

He picked up her hand in both of his. "It does feel like that. Since the moment we'd reconnected . . . " He kissed the top of her hand. "Easiest thing I've ever done. Falling in love with you again."

Poppy nodded. "C'mon, I'll tuck you in upstairs." She winked.

Geoff walked with Poppy as she turned off the downstairs light. He pulled her silently upstairs. "We're all alone up here. Just like New Year's Eve thirty-two years ago," he whispered into her hair.

# CHAPTER 33

# An Affair to Remember

⌢ᦞ

DONNELLY STREET, THE MAIN ARTERY *into downtown Mount Dora, could serve as a ski hill, if the charming New England–style community ever got snow,* I thought, as Poppy and Geoff made their way into town. A mile north from the quaint shops and restaurants in the heart of the village, and at the top of a large hill, the entrance to Waterman Village greeted residents. The gated retirement community attracted many snowbirds, quite a few of them from the Midwest. Miniaturized white picket fences lined this notable senior citizens' independent-living village, filled with charming homes and condominiums.

Jean and George Spencer lived in a two-bedroom condo across the street from a small park, accented with an octagonal gazebo. On the other side of the gazebo, a lush corridor of trees framed a small ravine.

"Jean?" George Spencer called out from the front sun porch. "They're here!" He folded the sports section of the *Orlando Sentinel* and laid it on the cushioned rattan sofa.

"Hi!" Jean Spencer walked from inside the townhouse to the porch. She brushed her taupe slacks with a linen kitchen towel, more from habit than to sweep off any condiments. She wore a freshly pressed white blouse and gold-flecked jewelry from Chico's—her favorite afternoon shopping destination.

"I hope the traffic wasn't too bad. And we're having your favorite dinner. I've marinated the tenderloin filets," Jean said as a greeting, and her graciousness blended the thoughts together so that they became a perfect verbal roux.

She turned to Poppy and smiled. "Hello, Poppy. It's so good to see you again."

"Hi, Jean. May I call you Jean?" Poppy hugged the petite woman.

"Of course." Jean's eyes sparkled. "Mrs. Spencer makes me sound so old. I love your blouse and jacket. So smart looking." Jean lightly touched Poppy's sleeve.

"Thank you." Poppy smiled.

"Hi, Geoffrey! Hi, Poppy!" George Spencer reached out his hand to his son. Geoff ignored the hand and wrapped his father in a hug instead.

"Hi, George!" Poppy hugged Geoff's father with a gentle half-hug on his shoulder.

"Come sit, please." Geoff's mother gestured to the aqua upholstered couch and pair of round sepia swivel chairs. "I've made some hors d'oeuvres."

A small plate of artichoke roll-ups and a bowl of mixed nuts sat next to a stack of coasters with Michigan logos on the square mahogany coffee table. Jean reached into a four-tiered wooden pyramid shelf filled with more than thirty antique glass and crystal pitchers and pulled one of the cruets out of the display.

Past the kitchen was the elegant dining room. Jean had set the table for four with sterling silver place settings. It appeared as though a six-course meal would be served. The table, enhanced by fresh flowers—soft orange freesia—looked like a living waterfall of color that complemented the slight melon tint in the white walls.

To the right of the display of glass, a built-in shelf with recessed lighting showcased Jean's collection of Northland fine china. The bright-red polka-dot pattern gave the room a sense of vitality. "It's Northland's Hungary pattern," Jean said to answer Poppy's question. She had not asked, but Jean's social insight detected the question.

Poppy leaned forward and glanced into the house. "Your table is beautiful." She smiled at Jean, who gave Geoff a glass of wine and a white linen coaster.

"I set my dining room table. Every day," Jean said, as though everyone did that.

"She's not kidding, Poppy." Geoff smirked. "It is *always* set like this."

Geoff took Poppy's hand. "She's been ready with everything since we'd discussed this with her a week ago." Geoff winked at his mother. "C'mon. I'll show you the rest of the place."

He led her down a hallway, past a dark wooden chest. "More collections." He pointed to the antique dresser where twenty colored paperweights adorned the top.

"So pretty." Poppy stopped. "I feel like I'm in an antique shop. Like when I shopped with my mom."

From behind them, Jean approached and rested her hand on the dresser, not so much for balance but perhaps to support the emotions the paperweights evoked.

"George and I've always bought a paperweight from the many different countries we've visited. We've traveled a lot." Jean glanced back toward George Spencer, her bittersweet expression a combination of happy memories and current limitations. Her face brightened as she said, "I like to collect them because they're easy to pack and not too heavy." *A mother's resourceful pride,* I thought.

Poppy picked up one of the globes—a blush-pink lotus flower centered by fluffy green leaves. "These are quite exotic, Jean." Poppy nestled the glass weight back into its spot and turned to Geoff's mother. "I imagine you and George cherish wonderful memories from your travels."

Jean rounded her palm over the top of the one closest to her. "We're very fortunate to have seen so many places."

As Geoff finished the tour of his parents' home, he paused in the guest bedroom doorway. "Here's where I stay when I come." He pointed to the twin beds and winked at Poppy. "Just like college."

From behind, Poppy put her arms around Geoff's waist. "Thank you for bringing me, Geoffrey. For sharing." Poppy's eyes filled. "Your parents adore you. Although, what's not to adore?"

~9

Geoff swallowed a bite of mint ice-cream pie. "Mmm, this is good, Mom."

He glanced at Poppy and gauged her emotions from her face. "So, as I said earlier, when Poppy and I broke up at Rollins, nothing was wrong. We were crazy about each other."

Jean set her fork on the plate, her eyes focused on her son's contemplative expression. "What do you think happened?" she asked gently.

Poppy inclined her head slightly toward Geoff. "Shortly before I broke us up, I'd asked Geoff what would happen next year. He talked about what *he'd* be doing at Rollins. I felt sort of irrelevant and made an assumption that he didn't care that much about me." Poppy looked at Jean and then at Geoff. Her ice-cream dessert melted on her fork.

"Well, you were both young," Jean said. "It's hard to know at that age what you have." Her voice soothed with an edge of softened practicality.

"Well, we know now." Geoff reached out his left hand for Poppy's.

Jean touched George's left hand. "Can I get you anything else, George?"

"No, thank you." He smiled at his wife. "You're so good to me," George said, a statement of fact.

Poppy and Geoff looked at each other. Poppy winked. *It's so beautiful to witness this kind of love,* she thought. *So tender.*

"Poppy and I marvel at how *both sets* of our parents have great marriages. Role models of incredible loving kindness. Respect for one another." Geoff's eyes watered.

"Yes, my parents have been married more than fifty-five years." Poppy raised her eyebrows, an open expression to give permission to judge. "We weren't able to make it work in the wonderful way that you two obviously have." Poppy smiled.

"Well," Jean began. "I don't really know what we did." She searched George's face. "We've never had a fight."

"Never." Behind George's glasses, the corners of his hazel eyes each collected a warm tear.

She wiped her mouth with her linen napkin. "I guess we're just lucky."

Sunday afternoon, after dinner with Geoff's parents the evening before, Geoff and Poppy drove past acres of Florida orange groves filled with emerging white flowers.

"Ahhhh, this is so pretty," Poppy smiled.

"Look over here to the left, Honch. Disney properties in the distance. Those pyramid shapes are the Swan and Dolphin Hotels. And that giant golf-ball-shaped globe is Epcot."

"Is that Cinderella Castle at the Magic Kingdom?"

"Yeah, I think so." Geoff reached his hand into the center console and picked up a Burt's Bees lip balm. He bumped Poppy's wrist as he pulled off the cap. "Excuse me," he muttered.

"Squeeze you? I barely know you," Poppy said playfully, and gasped. "Oh my God!" She shifted suddenly, her back to the passenger door. "We used to say that, *right?* When we were together. You'd graze my boob and say, 'Excuse me.' And my automatic response was 'Squeeze you . . .'" Poppy leaned back against the door.

"Ha. Yes, you did say that." Geoff laughed. "Another great Poppyism."

"Geoffrey! I haven't said that since I said it with *you.* Not since Rollins!" Poppy put her hand over her heart. "It came back." She snapped her fingers. "Just like that."

"You know what, Honch?" He caressed her knee. "I'll bet this will happen over and over." He signaled and merged onto I-4. "Like this morning."

He smiled at her. "After we'd made love, I lay back on the pillow and said, 'Oh man.'"

"And I said, 'Oh woman,' as if we'd said that to each other after making love every day for thirty-two years."

Geoff grinned. "So, we would've made love every day? For thirty-two years? Wow, that would've been great."

They both laughed. Poppy wiped her eyes. "I cry all the time." She sniffed. "But these are all happy tears." Poppy traced her finger around Geoff's ear. "No matter what we do, I'm so happy with you." Her hand caressed his shoulder. "Thank you for the visit with your parents. They're wonderful. So kind." She smoothed his hair. "Just like you."

"Yes they are wonderful. Having you there reconfirmed what I've always known. That you're the one I was always supposed to be with," Geoff said. "It's kind of like the scene at the end of *You've Got Mail*, where Meg Ryan says to Tom Hanks, 'I was hoping it would be you.'" He recalled it with a wide smile. A touchstone memory.

"I love that movie. And Meg Ryan and Tom Hanks were also great in *Sleepless in Seattle*. Do you remember that one?" Poppy inched to the edge of her seat.

Geoff looked up to his right. "Vaguely."

"Based on *An Affair to Remember*. Cary Grant and Deborah Kerr. One of my all-time favorites." Poppy touched her neck. "It's a classic, right?"

Geoff gently shook his head. "I don't think I've seen that one."

"WHAT?!" Poppy shrieked. "Seriously? You've *never* seen it?" She rested her elbow on the dashboard. "C'mon, they meet on a cruise and fall in love?"

"No, I don't think I know it." Geoff glanced in the rearview mirror.

"Oh my God." Poppy fell back against the door. "I'll explain it." She took a breath. "Deborah Kerr goes on a cruise and meets a player—playboy—Cary Grant. They're both engaged to other people, yet they fall in love. They meet Cary Grant's aging French grandmother, and she, of course, adores Deborah Kerr. The ship whistle blows; they leave the French grandmother. They pull into New York Harbor and make a deal."

"Did they fool around on the ship?" Geoff asked like a teenager.

"No, just a kiss, but Cary Grant decides to ditch his gigolo ways, get a proper job, and after six months, he will honor her—ask her to marry him. They agree to meet on top of the Empire State Building in six months."

"That was the deal?" Geoff smiled at Poppy, who gestured wildly with her hands.

"Yes. She breaks up with her fiancé, Ken. Cary—Nick—breaks it off with his socialite fiancée, and they prepare to meet up. On the day that she's on her way to meet him, Ken, her ex, says he'll do whatever for her, and in her rush to get to the Empire State Building, she's"—Poppy swallowed and squeaked—"struck by a car."

Geoff looked over at Poppy. "Honch?" He leaned forward to see her face.

Poppy waved her hand in front of her face, like a fan. "Then she's in the hospital..."

"Oh my God . . . you're crying? Just *talking* about this?" Geoff's lips parted.

"She's in the hospital and insists that Ken, her ex, never reveals"—she exhaled loudly—"what's happened to her. Meanwhile, Cary Grant is up on the top of the building in a . . . in a . . . thunderstorm, and is . . ." Poppy gulped and held her abdomen.

"This is a *riot*," Geoff laughed. "You can't even *talk* about this movie?"

"Stop." She panted. "So, she . . . doesn't show . . . because now she's in a wheelchair. He leaves at midnight. Six months pass. He drinks too much and paints. And now it's Christmas, and she's at the theater with her ex, Ken, and she"—Poppy whimpered—"she sees him there. He doesn't know why she stood him up, and so they see each other, and then . . . and then . . . he walks away." Poppy wiped her cheeks with both palms.

"You're just *talking* about this? Aww, God." Geoff grinned and shook his head. "This is wild." Geoff laughed.

Poppy exhaled and pursed her lips. "Christmas night she's home. Her assistant leaves her on the sofa—legs covered with a blanket. As the maid opens her door, Cary Grant is standing there with a present. He comes in. Tells her he thinks that *she* ought to be angry that he didn't show up six months ago as promised." Poppy rested her forehead in her hand. "And . . . and . . . he lets her know that *he* was upset that she didn't show up."

"So, did she explain what happened?" Geoff glanced over at Poppy.

Poppy shook her head. "He gives her the present, and it's the white shawl that'd been his grandmother's. His grandmother had wanted her to have it." Poppy's voice creaked. "She's sad—*that's* why her letters to the sweet lady had been returned.

"Deborah Kerr puts the shawl around her shoulders as Cary Grant grabs his coat and gloves, and is . . . ready to leave." Poppy sucked air in. "He's . . . at the door and stops. He turns to face her, and says, 'You know, I once painted you like this. The gallery owner was going to sell it to a woman who didn't have enough money, and when he . . . he . . . he.' Cary Grant starts to stutter, stops, and says, 'He told me that she was in . . . in'—and he's about to say wheelchair...'" Poppy's voice cracked.

"She was in where?" Geoff leaned toward Poppy.

"In the shop. And then Cary Grant puts his gloves and coat down and starts to ramble . . . about the shop owner and the painting . . . and then he scans the walls of her apartment..."

Poppy sobbed once. "And Deborah Kerr looks at him imploringly, as if she were saying, 'Oh God, he knows.' And Cary Grant opens a door to a room and, and looks around. And he's still babbling about the painting and the owner, and finally." Poppy heaved a heavy breath. "He opens—he opens the door." Poppy swallowed. "To her room—her room. And..." Poppy slurred as she gulped her breath.

"And there, there on her wall in her bedroom is *his* painting," She gasped. "And he stands there with his eyes closed . . ." Poppy slurred the word "eyes" with a gurgling sound, through her tears, which made it sound like "highes," and added, "And he has a look of torture. Such anguish. Sorrow. Such sorrow on his, his, face...," Poppy choked out.

"And...?" Geoff leaned forward on the steering wheel.

"And he rushes to her and asks why she hadn't told him. And she says she hadn't wanted to burden him." Poppy whispered. "And she says if he can paint again, she can..." Poppy's chest heaved a sob. "...She can *walk* again." Poppy held her breath after she said "again."

"That's how the movie ends?" Geoff raised his eyebrows.

Poppy nodded and opened the glove box. She removed a stack of light-brown napkins, then wiped the edges of her nose.

Geoff's eyes misted. "Just talking has you sobbing. I'll have to see it."

Poppy lay her head back and steadied her breath and closed her eyes. Only the sound of the highway, interrupted by her inhaling air in a slow, measured manner, filled the quiet car. The silence, the kind that comforts two people who know each other so well, cushioned Poppy and Geoff as the road unraveled before them.

Less than five minutes later, Geoff looked at her and smiled. Poppy's lower lip drooped—her breathing louder. *She looks so sweet,* he thought. *This woman I adore. Sleeping next to me, so peacefully. It's so right being with her.*

218

# CHAPTER 34

# Sibling Synergy

~◞

FROM THE BACK OF THE Poppy's house, I detected George and Molly's muffled voices. I joined them in George's room, where both siblings sat cross-legged on the bed. As if it were a Ouija board, they stared at the landline phone handset on the comforter.

"George and Moll? You there?" Their sister Kelly's voice sounded through the speaker. "Hold on. I'll conference Kimmy. Be right back," she chirped—professional.

"George, move over. You're hogging the whole bed." Molly pushed his shin.

"It's my bed," George grumbled and shifted toward the wall.

Kimmy's Chicago twang filled her brother's room. "Hi, you guys. This is great that we can all talk. Thanks, Kell, for setting this up."

"Sure," Kelly said. "So, George and Moll, where's Mom now?"

"She left a half hour ago to get him at the airport," George blurted out the update.

"In Tampa." Molly leaned in close to the phone to be included.

"So, Molls, what do you think of him?" Kimmy asked, using her oldest-sister status to start the dialogue.

"He's nice. I mean, I remember what you and Kell said to us last year when Mom and Dad split up." Molly curled and uncurled the edge of the pillowcase on George's bed. "That Mom wouldn't date any time soon."

"And she hasn't, Molly," George said as he waved a contradictory hand at her. "Not until she connected a few weeks ago with Geoff."

"I know, George." She raised her voice, even though they sat next to each other. "It's just that there's a part of me that doesn't *want* to like him."

"Uh-huh. I understand, sweetie," Kelly said, maternally. "So, Molls, can you tell if Big George and Val like him?"

"Yeah," George intercepted the question. "They totally like him." George noticed Molly's ponytail holder on his nightstand. He grabbed it and spun it on his forefinger.

"Okay, so see how this weekend goes. This is the second time you'll be with him, right?" Kimmy asked, keeping track.

"Yep," Molly nodded. "And they haven't seen each other in two weeks."

"Where's he *staying*?" Kelly blurted.

"Here," George said. "When Mom asked us if that'd be okay with us, we said yes. Then she said that when we're fifty years old, we can make our own sleeping arrangements," George scoffed. "She told us not to even *think* about trying that now."

Both of the Chicago-based sisters laughed.

"Of course we said it was fine." Molly rolled a loose thread from the sea-green down comforter in her fingers. "It's juuuuust . . ." Molly dragged out the word as if it were a hinge that needed lubrication "Different."

George interrupted Molly's echoing comment. "Mom told us Val was weird about it for us. But it's not like we're little kids or anything." George dropped the ponytail holder and slid his watch back and forth on his wrist.

"And besides, remember that Geoff was her first." Molly made air quotes when she said the word "first."

"Jesus," George muttered.

Kimmy laughed. "Oh my God. Kell, remember when Mom gave us *the talk,* before we headed off to college? She said she'd waited for Geoff. Someone who was good to her. Whom she loved and trusted."

"Totally," Kelly said. "And how she broke his heart."

"We've alllll heard about that again," Molly groaned. "I've received the same speech, even though college is two years away."

"The point is, Geoff was good to Mom. She obviously trusted him. He isn't some random guy from Match.com," Kelly snickered.

"Yeah, some dickhead." George grunted.

All four siblings laughed.

"Mom's favorite bad word." Kimmy chuckled.

"Okay guys, I have to get back to work. Text or email if you want to talk some more, okay?" Kelly asked.

"Me, too. Let us know how it goes," Kimmy said, her tone upbeat. "And don't worry, George and Moll. I can hear it in Mom's voice. She's really happy. And she'll always put you guys first."

"Exactly." Kelly mirrored her sister's message. "I agree with Kimmy. Mom sounds really good. She's not going to do anything that'll upset you guys."

George nodded as his tanned bare feet smoothed the comforter. "Thanks." George picked up the handset.

Molly thrust her chin forward to the phone in George's hand. "Thanks, K2."

George switched off the phone and tossed it at the foot of the bed. "So, we'll just have to wait and see."

"D'you know what's so weird, George?" Molly cracked her knuckles and made them sound like bubble-wrap popping. "It's like they've been dating for years. I don't mean to go all *Parent Trap* here, but do you think we need to protect Mom?"

"Molly, you knew a long time ago Mom and Dad would never get back together."

"Yes, I know *that*. What if she falls for Geoff more than he falls for her?"

"Then I'll take him out if he hurts Mom." George leaned back against his headboard and cracked a pencil in half. "I think Mom's really into him," he mumbled.

"*Pssshhhew.* Yeah, right." Molly picked up Nicky, who stood with her front paws on the side of the bed. "And did you see George and Val at dinner last time? It's like Geoff's been a part of the family for years."

"Jesus." George tossed the broken pencil toward his wastebasket. "I know."

"I'm pissed because Nickynoo likes him." She rubbed the dog's back as she curled next to Molly's thigh.

The Shih Tzu lifted her head. "You don't like that man with the silly moustache, right, Nickynoo?" The dog's ears went back as she swallowed and lay down.

"Let's just wait, Molly. You never know how this will play out."

"I know. I just don't want her to get hurt." Molly got off the bed and scooped up the dog in both arms. "But she does seem really, really happy, doesn't she?"

"Yep, she does." George tossed a pair of rolled-up socks back and forth in his hands. He looked beyond his sister. "I've never seen her this way."

"Me, either," Molly said, as she stared at the pool outside her brother's room. "What if they end up together and he's all authoritarian and man-of-the-house?"

"He better not pull that crap." George threw the sock roll at his mirror. "I won't take any shit."

I recognized that the four siblings had a synergy—an unspoken bond to cooperate with one another. Stick together. No matter what happened.

# CHAPTER 35

# Birds of a Different Feather

⁓

ACROSS FROM POPPY'S DESK, ON the kiwi-green couch in the living room, Nicky's head jerked up. The Shih Tzu had listened as Poppy had blurted, "Oh my Goddd!" as soon as the images had appeared on her computer screen.

The screen revealed a campus picture of Poppy and *her* Geoff at Rollins in 1978. Poppy, in a long-sleeved teal shirt and matching scarf, looked coy seated next to Geoff in khakis and his navy-blue ski team T-shirt. The email subject line read, *Look what I found.*

She hit Geoff's contact on her phone. "Geoffrey, I can't believe you *had* this." She squinted at the monitor. "And *kept* it."

"It was tucked away in one of my yearbooks." Geoff rocked back in his leather desk chair.

Poppy looked at the image on her screen. "We're on the ledge right outside the Theta House. It looks as though you've just pinched me." Poppy giggled. "You've got that sexy twinkle in your eye." Poppy closed her eyes. "I wonder why you kept it."

"Maybe so I could share it with you." He stood and walked to the oak tallboy dresser and picked up a 3x5 glass frame. He slid out a picture of a yellow Lab and blew dust off the top of the frame.

Once more he studied the photo. The memory of the two of them, more than thirty-two years ago, had become iconic. Treasured times. Times that had slipped into the mists of the lakes surrounding Rollins. Recovered now that the bits and pieces of their lives were beginning to blend. He glided it into the frame. "Now when you come here this weekend and meet Jonathon, you'll be able to see it."

⁓

At Geoff's dining room table, Jonathon sipped a drink through a straw. His shoulders hunched forward—the word "posture" not in his vocabulary this week—and he leaned into the drink. Intensely, he studied it as if looking for answers. Agile, his lean and wiry body displayed the transient youth that only the youthful choose to ignore.

The six-foot-three-inch young man rose when his father and Poppy entered.

"Hi, Jonathon. I've heard so much about you." Poppy leaned in to hug him.

Jonathon glanced at his father and sat down. "Should I be worried?"

Poppy raised her eyelids and suppressed a grin. "Your dad told me that he can never get you to stop talking."

Jonathon's mouth twisted into a tight grin. His cheeks flushed, and he looked down at the water droplets on the glossy table.

"That's right. A big talker." Geoff tapped Jonathon's arm. "Did you just come from working out?"

"Yep. Did some Romanian dead lifts." Jonathon exhaled.

"Weights, not dead Romanians?" Poppy suppressed a grin.

"No, not dead people." Jonathon gave a half smile and stared at Poppy.

Geoff placed a cat coaster underneath Jonathon's water glass. "Did I tell you Poppy's a professor at Ringling College?"

Jonathon looked at his father. "Some kind of art school or something?"

"Yes, it is. I teach several different psychology courses in the Liberal Arts Department." Poppy smiled at Jonathon. "So, what's your favorite college subject?"

A roseate flush surfaced on the twenty-year-old's cheeks. "Umm," he sighed. "Probably psychology."

"It's the second most popular college major. So what intrigues you about psych?" Poppy asked, nonchalant.

Jonathon shifted in his chair. "Actually, I like abnormal psych." He looked toward his leg jiggling beneath the table and then at his father with a sheepish expression—one that usually came with a confession.

"Really?" Geoff raised his eyebrows at his son. "I've never heard this before."

"You and every other twenty-year-old." Poppy tsked.

The three of them talked about topics familiar to all: TV shows like *Dexter, Star Wars, Star Trek,* and *Seinfeld.* Jonathon seemed resolutely subdued. Part manners. Part shyness around Poppy.

When either Poppy or Geoff asked Jonathon a question about his interests, his face had flushed. I wondered, *Does Jonathon's physiological reddening appear because he isn't used to sharing his thoughts and feelings aloud? Especially with a newcomer who asked questions his father never had.*

I'd watched father and son together—their easy way with each other, even though their temperaments differed. Geoff savored the opportunity to be curious and energetic about life, yet his son, with a robust internal curiosity, approached his life in a more languid way.

Geoff led Poppy outside to his second-story balcony. "Jonathon seems comfortable with you. More engaged than I expected," Geoff said after Jonathon had left to meet up with a friend. "I'm sure you noticed he's different from me. Quieter. A bird of a different feather," Geoff said, and swung their joined hands toward a sparrow that had perched on a tree.

"I love the sparrow," Poppy said, as if it were a childhood friend she'd stayed in touch with. "The sparrow reminds us that we're good enough. That we have our own gifts and talents." She rested her head on Geoff's shoulder. "It is a bird that flourishes in spite of life's adversities," Poppy murmured. "It's resilient. Like us."

CHAPTER 36

# Perennial Poppy

~⌇

THE FESTIVE AIR IN POPPY'S family room had spread to the outdoor patio, where sounds of iced glasses and cocktail conversation circled in the
sultry evening air. *An attentive and gracious hostess,* I thought, as I watched
her guests. The Empathic Bridge had lit up from the enjoyment, not only
because of Poppy and Geoff, but, moreover, from the demonstrative joy on
the patio.

At the edge of the pool, the spotlight under the surface of the water
provided ripples of illumination, as the surface moved with the gulf coast's
breeze. The soft light from the angelic glow from the votive candles reflected on guests there to celebrate Poppy's Friday night birthday, two days
before the Fourth of July.

I reflected on Poppy and Geoff—their first time ever giving a party
*together.* They looked like a couple who'd entertained together for decades.
Poppy picked up the wine bottle and held it up to the light—a few ounces
remained. She scanned the family room. As she walked around the counter toward the hallway, Geoff re-entered the room with two new bottles of
wine. *Thoughts in lockstep.*

Many of the partygoers commented that they'd never seen Poppy so
radiant.

"The love story of the century," they said. "She's just blossomed." And
the ladies' cheeks revealed happy parentheses, while their hands covered
their hearts—overcome with emotion. And the most common proclama-
tion that Poppy and Geoff heard over and over: "I have goose bumps."

On Saturday evening, the night after the birthday party, Poppy's parents visited and shared the leftovers of tenderloin buns, turkey buns, and
cheeses, along with a fresh salad Poppy had prepared.

Valerie, with Poppy and Geoff, looked down at the granite countertop.
She squared the stack of cocktail napkins, her unconscious way of making
things make sense again when she wanted to restore some order in lives
that had taken a detour.

Geoff joined Big George on the adjacent couch. From the other side of the room, in the kitchen, Poppy and Valerie talked about Monet's garden at Giverny. They reminisced about a trip in 1988, when George had driven through the French countryside wearing a French chauffeur's cap—just the three of them during the two-hour drive from Paris. Valerie beamed at her husband. For a few moments, Geoff and George sat in silence—the good kind of silence where the joy comes from listening to loved ones reminisce about magical trips in youthful bodies that weren't failing.

At the counter, Geoff rejoined the mother and daughter and dropped three more ice cubes in Valerie's glass. The clinking sound seemed to bring her back to the present.

"Thank you, darling." Valerie had smiled at Geoff. "I hardly slept last night. I was so amazed at how you two hosted such a wonderful party." She stared at them with a look that said she wasn't just making small talk. "It was so different. There was such an . . . energy. An excitement in the house. Upbeat. Just fabulous."

"Wow, Mom. You used the word 'energy.'" Poppy grinned. "That's so cutting-edge." She gently rubbed the top of her mother's shoulder.

"I mean, really . . . I can't explain it. You both brought such joy to everyone," Valerie murmured, and her eyes filled with emotion.

Geoff reached for Poppy's hand as they stood shoulder to shoulder.

Valerie noticed the tender exchange and centered her cocktail napkin under her glass. She looked up at Geoff—her eyes too blurry from emotions. "Geoff." She paused and looked into his eyes. "I especially want to thank you"—her voice cracked—"for bringing Poppy back to us."

Poppy's eldest two daughters, Kimmy and her family, as well as Kelly, lived in Chicago. Two weeks after Poppy's birthday party, I arrived at the grayish-white townhouse in the late afternoon. Nestled on a quiet maple-lined street, Kimmy's home was stroller-distance from downtown Downers Grove. Poppy's oldest daughter stood in her kitchen, in dark yoga pants, a workout top—a lime-green tank—and sandals. She gazed at her infant girl in her arms.

Kimmy laid the baby's head against her well-toned bicep and opened a drawer to retrieve a white kitchen towel. With a nimble move, Kimmy handed the cloth to her mother, put a pen in her mouth, and pulled out a large chart. "I'm just going to jot down the feeding times."

I watched the thirty-year-old mother and recalled the conversation Poppy had shared with Geoff about how Kimmy had persevered through an eating disorder when she was a teenager. It appeared that Kimmy had quickly developed the emotional skills needed to better manage the events of her life.

In her position as the director of exercise fitness, she oversaw more than one hundred instructors at a high-end Chicago health club. Kimmy mentioned that Oprah occasionally greeted her as she passed by. Poppy's daughter had made sensational progress, this healthy mother who deftly managed both herself and her full family life.

Geoff shared tea with Poppy's two-year-old granddaughter, Daniella. Poppy's second child, Kelly, just a bit over five feet, had arrived from work, her cherubic face framed with soft blond curls that fell just below her shoulders. Kelly's eyes—a cross between periwinkle and aqua with an abundance of dark lashes—sparkled when she first saw her mother and Geoff. Five two at the most, she tiptoed up to hug her mother and Geoff.

For the next couple of hours, Kimmy and Kelly shared their observations about the transition they'd recognized in their mother. Poppy held her youngest granddaughter and rested her cheek against Adrianna's head. She stroked the infant's back. *So human,* I thought. A maternal rhythm—up to the top and again from the base.

"Mom's usually happy, but this is a *different* kind of smile," Kelly said as she studied Poppy's face, like an artist when she draws a portraiture. "A smile that comes from deep within."

"The only smile I've ever known." Geoff put his arm around Poppy.

"Well, whatever the smile is, Geoff, I know Mom's different." Kelly stared at her mother, whose eyes teared up. Like a game of emotional tag, Kelly's eyes also filled. "Thank you, Geoff. You've made our mom ecstatic."

CHAPTER 37

# Perfect Timing

◦⁓◦

THE SELBY AQUATIC CENTER IN Sarasota, home to local, regional, national, and international competitions, featured one of the first pools in the country, called Myrtha, a fifty-meter-long pool with moveable bulkheads. I watched swimmers from all over the region warm up in the water, as arms and heads turned in a hypnotic rhythm.

Near the pool's edge, Poppy and Geoff sat. Poppy, in a light-blue tennis skirt and white Rollins T-shirt with a long tail she'd gathered in a flower-like knot at her waist, held a clipboard on her lap with the score sheet secured. Poppy crossed her legs, her pale-blue sandals already damp. "I love that you're here—timing with me. Thank you."

Under her red visor, her eyes reflected warmth, nostalgia, and an overwhelming sense of joy as she spoke with Geoff. "I've always done this alone," she murmured and looked at Geoff, as he adjusted his white-and-blue Rollins alumni hat.

He leaned forward on the chair, the lower half of his khaki shorts dampened from a swimmer's vigorous flip turn. "I *want* to be here with you. I love watching Molly. She has a powerful breaststroke. A strong competitor." Geoff sipped from his bottled water and looked at Poppy, and a concerned expression crept onto his face.

"You don't understand how special this is to me. To spend a day and a half here in Sarasota—timing for four hours at a noisy, sopping-wet venue." She slid her sandals on the puddled water on the deck. "I've never shared this . . . with anyone I care about, that is."

Geoff stroked her knee, a gesture to ward off tears. "Get used to it, Pops."

⁓◦

Molly panted at the edge of the pool in the lane next to Poppy and Geoff. She turned to squint at the digital scoreboard. On the clipboard, Poppy recorded the time of the swimmer in their lane and smiled at Molly. "Way to go, Molls," she mouthed.

Molly nodded a smile in acknowledgment, and water dripped from her tanned, muscular body as she rose from the pool.

"Nice race. You finished strong—held the other girl off." Geoff gave her a thumbs-up.

"Thanks, Geoff." She looked down. "My start wasn't great."

"I know." Geoff smiled. "But you looked confident when you got on that block. Really good focus. And you caught the gal in our lane and stayed out front." His voice was positive—filled with atta-girl praise.

Molly smiled at Geoff and headed to debrief with her coach.

Poppy rested the clipboard upright between their two chairs and relaxed against the hard plastic seat. "You know, Geoffrey, Molly's very different with you. When you cheer her on and comment on her swimming, she listens to you. I have *no credibility*. Mothers are always supposed to say, 'Good job.'" Poppy shifted to face Geoff. "I *do* know my daughter, however. She appreciates your comments. She respects you, Geoffrey."

"Well, I'm honest. She swam well. She won." Geoff glanced toward Molly, her towel draped over her shoulders. A swimmer's cape. "Did you see her in the zone before the race?"

Poppy reached for Geoff's hand. "This is different today. I've not seen this kind of confidence with Molly. Not until now." Poppy smiled. "I attribute that to you."

"It's us. *Our* energy." Geoff squeezed Poppy's hand. "In my mind, I expected Molly to win. Maybe she picked up on that." Geoff looked over at Molly as she laughed with her teammates.

"And timing. How many times have we synced our watches exactly? To the one one-hundredth of a second?"

"Twelve." Poppy wiggled her stopwatch. "Geoffrey that just doesn't happen."

"I'm not surprised we have perfect timing. Who's more in sync than us, Honch?"

# CHAPTER 38

# All Clear

~~

Two weeks later, on a Saturday morning in North Carolina, Poppy and Geoff chugged out on Lake Norman on *Big Daddy*—the twenty-two-foot pontoon boat and command center for the race committee at the Lake Norman Yacht Club. Poppy, Geoff, and a male club member paused in the center of the lake, where they, as committee members, prepared to drop anchor to set up the race course for the competition.

Geoff slowed the pontoon boat. He held his hand up to shield his eyes. "What'd you think, Charlie? This a good spot to set up the race course?"

A stocky man with thinning blond hair and wire-rimmed glasses, Charlie scanned the distance and looked to the north, to the direction of the prevailing wind. "Looks good. Plenty of room for good weather and leeward legs." He nodded.

"I'll throw out the anchor." Geoff shut off the engine and walked to the bow. "Pops," he said, as he turned. "Please grab that wind indicator, under the console."

She reached into the console and pulled out something that resembled a broken toy gun. "This?" She held up the wind indicator. Her deck shoes squeaked on the floor of the boat as she came forward. "I love that I have official duties." Poppy smiled.

Charlie removed his glasses and blew his breath on the lens. He looked pensive. "I can't believe you're leaving us." He scrubbed his glasses with the tail of his pale-gray T-shirt. "You've been here a long time, Geoff. What's it been? Twenty years?"

In a folding lawn chair, Geoff sat next to Poppy and affectionately rubbed her forearm. He rested his other arm on the chair's green vinyl webbing, which pulled against his skin, tickling. "Charlie, I've got a wonderful reason to leave." Geoff smiled at his friend and at Poppy. "I'm fulfilling my race committee duties. Today's my last day."

Poppy shifted slightly in her chair and turned to look at a motorboat passing a hundred yards away. She dipped her white visor lower over her eyes that now teared. *Oh dear God, this is torture. This morning, all those people in the clubhouse bemoaning his move to Sarasota. Annoyed I'm taking him away.* Her thoughts trickled out, her facial expressions in a tug-of-war.

On the slate's screen, I saw the Emotional Clock's hands at Four O'clock, Shame and Guilt.

*Why does every person immediately say how upset they are about Geoff leaving? Why isn't their first response, "Hey, Geoff, good for you, buddy. Glad you found happiness." Like I'm some sort of spellbinder who's hoodwinked him.*

As Poppy's last thought came to me, I felt her stomach twist in a mortar-and-pestle kind of grinding. She pursed her mouth and exhaled to settle her emotions. She shifted her gaze back to the two men, a faux smile affixed to her face.

Charlie stared at Poppy, his expression somewhat accusatory. "Really, today's the last time?" His cheeks flushed when he saw Poppy's fake smile vanish. He looked back to Geoff and spoke more slowly, his tone less harsh. "I know they have a good fleet of Scots at Sarasota Sailing Squadron." He forced a conciliatory smile. Charlie went to the bow to check the wind direction again. A redundant action to quell his awkwardness.

Poppy held a clipboard on her lap and turned sideways in the folding chair, her back to Geoff. She blinked back more tears.

Caught up in the excited charge in the air of a race day—the flirtatious dance in which the sailboats soon would engage—Geoff imagined himself out there as he'd been hundreds of times. His thoughts came out in rhythmic waves. *What a great day. I wish I could sail today. The right side of the course looks a little fresher. I see some puffs there.*

"We're good to go here, Charlie." Geoff gave a thumbs-up.

The two men went through the remainder of the starting sequence and signaled the start of the race. "All clear!" Charlie declared.

Geoff stood for a few moments until the fleet made their way upwind. "Isn't this cool, Honch?" He sat next to her, and his aluminum chair creaked. "That's how you start a race." He leaned forward and peeked under her lowered visor. "Pops?"

"I think I did this right." She handed him the clipboard without looking up.

Geoff took the board, glanced at it, and cocked his head to the side. "Is something the matter?" He bent down lower, his face beneath her visor.

Poppy shook her head. "It's no big deal. I'll tell you later."

*Geoff needs an empathy nudge,* I thought. I saw a dark spot on the water, a puff of wind to carry my nudge to Geoff. I wanted him to consider how his friends' responses might've affected Poppy.

Geoff lifted his head and stood—senses alert. With his hand on the rail, he looked out for a moment, past the boats, past the race course. *Shit. What's she upset about?* I felt Geoff's stomach lurch as his thoughts tumbled out. He lowered his glasses and peered at Poppy. *I bet it's because everyone says they're going to miss me. I didn't think about how it might upset her. It's actually nice to hear.* He stared at Charlie. *In the clubhouse earlier, what had Brent and Janie said about me moving? Was I sure I'd thought this through? Wasn't this a rash decision? Well, this is the* right *decision. I'm very clear. I've never been any more sure about anything in my life.*

Geoff's expression returned to that happy place when he'd waved to friends before the race had started. *I don't have any second thoughts. Is that what she thinks? That I'll change my mind and stay here? Not a chance.*

He sat next to Poppy and leaned over the aluminum armrest. Geoff took her hand in his and kissed it. "Thanks for sharing this day with me, Honch."

~~

Geoff idled his Explorer in the parking lot. He faced Poppy. "Are you upset about what Charlie said? What others said inside? About me leaving here?"

Poppy nodded, as tears sprang to her eyes. "I know they all mean well—you're beloved here. It's just the way they *say* it," she whimpered. "Like I'm a bad person."

"These longtime friends don't mean anything by it, Honch." He wiped away her tear. "They understand why I want to be with you."

"Geoffrey, I don't think you even *hear* it. 'Do you know how *lucky* you are? He's leaving behind his life here.'" She rubbed the corners of her eyelids. "And at church, I'll hear *another onslaught* of shaming, blaming comments. How much the church, the choir, will miss you." Poppy's voice squeaked in a high pitch. "How can I take you away? 'Don't you know how much he's loved and appreciated here? How many years he's—'"

"Whoa, whoa, whoa. Honch, slow down. I want to make this really clear." Geoff leaned forward and caressed her shoulder. "All that means is I have great relationships here." He unfolded her arms. "No regrets, Pops. I'm finally with the love of my life."

Poppy stared at him and searched his face for any sign of remorse or sadness. She sniffled. "And yes, I *do know* how lucky I am," she said, and nodded.

Geoff grinned and brought her hand to his cheek. "How lucky *we* are."

# CHAPTER 39

# Halos All Around

~~~

"ALL SET FOR LABOR DAY Weekend, Honch. I've booked tickets for me and Jonathon." Geoff stared into his computer monitor as he gazed at Poppy's face.

Poppy nodded. "We have seven more days to go."

Geoff nodded. "I know, sweetie. We'll look forward to a long holiday weekend. Our kids will get to meet one another. I just want to make sure that Jonathon's okay with me making the move." Geoff straightened a small stack of papers on his desk. "That he's on the right track before I leave North Carolina."

"Of course," she said as a flash of guilt registered on her face. "I wouldn't want you to do anything or make any changes until you felt sure that he's all set."

The conflicting emotion identified, I'd understood why Poppy wrestled with guilt. As someone who put her children above all else, including herself, Poppy would never want Geoff to leave his son in a vulnerable spot to join her.

"He and I have already discussed it, Honch. We haven't nailed down any dates yet, but I'll continue to feel him out. Make sure he's on board." Geoff jerked his head toward Jonathon's room.

"Absolutely." Poppy's eyes widened. "You're talking with a mom who gets it about kids. They come first."

Geoff lifted his chin, and his gaze settled on Lake Davidson. "We haven't said too much about this, and I'm not going to say when or where, but I have a perfect idea for our engagement."

"My stomach just flipped, Geoffrey. I'm in heaven with anticipation."

When they signed off from Skype, Poppy remained at her desk and leaned back in her chair. Her thoughts sifted out. An assembly line of uncertainty. Not about their relationship or their love, but about the timing. Would all of the pieces fall into place? *What if he decides to propose at Christmas? Then we'd have to wait a long time to get married. Plan the wedding, etcetera. That'd be, like, next summer, almost a year from now.* Poppy chewed her inside lip, her eyes watering. *Will Dad be here next summer?*

~~~

Seven days later, on a Friday afternoon, in Sarasota's regional airport, travelers spotted a waving square sign with *Soulmate's Son* written on it. Poppy held up the sign as Geoff and Jonathon exited the terminal at the Sarasota airport. Geoff shook his head and looked at Jonathon's hazel eyes for his son's response to the bobbing handmade sign.

"I want to be sure you saw my special sign." Poppy waved it in front of Geoff and Jonathon, whose face had turned crimson.

"I saw it. Pretty hard to miss." Jonathon smirked and glanced behind him. A furtive look on the off chance he might know someone in Sarasota to further his embarrassment.

"I'm so excited to see you guys!" Poppy beamed.

"Hi, Pops." Geoff encircled Poppy in his arms and kissed her on the lips.

Poppy reached up to hug Jonathon. "Molly and George are at home. They can't wait to meet you!"

Jonathon's long arms stretched out above Poppy's shoulders and made a partial circle, as if his arms weren't sure of the hug protocol for his father's college sweetheart and now modern-day love interest. In mid-hug, he lowered his head on his six-two frame, his smile in a permanent grin. A mocking grin. I couldn't tell if it was due to his own awkwardness or if it was the derisive look that many young adults and teens display when around their parents—parents who are sometimes out of touch with the young adults' reality.

On the short drive from the airport to Poppy's home, she briefed Jonathon on the weekend events. "All very casual, Jonathon." Poppy lifted her eyes to the rearview mirror to gauge his expression, which appeared to her to be part tourist, part college skeptic, and part pensive. She smiled. "George is *especially thrilled* to have another guy in the house."

"I'm looking forward to meeting them, too." Jonathon turned his head around and stared out the back window at the enormous statue—*Unconditional Surrender.* "Wow," he said, as he turned around. "That's some kiss."

"People pose there all the time. It's probably our greatest tourist attraction. It's modeled on the famous World War II photograph." Poppy, too, snuck a requisite glance at the statue as if it were a look tollbooth one were required to see every time they passed. "A sailor and a nurse in Times Square to symbolize the end of the war."

"You two have already posed there, right?" Jonathon smirked, seemingly entertained by his own musings.

"No. As a matter of fact, Mister Wise Guy, we haven't." Geoff leaned around the headrest to face his son, with an expression that said, "Mind your manners."

"But what a great idea!" Poppy giggled. "We'll have *you* take the picture."

"Oh, great." Jonathon blushed.

They pulled into the driveway and unloaded Geoff's roller bag and Jonathon's navy duffle. George and Molly came to the front door grinning, their looks a combination of curiosity and camaraderie. The familiarity of kids who'd grown up together playing on a league soccer team.

For the next hour, the overarching common thread became their well-established ability for eye rolling. Whenever they heard any references to the Poppy and Geoff story, the three of them, like synchronized swimmers, rolled their eyes in perfect unison. Jonathon, who'd had to endure the giddiness of his father and his father's college sweetheart all by himself, finally found a commiseration connection.

"Aren't they ridiculous?" George gestured to Poppy and Geoff, who held hands on the couch. "Jesus. Were they like this when our mom visited North Carolina?"

Jonathon nodded. "Yep, just like now." He stood next to George and folded his long arms across his chest. Two guys in lockstep.

"How many times have you heard *the story*?" Molly wiggled her face forward as if it were a zooming camera lens. "The Soulmates," she mocked.

"I've lost count," Jonathon quipped. His mouth turned into an upward curve.

"C'mon, let's go to the pad. I can't take much more of this." George tilted his head toward the garage and a let out a pretend disgusted sigh from his smiling mouth.

"Nothing like a video game to instantly connect kids, right?" Poppy rested her head on Geoff's shoulder.

"Like an international language teens share." Geoff stroked her back. "Video games and syrupy parents to bond them."

A half hour later, Molly burst in the kitchen in mock protest. "It's *so* not fair"—she whirled her head around to the two boys behind her— "for you two to gang up on me. I've never played *Halo* before. You guys have played hundreds of times."

"Just admit you suck." George baited his sister.

"We weren't really *even trying*," Jonathon snickered. "I only used one finger on the controller."

"You guys are mean. I'm *not* quitting." Molly refilled her ice water from the filtered spigot and lifted her chin with renewed confidence. "I want to try again."

"This is great." Poppy smiled at Geoff, as she separated romaine leaves into a large wooden bowl. "They're already at it. Like siblings."

Geoff balled up ground beef and formed hamburger patties. "This is a new phenomenon for Jonathon. He's relaxed. I can tell by his face."

⌒૭

Two hours later, after rushing through the grilled hamburger dinner where George and Jonathon continued their verbal assault on Molly's primitive video game skills, the three kids continued their game, *Halo*. Although Molly had improved in the few hours they'd played, George made sure to assert his gaming prowess.

"Molly still can't touch us." George grinned at Jonathon as the three marched out of the garage. "It's great to have some more testosterone in the house. Jesus, dude, you have no idea what's it like to grow up with three sisters."

"Oh, like you've had it rough being the only boy. Gimme a break." Molly threw a damp paper towel at him. George saw it from the corner of his eye and, in one motion, caught it, crumpled it, and tossed it into the trash bin.

Jonathon looked amused as he observed the brother-sister exchange. "I could play with my eyes closed. Maybe then you'd have a chance, Molly."

George high-fived Jonathon. "Nice one, man. It's great to have you here."

"Stop." Molly grinned at Jonathon. "Okay, fine. How 'bout we go swimming, then?" Molly squinted and made her eyes slit into a challenge. "Let's see how well you guys do against me in the pool. Underwater laps."

"You'll lose there, too, Molly." George guzzled his water. "C'mon, Jonathon. We got this." He motioned for Jonathon to follow him into his room.

In George's room, drawers banged shut. A conspiracy in the works.

Poppy and Geoff finished the dishes. With the damp kitchen towel on her shoulder, Poppy turned toward Geoff. "I wasn't worried about Molly and George, but Jonathon—he's quiet. I didn't know how comfortable he'd be. What do you think?"

236

"I didn't know, either, but look at them." He handed Poppy a china platter he'd just washed. Geoff smiled as he looked out the kitchen window to the lanai and the pool. After dusk, the only light glowed from the inside of the pool. On the ceiling of the lanai, the circle of light created a ringed prism, a rippled aura of three youthful lives filled with levity and laughter.

# CHAPTER 40

# Third Time's a Charm

GEOFF, TO HONOR HIS BROTHER on September 11, sailed in a regatta with a longtime family friend in Michigan. The next day, the day he'd envisioned for two months—the day his wildest dreams were fulfilled—was September 12, *a new day*. The day he proposed to Poppy.

I witnessed this one perfect moment of joy. It was one of those mornings when the air is crisp and light multiplies as it bounces off the water. In the bedroom, Geoff had pulled back the eyelet curtains in the lakeside cottage and breathed, "Look at this sunrise, Honch." With his right arm around her back, the satin Natori nightie silky against his fingertips, he spoke. "September 11 is significant. It is its own day. Just as this morning is the start of a beautiful new day"—Geoff nodded toward the sunlit window— "with this gorgeous sunrise." He smiled at Poppy as his eyes brimmed.

"Today marks the beginning of a chapter of a new life together . . ." He slid to a kneeling position in front of Poppy, a ring cupped in his left hand. "If you'll marry me." Geoff's tears dropped onto his cheeks. He gently held Poppy's hand as he slid the ring he'd chosen on her finger.

Poppy's eyes watched his hands slide the three-stoned diamond ring onto her finger—the culmination of one billion seconds of waiting. An idea created by two twenty-one-year-olds' naïve anticipation of a mercurial dream, from a college encounter—when only a mere wisp of the possibility of soulmates existed.

Poppy visibly shook—nodding at first—unable to speak. Tears rolled steadily down her cheeks like the previous days' raindrops. "Oh," she breathed. "Of course I'll marry you." She flung her arms around him. "I'm so happy, Geoffrey."

Thirty-two-years worth of emotion filled the lakefront room. With Poppy and Geoff, I experienced an exchange of an ethereal emotion. The kind of elevated emotional state about which musicians will forever write songs and poets will eternally record sonnets.

Most people dream of, yet rarely experience, this kind of moment. A moment that contains a lifetime of happiness, that makes time irrelevant.

A love. The kind of love the poets called "evermore" and the heavens weep for, when it happens.

~~~

In the evening, on their return from the sailing regatta—after they'd spoken to all of the kids and shared their engagement—the acute contrast in the US Airways boarding area in the Detroit airport made even me pause. Poppy and Geoff, as if they'd just been announced prom king and queen, floated in at a crowded Gate 43. They carried their roller bags, and also enormous the joy that exploded from them.

A love lost, and now found, could not be contained. Their expressions radiated smiles that would have made their cheeks, if they could speak, ask for a rest. They set their luggage upright next to a support column and giggled for no obvious reason. Poppy looked around at the crowded gate area and searched the faces, looking to share their bursting news with anyone. Like she was holding a sign that said, *Please ask me why we're so happy!*

Yet, nameless people sat on crumb-covered vinyl seats, their carry-on bags and backpacks next to them as warnings to find another place to sit. Men who traveled out Sunday night for Monday morning conferences. Their Shar Pei faces sagged under the weariness of the weekly grind. Harried families returning home, baby strollers and sticky-fingered runaway toddlers who'd skipped their afternoon naps to get to the airport on time. Restless, disengaged couples reading books. Nora Roberts for her, Tom Clancy for him. Romance vs. action.

Geoff took both of their roller bags to a quieter, adjacent gate area. "Do you want to try your parents again?"

Poppy nodded and thought of her dad. *I hope we plan a wedding date and he'll be there.* Her eyes filled with a different kind of tears, and I felt the opposite end of her emotional spectrum.

Through the Empathic Bridge, a memory surfaced in her thoughts of an eleven-year-old Poppy, playing the piano at a recital in the second-floor ballroom of the Women's Club of Milwaukee. Poppy imagined her then-forty-four-year-old father, George Terris, slowing as he climbed the stairs—two at a time—because he was a few minutes late. And the melody he'd heard—he'd explained to Poppy later—obviously performed by a professional pianist or a much older student, because it was *too good* for a young girl.

Her small fingers stretched and floated on the piano keys, right hand over the left as the familiar notes of Beethoven's "Für Elise" filled the hall. Poppy recalled herself as she glanced up when she saw her father in the doorway. A shiver of glee had run up from her heart to her hands. *Dad made it after all.* She'd tried not to grin because serious performers did not do that. But she couldn't help it.

She thought of herself as a nine-year-old, sitting on a one-mittened hand at Lambeau Field in Green Bay, Wisconsin, and staring into the Styrofoam cup at the dark chocolate residue from her third helping of hot chocolate. Her father, vibrant in spite of the below-zero temperatures in the Frozen Tundra, had worn different headgear from his current beret. A gentleman's fedora, a virgin wool plaid classic, burgundy, black, and white, and silk lined. With one arm around Poppy's right shoulder, and the other, gloved hand on her left arm, he'd vigorously rubbed. "You sure you're warm enough, honey?" he'd asked, his voice hearty and strong. Poppy nodded cocoa-lined lips and beamed up at her father. "I'm just great. I love this, Dad," she'd said and turned from his caring eyes to watch Bart Starr throw to number 86, Boyd Dowler.

Poppy, still remembering her youth, dialed her parents' number.

"Mom? Hi." Poppy's face relaxed into relief. "We've been trying to reach you." She cupped her other ear—an unsuccessful attempt to diminish the noise around them.

"Pops? Pops? Hi, sweetie." Valerie spoke loudly. "Is everything okay with you? Where are you? Are you home yet?" Poppy's mother, an archetypal mother, bombarded her with questions—continual inquiries without a break for answers.

In a full voice, Poppy said, "We're at the gate at the airport. We . . . yes, the trip was great. And Mom…yes, Geoff sailed well. Uh-huh." Poppy nodded to her mother's repeated questions and raised her eyebrows at Geoff— the *I-can't-get-a-word-in-edgewise* look.

"Mom, we wanted to tell you…yes, it's on time." She laughed. "And wait… yes, they were darling hosts." Poppy's laugh exploded out in a single burst. "I've tried to reach you also, because…yes, we rented a car." She shook her head at Geoff and held the phone for him to hear the continuous investigative barrage. She put the phone back to her ear slowly. "Mom, wait! I have to something to tell you. Is Dad right there?" Poppy nodded the confirmation to Geoff. "Geoff and I are engaged!"

"Oh, I'm so happy!" Valerie raised her voice to a near-shout. "George, honey, Poppy and Geoff are getting married!" A scuffled noise on the phone, and Valerie exclaimed, "Oh, we're both so thrilled. Here, Dad wants to say something." Another sandpaper sound, and George Terris came on the line.

"Pops? Hi, honey. I'm so happy for you," George Terris said—his robust voice belying his physical condition. "Really happy."

Poppy's eyes filled with fresh tears. "Thanks, Dad." Her lips cobbled together to make a smile. "We're beyond happy."

"Tell Geoff I say hi. That I congratulate him. Both of you. I love you, baby," he said, his tone a caress. "Okay, here's Mom."

"I love you, too, Dad," Poppy said, her "I love you" suspended in midair.

George Terris was highly empathic, I'd realized. Very sensitive to—*and of*—others. While Poppy may have wondered if her father had heard her loving response, I didn't worry. With George Terris' keen intuition, he knew the words she'd speak, even before she'd said them.

When Poppy ended the call, she stared at the cell phone in her hand. She traced the screen with her finger, as if to keep the connection with them a bit longer. Her lips seemed to fight with each other. A tug-of-war— joy vs. coming loss.

Geoff called his parents to share the news. Poppy's thoughts wandered. Her smile slid and softened into bittersweet. Her thoughts eked out. *I love those treasured afternoons with him. Tuesdays with Dad—Thursdays, too.* Her mouth curved upward at her play on Mitch Albom's book, *Tuesdays with Morrie.* She thought of her father's words when, before their trip, her father had shared business stories and successes. And where George Terris had smiled and said twice, "So proud of you, honey. Keep it up."

In the near-empty gate, Poppy looked up at Geoff, as he finished the we're-getting-married call with his parents. She caressed his shoulder, and her mouth curved into a solid smile from the timeline of emotions she'd just experienced.

CHAPTER 41

# Shadow of a Doubt

~

IN THE WEEKS FOLLOWING THEIR engagement, Poppy and Geoff talked every day—first thing in the morning, lunchtime, in the evening after work, and before bed. Plans slid into place like Chicago's Wabash Avenue bascule bridge, an automated drawbridge that seamlessly operates quickly and with little energy.

The night before Geoff left Davidson to tow *Misty* to Sarasota, Poppy murmured into the phone, "We must live the law of attraction, where things are easy—they flow and fall into place."

~

Poppy, Geoff, George, and Molly unloaded Geoff's belongings from both his car and his Geoff's now-famous sailboat, *Misty*. Several days earlier, Poppy cleared space on a storage rack in the garage for sails, water skis, and boating gear. In her room, she emptied five dresser drawers for Geoff's clothing. Next week, he'd make the final trip to their shared home.

At the kitchen counter, Poppy rubbed Geoff's back. "Was it hard to say good-bye to all of your friends at the yacht club?" she asked softly.

"You and I have been very focused on making sure Jonathon was settled physically and emotionally with my move, but I didn't give that kind of attention to my friends." Geoff slid onto the barstool and sighed. "It's really hard, Honch. Twenty years of memories. A long emotional journey. Losing Twig. Leaving the club."

Geoff rested his hands on his thighs as his back rounded into an exhale. "Walking away from sailing, getting *Misty*. Rebuilding her. Rejoining the club." Geoff looked out the dining room French door to the lush backyard beyond the lanai and pool. "And that wonderful time in 2003 that I sailed in the North Americans with Dad." Geoff looked down at the ice cubes in the bottom of the glass. "Winning again with *Misty*, and now, leaving Davidson." His voice cracked. "I've had a wonderful history with that place. Many long-standing friendships," he whispered.

As Poppy listened, swollen teardrops threatened to fall onto her black shirt. She shook her head. "I can only imagine how hard it was." Her lower lip quivered, and her thoughts emerged. *I hate to see him sad. I hope he doesn't come to resent me.*

From the side, Geoff stared at Poppy and sensed the shift in her energy. "Pops, I don't want you to think for a second I have regrets." He swiveled to face her on the barstool. "Without a shadow of a doubt, I'm exactly where I want to be." He jiggled her knee as if his motion could shake away her unwanted thoughts. "With you, the love of my life."

Via Skype in the following days, emotion emanated from both of them through pixilated sadness. The slate chronicled Geoff's events from earlier in the evening when he'd stopped in to say good-bye at choir rehearsal. It showed him holding up the college sweethearts picture from Rollins, as his quaking hand jiggled the photo. With emotion clogging his throat, he'd hugged the choir director and patted his back several times.

As if their minds and hearts were in the spin cycle of a washing machine, I felt the swirl of emotions from both of them. Just as everyone knows not to stop a washing machine during the spin phase, Poppy knew enough to allow Geoff to cycle through his emotions. Yet transitional space, like soaked clothing in the washer drum, is wet, heavy, and hard to manage.

Poppy wiped away another tear, and her diamond engagement ring caught Geoff's attention. She straightened, and her exhale signaled a renewed resolve.

As if the whirring sound had died down from the emotional spin cycle, Geoff leaned closer to the monitor, his expression solemn, *Uncle Sam wants you* serious. "I know, Honch, beyond a shadow of a doubt, that I want to join you there. Marry you."

# CHAPTER 42

# Eureka

~⁓

THE PINE TREE FORESTS AND lowlands of South Carolina, a blur of green-ish-brown along the I-95 corridor, gave motorists a lackluster landscape. Between Columbia, South Carolina, and Savannah, Georgia, the express-way seemed monotonous and made the two-and-a-half-hour drive drag.

Geoff's U-Haul labored along and passed dreary, often dilapidated roadside stands. The noise of the engine, the transmission, and the loud whine of the restrictive speed device—the engine's governor—and the slug-gish speed of the vehicle, eliminated the possibility of listening to the radio. With no CD player, the truck was beyond bare bones. The only luxury in the boxed vehicle was air conditioning—with depleted Freon. The U-Haul's in-terior emitted an aroma of sweat, cigarettes, and beer that seeped through the cab's congested vents.

The Empathic Bridge appeared as the same color as the scenery, a dull seaweed green. Even the sides of the bridge drooped and mirrored Geoff's mood.

He'd said good-bye to Jonathon. *Sort of.*

Even though Geoff had set up all the details for his son to stay with his mother until school resumed in two months, he could hardly speak. Geoff's arms had hugged his son—fingertips pressed against Jonathon's back—as if to imprint his heart on Jonathon's chest and leave it with his son. Geoff's upper body had shaken—convulsed. And from behind, I couldn't tell if he was laughing or crying. *But I knew.* Aching tears had racked his frame. As Jonathon hugged his father, his long arms had draped over Geoff's back like loose suspenders.

It'd taken Geoff one tank of gas and several hours to steady his breath-ing and regain his emotional equilibrium. His phone had rung, and al-though he hadn't heard it above the roar of the engine, he'd seen the cell screen illuminate with the caller's name: *Poppy.*

"Geoffrey? Hi. How did it go this morning?" Her voice softened. "With Jonathon."

"Hi, sweetie. What? I can barely hear you," Geoff bellowed. "It's so loud in here."

"Oh." Poppy cleared her throat and spoke louder. "How did it go this morning with Jonathon?"

Geoff glanced out his window and took a breath as he prepared to re-visit his tearful morning. "I couldn't even speak, Pops." He gripped the wheel tightly as the truck's steering wandered like a lazy eye. "It hit me all at once. I sobbed as I said good-bye to Jonathon. To the life I've known for twenty years." Geoff's voice cracked as he relived the scenario. "I hardly saw anything as I drove out of the gas station where we said our farewells."

"I'm so sorry, sweetie." Poppy put her palm on her throat. "I wish I could help. Be with you now."

"I know, Honch . . ." His voice cut out, as the emotional wound opened again.

"You know I'm with you. You're always in my heart, Geoffrey." Her words broke off.

"I love you, too, Pops." Geoff shoved the cell phone against his ear and shouted. "Sweetie? If you're talking, I can barely hear you." He exhaled a big rush of air. "This damn thing is so big. Takes up the whole lane. I only see with the side mirrors. There's no rearview mirror. People pass me all the time. I can't go more than sixty-five miles an hour. It's like driving in-side of a friggin' vacuum cleaner."

Poppy thought of a large Eureka vacuum cleaner on four wheels. I re-alized she had no prior experience or existing schema for the space and shape of the inside of a U-Haul truck, nor for the roads on which Geoff was traveling.

Her lack of a frame of reference added to her already high level of angst. Her inability to imagine him in a vacuum-cleaner-like truck brought her a feeling of disconnection. I felt her pulse quicken, followed by an eleva-tor lurch.

"Oh no. I'm so sorry." Poppy raised her voice. "Here I thought I'd bring some comfort. Make the drive a little less lonely for you." Facing the window to the street, Poppy kneeled on her living room couch and fingered the sea-green tassels on the drapes. "Where are you now?"

"Shit, I don't know. Somewhere above Columbia. It's really distracting for me to talk, Pops. I know you want to help, but there's nothing to do right now." Geoff shouted to be heard. "Just let me drive. Figure out the traffic."

"Okay, sure," Poppy said, a throwaway comment that filled in the uncomfortable space. She shuddered, upset that Geoff was upset, upset that she could provide no comfort, at the crossroads of people-pleasing and transitional space.

In frustration, he shook the cell phone in the air, as his face contorted into an Edvard Munch–looking silent scream. "I'll call you when I stop, sweetie, okay?" Geoff said, in a measured tone, his negative emotion not directed at Poppy.

"Sure. Drive safely. I love you," Poppy meekly called out. Her words, unable to anchor themselves, floated aimlessly in the noisy cab.

~⁀⁓

At noon on Saturday, Molly stood in the driveway as Geoff, who leaned halfway out the door to navigate, backed the U-Haul up toward the house.

"Hand it over." Molly motioned a hurry-up wave to Poppy, who reached in her Lululemon pant pocket for her cell phone. "I know you want pictures," she added, and rolled her eyes at her mother.

I felt a powerful mix of emotions that emanated from both Poppy and Geoff. The emotions squirted out like water through a nozzle on a hose—relief, first and foremost, followed by excitement, wonderment, exhaustion, and joy. The ten-hour drive, broken up by Geoff's overnight stay in Savannah, had helped him to process his transition. Time was an emotional balm. The twenty-four-hour span from Charlotte to Sarasota had allowed Geoff to leave behind some of his raw angst.

"You're here, you're here, you're here!" Poppy squealed, waving her *Soulmate* sign as she ran to meet the pockmarked white-and-orange truck. Geoff, like a folded measuring stick, uncrimped his body from the grimy cab of the U-Haul. Poppy rushed over to greet him as if he were a soldier who'd just returned from Afghanistan.

"Ahh, Honch." He straightened and arched his back. "God, I'm glad to be out of that thing." His arms stretched around her back. "It's good to finally be here, sweetie."

On her tiptoes, Poppy reached up and found Geoff's lips under his moustache. She closed her eyes, moisture at the corners. "Welcome home, Geoffrey."

~⁀⁓

Near midnight, they headed to bed after they unloaded the U-Haul, had dinner, and unpacked Geoff's clothing and home furnishings. Geoff, Poppy, and the two kids, George and Molly, were a study in efficiency. In less than two hours, they'd unloaded all of Geoff's belongings and deposited the empty truck at a drop site.

The light of the moon peeked in between two slats of the vertical blinds. Poppy blinked and nestled her head in the crook of Geoff's arm. "It's a good thing you brought both recliners. My kids love them." She lifted her head and pushed back her hair. "I still can't believe you're here for good," she murmured, as she stroked his chest.

"Me, too, Honch. The drive in that truck felt brutal." He caressed her shoulder, and his eyelids fluttered shut.

Poppy propped herself up on her elbow and stared at the moonlit silhouette of her fiancé. "Do you realize that we get to sleep together from now on?"

"Mm-hmm." Geoff stroked her hair, and his half-asleep voice whispered, "G'night, Pops, I love you."

~◞

The clock read 4:17.

The Empathic Bridge was now a sickly yellow-green. It'd been a seaweed green during Geoff's time in the truck and had changed to an Oz-like vibrant emerald green when he'd wrapped his arms around Poppy upon his arrival.

I jiggled my slate. *Is there a problem with the color output of the bridge?*

Suddenly, I felt Geoff's heartbeat race—an elevator lurch. He blinked, his eyes wide. He turned to gaze at Poppy and saw her sleeping profile as she lay on her back, her dark hair splayed on the white pillow. The moonlight cast enough ambient light through the vertical blinds to show the contrast.

"Pops, you awake?" Geoff whispered.

Poppy, who had the instinct to wake on demand—the built-in sensor of mothers—sat upright. "What is it, Geoffrey?" she also whispered, an edge of alarm in her tone.

"I just woke up and felt"—he gulped air— "the weight of all of this. The move and all. I gave away a lot of my stuff. Even though it wasn't sentimental, it was still *my stuff.*" His sienna-colored eyes produced tears that rolled onto the edge of his pillow. "I mean, I appreciate that you made space for me."

He groped for her hand on the top of the comforter. "I have my clothes, but I feel like . . . like . . . I don't *exist* anymore. That anything that was mine is *gone*. I look around, and I don't see any sign of *me* here." Geoff heaved a sob.

"And I wouldn't change anything because I'm excited to be here with you." He squeezed her hand. "To share my life with you forever," he whispered. "But there's nothing here that says *me*."

Even though she'd been startled awake, Poppy remained calm, her heart rate normal.

At first, Poppy said nothing. She stroked his shoulder and wiped his forming tears before they hit the pillow. With her usual tendency to tear up whenever she witnessed another's tears, I found it surprising that Poppy didn't cry.

As I watched the two of them lay there—Geoff prone, as Poppy caressed his shoulder in rhythmic strokes—I realized the powerful emotion from Geoff. The feeling, the raw fear of losing himself. Poppy displayed what Phillip referred to as *Unconditional Loving Detachment*. The ability to be fully present, yet not hijacked by any fear. Like a huge, calm empathy container that's safe.

"Go on," Poppy urged him gently.

"Who am I here, Pops? Yes, I'm your fiancé and college sweetheart. But when I arrived here yesterday for good"—his body shook—"it felt overwhelming. The realization that I've walked away from everything that defined me, my son, my relationship with him. Friends I've known for twenty years." His raspy voice choked out the last few words.

Poppy placed her hand on top of his and held it still. Steady. "Geoffrey, you won't stop being a father any more than you'll stop being a sailor, performer, singer, or friend." She leaned forward so that the light from the slatted blinds now shined more directly onto Geoff's pillow.

"I know, Pops. I know. It's just that . . ." He waved his other hand aimlessly in the air. "I look around here, and even though you've shared everything with me, there's no physical evidence of me. No old photos, no—" Geoff's voice broke.

"Oh my gosh, sweetie." Poppy sat up straight. "Of course we'll place your things here. Photos, sailing artwork. Pictures. Family legacies. The Fairbanks rocking chair. And your special trophies. We'll put these items and important symbols out, wherever you want them, okay?" Poppy smoothed back the hair on his forehead.

"Okay." Geoff sniffled with a childlike nod, as if Poppy had just opened the closet door and proved there was no bogeyman.

"And we'll go to the Sailing Squadron today. Introduce *Misty* to her new home. Maybe even take her for a sail on Sarasota Bay." Poppy brightened and now sat cross-legged on top of the bed. She shifted her hips. "Geoffrey, believe me. I know all about identity and connection. I understand the need to be—*and feel*—really connected here."

Geoff swallowed and wiped the corners of his eyes with the pillowcase.

"We can join the church choir if you want, too. I can hardly sing but can pull off lip-synching like a pro." Poppy leaned forward so Geoff could see her smile.

"Okay." He nodded and steadied his breathing. "That'd be good. I'd like to see the photos out. Like on the family room table. Of Twig and me. And my mom and dad. Maybe even that replica of *Misty*." He looked in Poppy's eyes, his expression asking if that'd be alright.

"Yes, the *Misty* model. Of course," Poppy said, her tone like a museum curator's. "We'll put her in a *safe* place."

Geoff turned toward Poppy and leaned on one elbow. "And maybe the hand-painted blue-and-white bowl from the '91 Carolina Districts."

As Geoff's demeanor shifted, I realized that his ability to access cherished memories from his successes reinforced core parts of his identity.

The clock read 5:03.

My slate illuminated: *Eureka! When one diffuses those discordant emotions by archiving positive memories, hope topples fear.*

# CHAPTER 43

# Hearts at Home

~⁓

THE EMPATHIC BRIDGE SHINED THE color of a lush field of lavender in the Provence town of Coustellet, proof of Geoff's acclimation to his new life. The feeling of home in his heart.

In a few hours Geoff would return from a business trip after visiting a customer in Miami. The "meet Geoff" party at Valerie and George's home the next day occupied both of their minds. And hearts.

Poppy, just back from teaching at Ringling College, paused in front of the belongings the two of them had integrated into their home. There was the blue-and-white bowl, a meaningful sailing trophy. A large watercolor of a Flying Scot hung on the most prominent wall of the family room. Geoff's framed photos, intertwined with Poppy's, gave the room a new dimension. A completion of a family. As if something or someone long lost, almost forgotten, had walked into the home and had opened the windows and curtains to a brand-new view. A new perspective.

And in the bedroom was the heirloom family rocker that had been in Geoff's condo in Davidson, to set a tone of fulfillment. Of a legacy once lost. Sweetly and irrevocably reappearing. All of the items that indicated *Geoff* and looked as if they'd been there the whole time.

~⁓

*Glowing.*

Every one of the forty guests who entered Valerie and George's home on Thursday night used that word to describe Poppy. People who'd known Poppy as upbeat and happy commented on the distinct intensification in her radiance. She not only looked radiant, many told her she looked "ten years younger." And "so happy."

After the last guest departed, Poppy and Geoff stood in the large walkway between the ten-by-twelve dining room—now used as an elegant bar—across from the living room and family room. The fireplace mantle displayed antique vases and plates. Blue-and-white china figurines quietly told stories of artisans who'd developed their craft throughout life-times and throughout history. A collection of Delft, Japanese Imari, and Staffordshire, displayed in two massive wooden corner display units in the living room, conveyed a silent and enduring testament to Valerie's gift for interior design.

During the energy-filled party, I saw myself as novice Jesse, when I'd just started out as a choreographer at Rollins. When I'd watched them as they jitterbugged in Mayflower Hall at the Phi Delt House, Geoff joyously swinging Poppy around. And both with longer, floppier hair, and hands entwined in a seamless grip. The hair had been longer, yes, yet the dynamic was the same. They had flowed and floated, as sorority and fraternity friends watched with an innocent fascination. And tonight, although not dancing, onlookers had watched them with fairytale wonderment.

Even Poppy and Geoff's parents meshed beautifully. Jean and George Spencer and Valerie and George Terris shared similar values and characteristics: poise, graciousness, and kindness were at the top of the list. All four individuals deeply understood every loving nuance of their respective mate. They were part of a generation that inherently believed that caring for loved ones came without thought—and was the singular most purpose-ful thing in life.

George Terris sat on the sofa, crossed his sockless, Gucci-clad left ankle over his right knee, the crease in his battleship gray trousers still evident. He wore a champagne-pink dress shirt under a nubby cadet-gray textured silk blazer, and a dark-navy beret with a custom-made ear covering, with a flap to both conceal and shield his left ear. The beret, once a keepsake of a life well-lived, camouflaged the visible signs on his head of fifteen rounds of radiation.

Poppy's thoughts snuck out. *Maybe Dad can make it to our wedding on February 19. See us get married. Maybe even walk me down the aisle? Even though we're about to lose Dad, maybe we can bring some bright relief. A little joy in his battle.* Poppy's lips quivered as the next thought came. *Please don't let him suffer any more. I want him to feel good.*

Poppy went over to him and sat on the edge of the couch, re-summon-ing the bliss of the evening. "Hi, Dad."

Her father began to shift to allow Poppy room to sit.

Poppy rested her hand on his arm. "Don't move. I just wanted to say hi." She feather-kissed her father on the cheek. "I love you, Dad," she whispered in his good ear.

George's green eyes sparkled, a magical instant where the joyous energy of the party, and the love of family and friends that had surrounded him with the connection to fond memories and joyous events, offered him a reprieve. A moment of intimate normalcy.

Poppy's father smiled and lowered his left hand—the always-protective sentry—and reached over to hers. A strong hand that'd always been there to protect her. "Hi, honey." He patted her hand three times. "I love you, too, baby."

CHAPTER 44

# Baggage

⤙

IN FRONT OF THE SIX-THOUSAND-GALLON Mote Marine Aquarium on the concourse level of the Sarasota airport, Poppy bounced lightly on her toes, as if she had two-inch hydraulic lifts embedded in the balls of her feet. She loosely held her *Soulmate* sign between the two fingers of her left hand, the one with her cherished new engagement ring. The ring with the third-time's-a-charm three diamonds.

I furrowed my brow as I stared at the color on the Empathic Bridge. One side of the bridge was a vibrant green—expressing love in action— and the other side was a dingy yellow. Like it'd been washed in dirty lake water.

My slate made a notation: *My speculation is an imbalance. It appears Poppy's very excited about Geoff's arrival; however, Geoff feels some discord.*

"Discord?" I muttered. My thoughts went immediately to choreography nudges I might've forgotten. After all these years, I still had a somewhat raw—and guilty—memory about how misguided my strategies were when they'd first met. All the things I could've done but hadn't. All of the assumptions I'd made that they hadn't needed a choreographer. And of course, my focus on myself. My own desired success. I cringed now at my own memory, the shallowness of the inexperienced self.

I looked at Poppy, who was still smiling, like Christmas had already arrived for her.

The slate's screen looked like a Vegas slot machine. Rows and rows of words spun on the slate. *Geoff appears to be on edge. I'm still searching for cause. On the Emotional Clock, he's at Two O'clock: Anxiety.*

I focused on Poppy. She thought of her first airport meeting with Geoff nearly seven months ago. When Geoff had sauntered—more a walk of joy— up the ramp of the concourse to the main terminal of the Sarasota airport. When she had bounced up and down and held the *Soulmate* sign.

She spotted Geoff, who walked toward her, and the levels of her energy now rose even higher than the first airport meeting, if that was possible.

Geoff trudged like a caveman hauling a woolly mammoth back to the tribe. He'd finished his pre-Christmas business travel, and instead of looking like himself—the cheerful Geoff Spencer—he had a tinge of, well, Lee J. Cobb during his Broadway appearance in Arthur Miller's *Death of a Salesman.*

Poppy's sign bobbed and her bounce increased, until it turned into a little run to the authorized entry point. "Hi, Chief! I'm so excited to finally have you home." She enveloped him with a hug and closed her eyes as she rested her chin against his shoulder. Her sign squished against his full backpack.

Geoff's eyes darted around the concourse as though he was looking for cover. "Hi, sweetie. Let's move." Geoff steered her elbow forward.

Poppy moved toward the side to allow others to pass by. "How was your trip?" she asked, and she tried to match his quick pace—dangling the *Soulmate* sign in front of him again.

Bad thoughts toppled one upon the other as he walked with Poppy through the airport. As a sales manager, trained to evaluate, he did a postmortem on all his trips. He mentally went through his checklist, and the recall seemed heavier than his baggage: a harried Geoff as he'd driven around the Baton Rouge airport at ten thirty that morning; Geoff as he'd tried to find a gas station to return a rental car with a full tank, no drop-off attendant at the rental hub and no terminal shuttle service, which meant he had to haul all of his gear to the departure gates by hand.

The vivid memory throbbed with the aggravations of flight delays: the jammed-packed waiting gate at Baton Rouge Airport; a cramped CRJ700, a small regional jet; a late arrival in Charlotte; and his bag, the last one in the gate-check queue.

Dashing through the airport in his dress loafers, he'd had no time for Charlie, the shoeshine man who always noticed and said, "Hi, sugar," to the pretty women in the concourse. To catch his connecting flight, he'd sped past the US Airways Club, where he would've stopped for a moment of respite and a quick nibble. *If he'd had the time.* And even though he ran, he was still the last one to board the plane for his flight home to Sarasota.

He stopped picking through the wreckage of his recent trip long enough to recognize that Poppy was walking beside him. "Long. And not fun." He grunted.

Geoff walked faster, and as he did, he thought of the flight attendant who'd spilled Coke on his white shirt as she leaned across his aisle seat to the window passenger, who had his ear buds in, bursting out heavy metal. Geoff frowned as he recalled the parents who'd let a toddler behind Geoff's second-to-last-row seat open and close the tray table. It pounded against the back of Geoff's seat the way his head, and the veins underneath his skin, had pounded.

When he was close to home and his Poppy, the final indignity surfaced. The grand and mischievous sprite of all travelers had pounded a brass nail into the final leg of his travels. Geoff had to sit on the plane at the gate in Sarasota for an extra fifteen minutes as he waited for a gate agent to release the *prisoners*—passengers.

All of these images collided with one another in Geoff's head. Seven hours of travel. Geoff ignored Poppy's sign, his intense focus on the parking lot. One more piece of the puzzle in his are-we-home-yet picture.

"Did you park right outside baggage claim?" he muttered, more of a command that implied she better have.

"Yes, it's over there." Poppy pointed, and both her sign and her expression drooped. She tried to walk faster until eventually she was run-walking.

I felt her retreating heart. Her silent and immediate thoughts now formed the words and tumbled out. "You don't seem happy to be home." She looked at Geoff, and at her fast-moving feet, which appeared to tap out a beat that said, *Where's the fire?*

"I thought after being gone for the week, you'd be more excited to see me."

"I am, Poppy. I just want to get home." Geoff's words hit the air like water on hot asphalt. "I'm tired of traveling."

His sharp response sent her imagination into overtime, and it promptly spun out every kind of calamity and tragedy. A speeding list of thoughts that could not keep up with her feet and left a trail of uneven, dark-yellow and gray mists in the air.

*Even though traveling was hectic for him, shouldn't he still be happy to see me?* Poppy thought. *Maybe he didn't miss me? Maybe when he stopped off in Charlotte, he missed being there? Maybe, like I thought back in college, he doesn't care that much.* Poppy's thoughts piled up like Christmas bills in January, as she swooped down toward the right side of the Emotional Clock.

"So, how was your day?" Geoff asked a forced question. Polite, with an edge to it.

"Good. I finished up grading final exams. I saw two of my elderly clients this afternoon." Poppy got in the driver seat and started the car as she waited for Geoff to close the door to the back, where he'd stored his backpack and luggage.

*Jesus. Small talk? We're doing small talk?* Poppy's thoughts picked up pace and matched her heartbeat.

Geoff got in, sighed, and closed the door. Neither said anything until they'd reached the light facing the Ringling Museum—almost a mile from where she'd parked.

The entire Empathic Bridge morphed to a dull yellow, the color of a neglected swimming pool with low levels of chlorine and alkaline.

"So, what'll we do for dinner?" Geoff looked out his passenger window as he asked the question. He didn't look at Poppy, and I thought, *His way to clear his head and not taint Poppy's good spirits with his crummy day.*

"I thought we would have salmon for dinner. If that's okay?" Poppy said, her voice unsteady.

"Sure, that's fine." Geoff looked out the windshield and shook his head slightly at the tourists posing under the massive Unconditional Surrender statue. *More travelers. I'm still friggin' traveling. I just want to get home, unpack. Unwind. Argh.*

He looked at Poppy, who stared straight ahead, her hands at ten and two on the steering wheel. The joy of Geoff's arrival now squashed by his disharmony.

*Shit. Now she's probably upset because I'm not bubbly like she is. Or rather, was.* Geoff thought as he ventured into Four O'clock, Shame and Guilt.

Packed with his baggage from the flight, a heavy bone of guilt was lodged tightly against his lungs and his heart.

I felt Poppy tremble a little as they pulled in the driveway. She hurried to the back of her car to help with the suitcase.

"I got it," Geoff barked. "Just go unlock the door," his irritated voice commanded. "Please." He leaned dramatically back when he opened the back hatch, as if the door might somehow lash out at him.

Another heave of emotion, and Poppy's thought came out as a silent moan. *I just wanted to help.*

Geoff looked at Poppy, as she rummaged in her purse at the front door. Nicky, in the window, barked incessantly. His thoughts came out in a rant. *Just find the fucking keys in that black hole you call a purse, so I don't have to wait outside for another fifteen minutes while you dig around, and try not to ruin your manicure. Argh.*

My slate, in an attempt to lighten my spirits, imitated a Sotheby's auctioneer: *Do I hear Five O'clock from the man with the moustache? Yes, we have Five O'clock, Anger on the Emotional Clock!*

I swooped up the vaporous image from my slate and stuffed it into the planter at the front door. "Not funny. I need to get them to Six and quickly to Seven O'clock, Relief."

My slate displayed a sentence on the screen: *If it's any help, Poppy's keys are in the bottom of Poppy's bag.*

Poppy finally located her keys and opened the door. She stepped aside and let her angry fiancé pass through first.

Geoff wheeled in his bag, sloughed off his backpack as if it'd been filled with a dozen bricks, and dumped it next to his desk. On top of his desk, he glanced at a neat stack of unopened mail that Poppy had sorted by envelope size. He removed his cell phone, wallet, keys, and laptop and looked down at his ankles, where a wagging dog with a stuffed animal in her mouth—her show-and-tell toy—gently scratched at his feet.

"Nickynoodles. Hi girl!" Geoff knelt down and smiled for the first time since he'd gotten off the plane in Sarasota. "Ooooh, you want a belly rub?" He spun her rear legs like a dial and brought her closer to him. "Come here." He stroked the Shih Tzu's tummy and patted it a few times before he stood.

Zippy, Geoff's cat, silently came up behind Geoff and rubbed against his trouser leg both to mark Geoff as his and to welcome him home. "Hiya, Zip." Geoff left the pink belly of the dog and picked up Zippy. He cradled him upside down like an infant. Geoff kneaded his knuckles into the cat's ears, and the cat leaned into the massage as if he'd been waiting for this moment for weeks.

In the kitchen, Poppy pulled out a glass baking dish, and her nerve-racking interior monologue made her quiver. *So he's capable of showing enthusiasm for our dog. And cat. But not me. Maybe he doesn't love me as much as I love him.* She looked out the window into the backyard and stared at the fence. Her thoughts quickened. *Clearly the case. Nothing to do about it. You can't make someone care.* She shook her head to herself, and with a final tight squeeze of lemon onto the salmon, her last thought appeared. *I guess reconnecting with me is not important to him.*

Geoff hadn't noticed Poppy's whereabouts. He dragged his luggage into the bedroom, where his thoughts came out like dictation: *Luggage. Unpack. Sort dirty laundry. Change. Put suitcase away. Finally relax.* He looked up from his nearly empty suitcase on the luggage rack and just then realized Poppy wasn't nearby. *Maybe relax, if I haven't upset her too much. Shit.*

Poppy walked from the kitchen and quietly and stood in the bedroom doorway, under a sprig of red-and-green mistletoe, just as Geoff zippered the side pocket of his carry-on bag. He hastily picked up her love note from the bottom of the suitcase and clumped it together with his boarding pass, and gas and rental car receipts. He placed the pile on top of the wooden dresser.

He saw Poppy in the doorway and noticed the cold Propel bottle on the dresser—the one she'd had waiting for him in a cooler pack when she'd picked him up at the airport. *Dammit. Don't leave the bottle on the dresser. It might leave a ring.* Geoff's thoughts rushed out as he placed the condensing bottle on the receipts with the folded love letter on top.

Poppy's eyes filled with tears. *He didn't even acknowledge what I'd written. He hasn't even kissed me.* She wailed in her head and zoomed to Despair— Three O'clock—on the Emotional Clock.

Still in the doorway, her hand on the doorjamb, she cleared her throat. "I sent your mom and dad that package of art materials. They should get it tomorrow. And I got your shirts from the cleaners. And picked up the Claritin-D you'd wanted." Poppy looked like she was waiting for a gold star. At the very least, she wanted recognition that she was something other than his chauffeur.

"Thank you," Geoff said, his back to her. He groped the outer pockets of his suitcase.

She turned as if dismissed.

Geoff put his suitcase in the garage, placing it in the empty slot next to Poppy's. He wouldn't need the suitcase for business travel again until January. As he passed Nicky on the couch, he stopped and slowly petted her head. He booted up his PC and sat down at his desk, unaware of the hand-made Santa dressed in furry white that sat on a shelf above his computer. He sorted through the mail and tossed the envelopes in a haphazard pile on his desk, like a sloppy Blackjack dealer flipping Bicycle cards.

"How're Molly and George?" Geoff called out as he clicked through emails.

"Fine." Poppy's chopping got louder, as though to deafen her stormy thoughts.

*Shit. The other F word.* Geoff took off his glasses and stood from the chair. *When things are anything but fine.*

He came around the breakfast bar into the kitchen and circled his arms around her waist. "Pops? What is it, Honch? Talk to me."

Her body trembled. "I just feel like," she sniffled. "That you're not hap-py with me. That you have some regrets. Maybe I don't matter enough." She turned and looked at him, her eyes brimming. "Just like back at Rollins when I didn't think you cared enough for me. Maybe I'm not enough for you." Her last words squeaked out.

"Wait a minute. Pops?" He lengthened her name. "What are you talking about?"

Geoff took her hands in both of his and led her to the barstools. He sat and positioned her right in front of him, facing him—like she had to stand on that exact spot. "I love you. Adore you. I've left my whole life to be with you, Honch. I'm crazy about you. You *know* that." Geoff tilted his head as he caressed her arms.

"Well, I'm just so excited to see you. To be with you." Her tears plopped onto her cheeks and ran onto her trembling lips.

"Sweetie, I'm not excited about *anything* or *anyone* right now. I'm tired of hotels and airports and planes and schlepping crap. There's no relaxing. No time for reflection. No time to think about coming home to my beautiful fiancée." He wiped her cheek with a finger.

Poppy nodded.

"I can't be all lovey just like that." He snapped his fingers. "When traveling is so abusive. Like today." He laced his fingers behind her back and gently rocked both of them.

Poppy bobbed her head, still wanting to clarify her position. "Yes, but even though I have stresses, I'm always happy to be with you. I feel like you have regrets—that you're not happy to be with me."

Poppy's eyes refilled.

Geoff's mouth dropped open. "Pops. I'm not thinking *any* of those things." He shook his head. "You've gotta stop filling in the blanks."

Poppy nodded. "Okay. Well, tell me, when are you available to be all . . . all, lovey?" She smiled like she'd been told to practice a good smile, a *lovey* smile, on command.

"Right now." He pulled her closer. "I'm here now." Geoff's dimple assured her.

"I think what it is, Geoffrey, is that I'm so happy. So in love with you."

She looked down. "And maybe it's emotional baggage revisited. Like when we were in college and—because of propriety and social expectations—I didn't believe I had permission to come right out and say what I wanted to say." She searched his eyes. "But we can be open. Honest. And have the loving courage to say anything."

Poppy rested her wrists on his shoulders.

"Yes, we do." Geoff smiled.

"When you're away, I feel your absence. In here." She patted her heart. "So when I see you at the airport, I want to reconnect with you right away. It's my old stuff that creeps in." She shook her head, as if to stop going backward. "But we're not in college anymore—we've learned and grown. I'll do *anything* to cherish and savor us." Her voice broke at the end.

"And I'm just thinking, *I want to get the hell out of airports, baggage claims, and cars, and be home. Then I can reconnect.*" Geoff held her hips and angled her body back about a foot—a look-you-straight-in-the-eye posture. "No more filling in blanks, okay?"

"Okay, but share your thoughts with me." She held up a teasing warning finger. "Even if they're not lovey. When there's silence, I automatically fill in the blanks. You can talk about car transmissions for all I care. And I *will* care because it's the man I love talking," Poppy playfully admonished him.

"I don't care that much about car transmissions." Geoff smiled and pulled her back into an embrace. "Pops, I've always loved you. You're my, my soulmate person." He grinned at his made-up endearment, as tears rocked at the corners of his eyes. "I so look forward to Christmas. Our first Christmas together."

The Empathic Bridge, now clear of its dirty swimming-pool color, vibrated a magenta red. Poppy and Geoff had turned the corner from the cracks on their emotional sidewalk. The bridge turned a lovely Hermosa pink and revealed the nurturing calmness of two people who lovingly work together. Something they hadn't had the capacity to do thirty-two years ago. Nor had I had the wisdom to understand what they'd needed when we were at Rollins.

Watching them, their arms around each other, I realized that they had the ability, by themselves, to overcome obstacles. To scrutinize and discuss those hard emotions. To address concerns immediately. To understand each other's soul. Back at Love, Twelve, on the Emotional Clock, they'd resolved their misunderstandings in less time than it'd had taken for Geoff to unpack his baggage.

# CHAPTER 45

# Picture Perfect

~

GEOFF SAT AGAINST THE CARVED ivory four-poster headboard—stacks of unwrapped presents with Post-it notes and paper bags strewn around him. Each bag had a family member's name on it—including the pets, Nicky and Zippy.

"Do you plan to fill *all* eleven of the stockings out there?" Geoff pointed to the family room area. He stared at the gift-laden piles on the bedspread where Poppy had set up a Christmas staging area.

"Mm-hmm." Poppy tossed a wrapped squeaky toy, its package misshapen, into a bag marked *Nicky*.

"And *when* do you plan to fill them? It's almost five O'clock, and we have to be over at your parents' Christmas Eve party at six, right?" Geoff looked at the nightstand clock and back at Poppy.

"Six, seven, eight," Poppy mumbled, her index finger sorting multicolored keychain flashlights on the spread. "Where is the...?" She lifted the fringed throw pillow and retrieved the tape dispenser. "Yes, we'll fill them when we get home and everyone's asleep." With one hand, she held down two sheets of gold-and-burgundy Christmas paper, and flicked off a piece of tape with the other.

"Except *us*. *We* won't be asleep." Geoff looked at the ceiling and shook his head. "Oh God, we'll be up all night, won't we?"

Poppy tossed the wrapped present toward a finished pile at the edge of the bed. She inched on her knees toward Geoff, careful not to topple the assembled line of waiting-to-be-wrapped gifts. "I love you, Geoffrey." She kissed his dimple. "It'll be okay. Have I mentioned this is my favorite day of the *whole* year?" She grinned. "And our first Christmas together." She sat back on her ankles.

"I love you, too, Pops." Geoff counted the paper bags with eye blinks. "You have fourteen bags here, only twelve stockings. "Who are the other two bags for?"

"Mom and Dad." Poppy's mouth quivered as if her lips couldn't decide whether to turn up or down. "I always do Santa for my parents," she whispered, and stared at the bag marked *Big George*. Her tears came as she stuck tape onto Christmas paper, a three-part movement of tape, wipe, and sniffle.

Geoff rubbed her knee. "You're so thoughtful." His eyelashes dampened as empathy took over.

I felt Geoff's stomach sway almost like a swinging rope bridge. His thoughts came to me. *I know she's thinking of her father. It might be the last Christmas with him.*

Poppy thought, *Enjoy the moments with Dad right now.* She looked back to Geoff and exhaled. "So, you'll help me later?"

"Of course, Honch." Geoff sat up and pulled her close. "We're a team."

Poppy dangled her arms on top of his shoulders, and a strand of green velvet ribbon fell from the spool still in her hand. She closed her eyes and hugged him.

Geoff ran his fingers in his hair and gazed at the strewn gifts. "It's like looking at an aerial view of Manhattan." Geoff chuckled. "When George and Molly said you go overboard for Christmas, they weren't kidding."

Poppy gave a sheepish grin. "I own it." She shrugged and backed off the bed on her knees. "I'm excited to have you see my dad's Christmas pants for the first time." Poppy brightened.

"That's right." Geoff opened his closet door and took out the dry-cleaning bag with his white shirt. He scrunched up the plastic to the top of the hanger. "I can't believe I had the same pants back in college."

Poppy paused at her jewelry chest and closed her eyes. She thought back to December 1977 when she'd said to Geoff: "My dad has those same pants—wears them once a year. On Christmas Eve."

Poppy put on her ring and closed the chest drawer. "This is the ring I told you about." She held out her hand to Geoff. "Dad bought this ring for me twenty-five years ago. He gave me strict instructions. 'I want you pick out a good piece of jewelry for yourself—not the kids.'" She held out her right hand and stared at the ring, the distinctive ring like a beacon. A symbol to remind Poppy that she wasn't just a mother or a daughter. She was a beautiful lady who ought to be appreciated.

With the cuff of her velvet sleeve, Poppy buffed the amethyst stone. "I think this ring will always remind me of the Tuesday and Thursday afternoons I spend with my dad." Poppy leaned on the closet door. "I love our time together. We discuss everything. My art therapy. Coaching clients. My classes, and some of the topics I discussed in my classroom."

Poppy held her shoe in her hand. "We even talk about God, Heaven, and the afterlife."

At the foot of their bed, Poppy slipped her heels on and sighed. "And *even* mindfulness, Geoffrey. My dad read my blogs about mindfulness and didn't dismiss the topic as some airy-fairy thing. My almost eighty-nine-year-old wise dad gets it."

~~~

Christmas Eve at Valerie and George's had been stunning and festive. All of the senses were piqued: the twenty-seven candles, some cinnamon-scented; Valerie's handmade crystal-and-jeweled ornaments; and the delicacies on the Christmas buffet, including Molly's special chocolate chip homemade cookies. Aside from the visual splendor, the voices of background Christmas music provided the perfect ambiance for joyful voices big and little—four generations of love.

When Poppy had asked the bartender, Duke, to take a picture, her thoughts had immediately accompanied her request: *Please don't say you won't be in the photo, Dad.*

And as if on cue, George Terris had waved his hand. "You don't need me in the picture."

"Yes, we do, Dad. *Please*," Poppy had said, softly.

As Duke steadied his hand, Poppy's thoughts had flashed in sync with the camera flash. *The man I love next to me, surrounded by my wonderful children, family. Four generations here. My parents. This is probably Dad's last Christmas. Bittersweet. Hard to smile.*

~~~

The energy in the Christmas morning family room revealed a study in excitement—the joy of the gifts, both given and received. The little ones and the dog, consumed by the gifts they'd received, tore off wrapping paper with great physicality and dramatic flair.

All of Poppy's children and granddaughters, with help from their aunts and uncle, had opened most of the presents, while Poppy and Geoff scooped up ribbons, paper, and tissue to clear a path to walk.

When the little girls had finished opening their gifts, they stood and crawled like conquerors who'd just taken a hill, their bare feet tramping their way to the top of a pile of wrapping paper and cardboard boxes. Their round cocoa eyes wide, searching all four corners of the room with an *is that it?* look.

My slate projected an image of Adrianna's pacifier, buried beneath the mound of trimmings. Before my slate even posted a warning, Kimmy, still talking with animated nods to her siblings, groped blindly under the heap and produced the pacifier. A mother's knowledge of her child's needs.

I'd watched as each of the children peered into the velvet recesses of their stockings, the ones that Geoff had helped Poppy—as Santa—fill.

New presents appeared under the tree, brought in from Poppy's closet and a red lacquer basket in the living room. This time, the trimmings were far more glorious. Lamé satin bows; wide, rich velvets; silk-wired damask; and gilded cards. Even the wrapping paper was triple-thick and glossy. Elegant and fancy, the gifts were almost too pretty to open.

In the kitchen, Molly inhaled the hickory aroma of Wisconsin-made Neuske's bacon, and at the same time, she leaned away from the skillet and crackling bacon grease.

Nicky announced Poppy's parents' arrival with several barks and quickly circled Valerie's ankles, as she spun in wearing red palazzo pants. George Terris helped Valerie up the front steps, as he carried three large gift bags with red velvet bows tied on the handles.

After exchanged kisses and rounds of "Merry Christmas," Valerie set her sequined purse on the counter. So many things about Valerie sparkled: her clothes, her jewelry, her smile. She turned to her daughter. "Honey," she said half-scolding, "you shouldn't have done so much, with the stockings you left last night."

Poppy smiled. "You say that every year, Mom. Besides, Santa brings the gifts."

"Merry Christmas, Val. Big George!" The grandchildren made a chorus of greetings.

Poppy and Molly, as elves, distributed presents to each family member.

A radiant Poppy walked over to Geoff's chair and turned the box to read the nametag. "And this one is for you, Geoffrey."

Poppy glanced back to her father as he held the gift she'd handed him. George Terris used four fingers to peel off the wrapping layer. He lifted the lid from the box on his lap. "Oh! I like this." He rubbed his hands on the long soft cotton sleeves of a shirt. "You put my initials on there." He looked up at Poppy. "Very nice." He waved his hand toward his daughter, and in a tone reserved for when he was surprised, he said, "You're something else."

"I got one, too." Geoff said, and held up a bright-red shirt with his monogram, *GTS*, on the front.

The present opening picked up pace. The *oohs* and *aahs* and thank you's all spilled over one another in a melodic round. As elated voices, tissue, and paper spread like air-popped corn, Poppy handed Geoff a carefully wrapped box.

"Honch, you've already given me so many things." Geoff looked up from the gift she'd placed on his lap. "You're so busy as the elf, you haven't opened the gifts I have for you." He reached below to the side of his chair. "Here, Honch. Please open this now."

Her lips parted as she stared at the square box. "Thank you, sweetie." She gently unfastened the gold ribbon and slid her finger underneath one end of the fold to unstick the tape. She removed the box and shimmied the lid. "Oh, Geoffrey. It's beautiful." Poppy lifted the silver and clear-jeweled watch from the little pillow in the box. "I love it," she whispered. "And you."

As she put it on, Geoff reached inside the bottom of the box and produced a hand-written note. "Here, Honch. Read this, too."

Poppy's hand shook as she held the note. Her eyes blurred the words he'd written.

> *My Dearest Poppy,*
> *Denied time together for so long, I thought it only fitting that on this—our first Christmas Day together—I give you the gift of time.*
> *Even though we did not have the chance to share the joy of having children together, may we cherish the time with the children we now share, to make up for lost time.*
> *I love you, Poppy,*
> *Geoffrey*

She softly brushed her salty lips on his dimple. "Thank you, Geoffrey. I love you." She leaned on the arm of the recliner. "And you open this one." She lifted the box she'd placed on his lap.

The Empathic Bridge, which had glowed a bright crimson all morning, suddenly turned a rich Christmas green, the color of expressed love in action.

As I watched the two of them now, Poppy's brown eyes glistened like the inside of a Godiva truffle, as he lifted the tissue-wrapped framed photo.

With both hands, he stared down at the 11x14 photo of Poppy as a college senior. No thoughts emerged from Geoff. Only a pure, raw flood of emotion. His chestnut eyes filled quickly and dripped uncontested tears onto his shirt. "It's my Poppy," he whispered.

He inhaled, and it sounded like a gasp. His thought slipped out. *I can't even speak.*

"Excuse me," he mumbled as he made his way back to the bedroom.

"What's the matter?" an intuitive Kimmy mouthed to her mother.

"I'll be right back." Poppy stood and gave her daughter an it'll-be-okay smile.

Geoff sat on the edge of the bed, the photo next to his thigh. He blew out an exhalation of emotion and glanced again at the picture of Poppy in a green silk blouse. Her twenty-one-year-old warm caramel eyes reflected the sun and palm trees.

"Sweetie?" Poppy sat on the other side of the photo and caressed his shoulder. "I didn't mean to upset you."

"I know." He nodded. "You didn't, Pops. I'm just overwhelmed." His last word came out as a whisper. "I can hardly contain the love I feel. It's so wonderful to share all of this. This Christmas as a family with you. Eight short months ago, I found you." He blinked watery dew from his eyelashes. "And now. All that we now have. All the goodness and happiness in this room." His voice collapsed into a sob.

"I know." Poppy's voice quivered and her fingers trembled.

From the inside of Poppy's being, I felt a sensation, a surge of feeling. What I can only imagine as love. With the side of her pinkie finger, she dabbed his cheek and redirected a tear from his cheek to her hand.

"And to open *this.*" He picked up the frame and held it like a chalice. A Holy Grail. "It's like an iron stamp that you're mine again." He looked at Poppy and dabbed his finger at a tear on her cheek. "Like when I first heard your voice say, 'Hi, this is Poppy.' And when I got your love note with your name on it before we'd even seen each other. The promise of you—*always there.* Those things . . . the small physical signs . . . mean so much. It's proof that you're real. That I didn't imagine all of this."

"You haven't imagined this."

"And"—his whispered voice cracked—"to open this gift and see *you*. *My* Poppy. This girl I'd lost. I was certain you were gone from my life forever." He swallowed into his emotional vortex. "And to realize that you'd come back into my life. Like I got the thirty-two years back—as if I'd never lost you." He touched his hand to his heart. "That you were here all the time."

I remembered her excitement when Poppy thought of the perfect gift for Geoff. How she'd gotten up and hurried to her closet. She'd lifted the photo and stared at the image of herself as a twenty-one-year-old girl who'd already met her first lover. The Poppy that still loved Geoff, even though he hadn't known it then.

## CHAPTER 46

# Do-Over

~

JANUARY BUZZED WITH WEDDING EXCITEMENT, and my slate joined in the buzz by projecting statistics on wedding guests. *Ninety-eight percent acceptance rate to date.*

On their green sofa, with Nicky on a stack of pillows next to them, Poppy and Geoff checked off the names from the ecru response cards.

"Do we have a quorum of Thetas for the Candlelight?" Geoff peered over the top of his reading glasses, the look of a CPA verifying the accuracy of a tax return.

"Yes, Geoffrey." She tilted her head and gently kissed the corner of his moustache where it brushed against his dimple. "We'll set the record straight. I promise." Poppy straightened up and saluted.

"I know we laugh about it, but seriously, Honch. This is a big deal to me." He removed his glasses. "That Candlelight convinced me you didn't care about me."

"I know." Poppy shuddered. "I still feel shame about that time thirty-two years ago." Her words melted together. "I felt irrelevant." Her pupils began to swim. "It still hurts me to go there."

"I don't want you to feel badly. The once-denied Candlelight is for *me*. A loop I want to close." Geoff looked into her eyes and nodded.

Poppy exhaled. "It amazes me that I can't remember my own graduation. The heartache I felt with our breakup and the Candlelight. I hadn't even wanted that damn ceremony to begin with." She tsked. "I know enough about psychology and defense mechanisms to know that the trauma of thirty-two years ago—our breakup—has caused me to repress it."

"I remember the hurt, too, Honch. And it's weird that *I* remember your graduation. And details, too, like when I saw your parents there." He stroked the top of her hands with his thumbs. "That's why this Candlelight is so important to me," Geoff said, his voice reduced to a whisper.

I felt something old—the lurch of that crushing 1978 memory, as Poppy begged her friends not to open the courtyard door to spread her engagement news to Geoff's fraternity brothers. I recalled the agony in Geoff's eyes, when the right side of the Emotional Clock had revealed combined feelings of Anger and Despair. And Poppy's eyes had swum with shame and guilt, a stark contrast to what any other Candlelight should've evoked. Their two hearts and souls had filled with pain.

Three weeks later, the rehearsal dinner, hosted by Geoff's parents, Jean and George Spencer, at the Bird Key Yacht Club, caused the Empathic Bridge to pulse with a brilliant shade of indigo. Perfection. Many of the women used their white linen napkins to dab the corner of their eyes after the toasts, including one from Ernie, Geoff's college roommate, who announced to everyone that he'd just stepped back in time with Poppy and Geoff.

Ernie's blue eyes shined like aquamarine gemstones. His brown hair, just a shade darker than college and combed short, revealed a slightly receding hairline with a dusting of gray at his temples.

Yet it was Stacy, Poppy's brother, who, during his toast, reminded the guests of the first words he'd spoken to Geoff when he'd met him at their Wisconsin home in 1977: "Welcome aboard!" Dressed in a cerulean-blue blazer, a pink dress shirt, and Hermès tie, Stacy lifted his wineglass in the air. "I'm proud to call you my brother-in-law. Please raise your glasses to Poppy and Geoff." Amid the clinking of glasses and a chorus of "Hear! Hear!" Stacy had continued. "May we all continue to share in the joyous energy of their love."

After dinner, Geoff whispered to Poppy, "Can we have the Candlelight do-over now?"

Poppy kissed his cheek in answer and gathered seven of her sorority sisters in a circle, including her mother, who'd been a member of Kappa Alpha Theta at Rollins. The women sang and passed around an ivory candle. "That's how it is with Theta love; you want to pass it on," Poppy sang along.

The candle left Poppy's hand, and as she passed it around the ring of women, I thought back to thirty-three years ago, when I'd first witnessed this ritual. Arrogant and clueless, I'd mistakenly thought at the time that the ceremony was honoring Geoff. I recalled my desire to excel as a choreographer. I'd completely lost sight of my purpose—to manage their relationship.

As I considered the significance of the Candlelight ceremony at Rollins thirty-three years ago, I remembered my initial feelings of relief. *Oh! They've worked it out.* And to my horror, I'd discovered along with everyone else that Poppy's engagement had not included Geoff. It was still fresh in my mind—the image of Geoff's fraternity brothers on a late Sunday afternoon, as they dangled tanned legs and sipped beers on their balcony overlooking the Theta courtyard. I thought back to the excited innocence of the young men and women present that day, all of whom had wondered which magical couple would leave paradise and start a life together.

When Poppy had blown out the candle in 1978, some had seen the ritual as an excited declaration. Others, especially Geoff, had seen it as an extinguished love. Their romantic fate sealed.

I recalled Poppy's face, and at the time I had not understood her look— her vacant smile. The kind that was detached but polite. Appreciative. As if she was stumbling through the motions like an out-of-town bridesmaid stuck in a receiving line at a wedding reception. I had erroneously thought Poppy's expression in the Theta living room merely reflected an awkward, youthful shyness.

Also inexperienced, I hadn't had the ability then to read facial expressions. I hadn't understood the clash of emotions she'd surely felt: feigning excitement, wanting to follow sorority rules, but knowing deep inside that something was terribly wrong. And I imagine she'd felt a fearful hollowness—the emptiness of a passenger on a runaway train she couldn't stop.

She had no communication tools, nor did she give herself permission to address the sudden end of her relationship with Geoff. She didn't understand how to process her emotions. Instead, she'd stayed on the train to wait for the next station to be announced.

And Geoff, who'd incorrectly believed for more than thirty years that Poppy had thought so little of him—that she'd been taunting him with the ceremony—had been left with a deep emotional scar. Like a black marble that rolled around the edges of his heart, this redo of the Candlelight offered him the chance to scoop out the foreign object so that it would no longer darken his memories.

He'd already forgiven; he already understood the misperception. Now, tonight, as he watched Poppy and her sisters, their excited hands passing around the candle, their eyes sparkling, and their laughter bubbling up, he could let go.

With his arm atop the mahogany lacquered surface, Geoff grinned from the corner of the bar. His eyes, like soft balls of fudge, glistened as he clapped his hands twice and approached the sorority gathering. "Thank you, ladies, for the do-over ceremony." Geoff smiled at the seven women and draped his arm around Poppy. He pulled her to him. "I got you back, Pops. *Officially*," he whispered, and brushed his lips on her hair.

# CHAPTER 47

# I Do

〜

On Pineapple Avenue, the First United Methodist Church's red brick tower and luminous white steeple stood like a beacon in downtown Sarasota. The church, built in 1891, was the oldest church in Sarasota County. The entrance, flanked by six large columns, led to an unexpectedly modest narthex. Many visitors showed surprise when four church doors opened to a massive sanctuary that seated twelve hundred.

The sanctuary offered congregants a breathtaking view. The magnitude of the formal worship space, the grandeur of the altar and chancel, and the fourteen stained-glass windows that lined the sides of the sanctuary made the church a stunning showpiece for the community.

With fewer than seventy-five guests at their wedding, Poppy and Geoff had chosen a more intimate setting for their ceremony—the chapel. A few steps from the front door of the church and opposite the sanctuary, the chapel proved the ideal size for their wedding. The right side of the chapel had its own display of beautiful windows—rich colors that caught the morning sun.

Reflections of sunlight created an echo, a secondary image, of a magnificent watercolor on the adjacent white wooden wall. The windows depicted a plow, a carpenter's hammer, a nurse's cap, and a mason's trowel—a story that revealed the ways in which men and women serve God, described in an exquisite visual narrative. It was a rich and effective storytelling method that predated movies, TV, or the internet.

The wood grains in the dozen or so pews on either side of the red-carpeted floor—sunny oak—added to the warmth of the room. The ivory-painted side of each pew, shaped in the form of a harp, made the entrance to the pew even more welcoming.

On either side of the chancel, two wooden stands held three-foot-tall vases filled with ivory calla lilies, soft white lilies, and cream-colored silk poppy flowers.

In a rear pew, I savored the beauty of the windows. Geoff waited in the conference room—a makeshift area where grooms and their attendants prepared for the big event. Poppy, in the room next to the ladies' room, squeezed her daughter's hands in excitement in the bride's dressing area.

I stared at the stained-glass image on the east wall—an angel in prayer. *It's the end of one journey and the beginning of another,* I thought.

My slate jiggled on the pew next to me. On the screen were these words: *Maybe they were only meant to be together now.*

My own thoughts trickled out. Had I choreographed them as I was supposed to? They may not have appreciated one another had they not had other marriages and divorces. Without the contrast to the best versions of themselves, they may not have experienced the gratitude for their relationship that they now feel intensely.

*And Poppy often comments that she feels so blessed with her children. She wouldn't have changed a thing. Of course, Geoff feels the same way,* I thought.

As I sat in the pew, I recalled how once Poppy and Geoff had spoken about the possibility of me. They'd said, "We feel as though someone has orchestrated perfect moments in our lives." I smiled at their innocent suggestion.

I stared at the carpeted steps that led to the small altar where three vertical windows illuminated the back wall with cobalt blue, maize yellow, emerald green, and bright pink. Etched in the glass below the golden cross were the words "We Are the Branches."

Jean Spencer walked beside her husband. Dressed in an ivory silk jacket, embroidered with delicate cherry blossom flowers, Jean looked elegant. The Chinese butterfly knots, in soft-pink brocade, created a stylish, if inefficient, button. Each fastener looked like a flower's delicate spring bud.

She slowed her usual purposeful gait to match George Spencer's. Her deep-brown eyes scanned the foyer for a suitable chair. She placed her hand on his shoulder as he lowered himself into a blue-and-beige-striped wingedback chair. She sat next to him at the edge of a quilted sofa.

I turned to watch them in the narthex. Dr. Spencer's silken white hair, combed neatly to one side, showed sheer strands of silver on his full head. Like the groom, groomsmen, and attendants, the fathers wore gray flannel trousers, a white shirt, and, on their lapels, an off-white calla lily.

George Terris dressed like the other men in the wedding party, save for his tie and the navy beret he wore to camouflage the visible signs of cancer. George's tie—the exact color of Poppy's dress—was fuchsia with thin pale green stripes. He gestured for Valerie to sit next to Jean Spencer on the couch, while he sat in the matching straight-back chair across from "the good doctor," as he called Geoff's father.

Valerie, in a magenta silk blouse and flared black silk pants, a black silk Chanel flower near her shoulder, leaned close to Jean and whispered. Their hushed voices teemed with excitement.

I watched the start of the procession as the organist played Johann Sebastian Bach's Air. The organ mimicked the baroque sounds of gentle violins.

I turned away from the procession and watched Poppy's father, who stood when his granddaughters appeared, followed by his daughter. My breath caught when I saw Poppy—whose eyes filled the moment she met her father's gaze.

Poppy was thinking about a father-daughter dance she'd attended as an eleven-year-old, her father healthy and strong. And then George Terris in white tie and tails when she made her debut at nineteen, his white gloves adding to his robust demeanor. And in this moment, she thought about how this would be the last time she'd take his arm as her escort. I saw in the bride's face a bittersweet expression, memories lingering in her eyes, her lips straining to override the past. An attempt to smile.

Kelly, her flaxen hair in an updo, had also caught Poppy's expression, and before she approached the aisle, she turned back to her mother and shot her an exaggerated smile, her star sapphire eyes twinkling in love. "Don't cry," she mouthed.

As Poppy and her father stood in the doorway to the chapel, George Terris placed his right hand on top of Poppy's hand, now tucked into his elbow.

"You look beautiful, honey." Her father beamed and wrapped Poppy in the greatest wedding gift a bride could want: a father's love. Unconditional love. A transition from an enduring love to a new journey. To enter into the arms and world of a husband's adoration. A discovered love. *A rediscovered love.*

The organist transitioned to Pachelbel's Canon in D, and the father and bride paused momentarily as the chords began to swell. Poppy gazed up at her father. "Thank you for being here for me—*with me*—Dad. I love you."

He squeezed her hand closer to his side. "I know, baby, I know. I love you, too," he said, his words barely audible. Not because of his frailty, but because he wanted only Poppy to hear it. "I know, I know," were words I'd heard many times from George to his daughter. The four words a signal to Poppy that she didn't need to say anything. No words were necessary to describe their deep, loving connection. Their intuitions were linked.

Many of the guests turned to look to the back of the church and waited for the customary cue to stand as the bride entered. A collective but muffled *whoosh* sound emerged under the organ processional music as guests rose to their feet. Kelly, Kimmy, and Molly—the maid of honor—all wore black-and-white taffeta and crinoline dresses with a fuchsia flower that perfectly matched Poppy's dress. They each carried a single ivory calla lily, surrounded by greens and tied off with a fuchsia organza ribbon. The daughters all beamed at their mother in the entranceway.

The groomsmen, Geoff's lifelong friends, both Hollywood handsome, and Poppy's son, George, all in gray flannels and navy blazers with navy ties that had pink turtles on them, waited at the altar. At six foot two and dressed the same, Jonathon, the best man, stood a bit taller than the others.

*Poppy's lovely,* I thought. *Radiant.* The fuchsia taffeta dress—stunning. The Italian satin and Swarovski-jeweled silver belt looked like a train, a large bow and trailing ribbons extending the length of her dress.

As Poppy's gaze caught Geoff's, the Empathic Bridge suddenly swelled and sent beams of crystallized white all around the chapel. Poppy wrestled with her bittersweet expression in the doorway as she took her father's arm, as if she was trying to coerce her mouth to diffuse the bitter part of bittersweet. Yet as she saw Geoff, her eyes glistened. Her unencumbered smile said, *There you are!*

My focus shifted to Geoff, as I wanted to see Poppy through Geoff's eyes.

With an ivory poppy flower on the left lapel of his navy-blue suit, his hands folded over each other in front, his eyes capturing only his bride. Geoff's pupils dilated, involuntary evidence of his adoration. On his left cheek, the dimple trembled as if it was trying to steady itself on the edge of a balance beam. In that moment, when their eyes locked, everything and everyone else in the room disappeared, except for the Empathic Bridge, which swelled in size and encompassed the entire chapel.

Like a powerful magnet, the shimmering bridge absorbed colors from the stained-glass windows and created an even more magical aura.

The ceremony had the feel of a first-time wedding—the innocence obvious, as if they were twenty-one-year-olds.

Poppy and her father walked down the aisle as the chords of Pachelbel's Canon filled the room. Poppy and Geoff's hearts beat faster as she drew closer and stopped next to him at the altar.

The minister, dressed in a white brocade robe with hand-stitched and embossed church symbols on it, stood at the small altar and faced the wedding guests. In front of him, Poppy, her father, and Geoff formed an intimate half circle.

The minister, Reverend Eugene Perkins, a genial man with a modest build, adjusted his wire-framed glasses. He cleared his throat and began.

"Dearly beloved, we are gathered here in the presence of God to witness and bless the coming together of this man and this woman in Holy Matrimony." The minister smiled, and light reflected off his glasses. "Who gives this woman to be married to this man?"

In a strong and solemn voice that belied his physical vulnerability, George Terris announced as if reading a decree, "Her mother and I do. For the third and final time."

*Did he just say what I think he said?* I wondered over the uproar of laughter that erupted from the guests.

*The minister paged through the Bible as if looking for what? A script?*

"Err, um, let us pray." The minster attempted to recover. From the pews, guests still giggled, elated by George Terris' declaration.

As part of the wedding ceremony, Poppy's brother, Stacy, shared the scripture reading with Poppy's daughter Molly. Stacy lowered his tanned face as he held the Bible for his niece to begin the reading.

In her black silk stiletto heels, on which she teetered at almost five feet ten inches, Molly began, "This is a reading from the first chapter of John 4:18. 'There is no fear in love. But perfect love drives out fear . . .'" When she'd finished her part, Molly gently eased the book closer to her uncle.

*It's all about courage,* I mused.

Geoff took Poppy's hands in his and tenderly caressed them with his thumbs. His monogrammed sterling-silver cufflinks sparkled; the right one read *Honch*; the left, *Chief*—their college nicknames. Geoff's eyes connected with Poppy's, and his voice, stalwart and confident, began.

"Poppy, never in my wildest dreams could I have imagined that I'd stand here with you, now, to become your husband. Our love for each other is so strong. After all those years apart, we are still crazy about each other. And I will always love you."

Poppy's smile stretched across her face. She gave an excited shudder.

"I am grateful we have our family, our friends, and God to bless us here today. I can't wait to start this wonderful adventure with you, Poppy. My heart's one true love."

The minister shifted to face Poppy. "Poppy, your vows to Geoff."

"Geoffrey, a man's unconditional love I discovered from my father and grandfather. And thirty-three years ago, I also knew it and felt it from you," Poppy began. "And for the past 299 days, since last April 26 when you'd first called me"—she grinned at Geoff—"you have opened my heart as you did at Rollins. And you've retouched my soul. You've brought much laughter to my spirit. I continue to cherish your love." Her voice faltered and revealed the depth of her conviction. The pupils of her eyes seemed to float beneath a watery surface.

Geoff gently squeezed her fingers once, signaling a surge of confidence.

She continued, her voice strong. "Geoffrey, I'm grateful every day and feel blessed that you have made us a *we*." She drew out the word "we" to emphasize its importance to her. "And an *us*." Poppy smiled, as her eyes twinkled. "And as I often say to you, Geoffrey, I love you more today than yesterday." She gazed into his eyes. "You were my first love. You are my last love. You are my forever love. You're my soulmate person."

I grinned at the memory of when Geoff called her that last fall when he returned from a week of travels—when she misunderstood his lack of energy.

Jonathon, the best man, reached into his pocket for the rings. His face suddenly flushed as he pulled out only one ring—the groom's ring—a simple gold band with a rope design. His forehead wrinkled and his lower lip drooped. Stunned, he scrunched his eyes like a jeweler with a loupe.

I stiffened in the pew. *Only one ring?*

And just as suddenly, a wry smile emerged on Jonathon's face. Poppy's wedding band was tucked perfectly into the interior of Geoff's ring—one inside the other. A perfect echo of their hearts.

"And by the power vested in me." The minister smiled and raised his voice. "I now pronounce you man and wife. You may kiss the bride."

Geoff circled his arms around Poppy's waist and leaned his head to the right. She did the same and tilted her chin up. As he'd done hundreds of times, his lips met Poppy's. Yet this was the first time he'd kissed her as his wife. Poppy's lashes touched her cheeks, and even through the sacred kiss, her smile never left her lips.

I remember their first kiss—in the loggia between their two houses at Rollins. Geoff's strong fingers had lifted Poppy's chin thirty-three years ago, just like now. And Geoff had had the same gleam in his eyes as he inched toward her face and pressed his lips into hers. The gleam that laughed and danced with joy.

The minister raised his robed arms. "I present Mr. and Mrs. Geoffrey Spencer."

With her hand in his, Poppy and Geoff both turned to loving applause. Geoff pulled her closer and kissed her again to the sounds of enthusiastic appreciation from the guests. His dimple flexed as he whispered into her ear, "We did it, Honch."

As the bride and groom stood at the altar and faced the guests, whose applause showered them, I wondered if they, too—especially the seven Thetas—believed they'd just witnessed the completion of a love story that'd been interrupted—put on hold—for thirty-two years. That magic now condensed into these joyous moments.

I moved toward the front of the altar and stood before Poppy and Geoff. I felt their love create a shift in energy between the three of us, like a warm breath of sun and wind billowing a sheer curtain in an open window. *I think they see me,* I thought.

"Honch, do you see what I see? Like, a being. *An angel?* A soft glow."

Like a dream where images and otherworldly beings appear, I realized the aura of lightness in the room didn't emanate from the chandeliers or soft candles.

The aura—love.

And for a timeless moment, the three of us had the sensory ability to see it. And *feel* it. Like a two-way mirror, now transparent. A light turned on. *On the other side.*

"Oh, Geoffrey." Poppy's breath caught. "What do we see?" she asked, her voice a murmur.

This powerful energy of love now choreographed our respective awareness. In awe, the three of us acknowledged what we'd experienced—the seamlessness of time travel, one billion seconds, softly swept into this one moment.

As the bride and groom studied me—took me in—I smiled.

And as we walked from the chapel sanctuary, we watched the being who'd apparently orchestrated our union, and the glow of the being left our wedding ceremony and moved to the doorway into the almost-setting sun.

On the steps that led outside, we glanced back and saw the narthex clock that neither of us had noticed before. As if acknowledging the fulfillment of our timeless love, this aura—*this being*—suddenly swung the hands from Six O'clock to Twelve O'clock.

We heard a faint chime, familiar to both of us at once, the glorious sounds from the abbey in Mondsee near Salzburg, where Maria and Captain von Trapp married.

# About the Authors

Poppy and Geoff Spencer transitioned from traditional roles in the business world to write their story and share the insights they've learned as relationship experts, "Millennial Translators," speakers, authors, and radio show hosts. Poppy brings experience as a psychology professor, sales and marketing director, registered art therapist, and a Licensed Certified New Life Story Coach who specializes in the Myers-Briggs Type Indicator; Geoff as a sales professional and Licensed Certified New Life Story Coach. They live and love on the Gulf Coast of Florida.

# Acknowledgements

~⌒

WE ARE GRATEFUL TO THE community of Rollins College for providing us with the magical setting where this story began. We thank Jack Canfield and Patty Aubrey for their master coaching and the inspiration that guided us on our adventures; Steve Harrison and his Quantum Leap team for guiding us on the publication and marketing of our book; Maxwell Billings for his wonderful design and illustration of our book cover; Brené Brown, for the reminder to have the courage to embrace vulnerability; Dr. Nancy Kalish, for her research on rekindled romance; Ringling College of Art and Design and Dr. Larry Thompson for infinite inspiration and support; Esther and Jerry Hicks for their teachings on the law of attraction; Ted Andrews, who taught us about the wisdom of creatures; Dr. Martin Seligman and David Pollay and the International Positive Psychology Association, for their positivity and inspiration; Dr. David, Krueger, for his wisdom and coach mentoring; Cathy Malchiodi, the "queen" of art therapy; our editor, Lindsey Alexander; our friends in the Davidson community, the dear friends at our "University Schools" in Cleveland and Milwaukee; our Milwaukee family and friends; the Sarasota community. To our friends around the globe who've said, "You should write a book." We thank you for your loving encouragement and ongoing support. And to our dear readers, thank you for sharing the ride.

We thank our parents for their support on this wonderful journey. Lastly, we thank our children for their loving patience every time they heard our story. We love you.

Made in the USA
San Bernardino, CA
29 August 2017